INSIDE

BIG BROTHER

GETTING IN & STAYING IN

JEAN RITCHIE

First published 2002 by Channel 4 Books
an imprint of Pan Macmillan Ltd
20 New Wharf Road, London N1 9RR
Basingstoke and Oxford

Associated companies throughout the world

www.panmacmillan.com

ISBN 07522 6507 5

Photographs on plates 1, 2, 3, 16, 17 and 32 © Channel 4 Television; plate 4 – courtesy of Mr and Mrs Sibley; plate 5 –
top photograph courtesy of Mr and Mrs Sibley, all other photographs © Channel 4 Television; plate 6 – top right ©
Channel 4 Television, all other photographs courtesy of Sandy's wife, Claire Davidson; plate 7 – top three photographs
courtesy of Sandy's wife, Claire Davidson, all other photographs © Channel 4 Television; plate 8 – top two photographs
courtesy of Jackie Roberts, all other photographs © Channel 4 Television; plate 9 – top right, middle left and bottom right
courtesy of Jackie Roberts, all other photographs © Channel 4 Television; plate 10 – top right © Channel 4 Television, all
other photographs courtesy of Mrs Ann Bruce; plate 11 – top left and top centre courtesy of Mrs Ann Bruce, all other
photographs © Channel 4 Television; plate 12 – top left © Channel 4 Television, all other photographs courtesy of Mr and
Mrs J Regan; plate 13 – top three photographs courtesy of Mr and Mrs J Regan, all other photographs © Channel 4
Television; plate 14 – top right © Channel 4 Television, all other photographs courtesy of Sylvia Lawler; plate 15 – all
family photographs courtesy of Sylvia Lawler, photographs from Big Brother © Channel 4 Television; plate 18 – top left ©
Channel 4 Television, all other photographs courtesy of Pete Davey; plate 19 – top three photographs courtesy of Pete
Davey, all other photographs © Channel 4 Television; plate 20 – family photographs courtesy of Alison's mum, Maria,
photographs from Big Brother © Channel 4 Television; plate 21 – bottom left and bottom right © Channel 4 Television, all
other photographs courtesy of Alison's mum, Maria; plate 22 – top centre © Channel 4 Television, all other photographs
courtesy of Jackie Budden; plate 23 – top left and top right courtesy of Jackie Budden, all other photographs © Channel 4
Television; plate 24 – top left © Channel 4 Television, all other photographs courtesy of Mr and Mrs Ellis; plate 25 – top
left, centre and right courtesy of Mr and Mrs Ellis, all other photographs © Channel 4 Television; plate 26 – courtesy of
Yvonne Gordon; plate 27 – top left and right courtesy of Yvonne Gordon, all other photographs © Channel 4 Television;
plate 28 – top right © Channel 4 Television, all other photographs courtesy of Maxine Smith; plate 29 – top left, centre
and right courtesy of Maxine Smith, all other photographs © Channel 4 Television; plate 30 – bottom left and right ©
Channel 4 Television, all other photographs courtesy of Mr and Mrs Culley; plate 31 – courtesy of Mr and Mrs Culley.

A CIP catalogue record for this book is available from the British Library.

Designed and typeset by seagulls
Printed and bound by Mackays of Chatham, plc, Chatham, Kent

O₂ sponsors Big Brother

This book accompanies the television series Big Brother,
produced for Channel 4 Television by Endemol UK Productions.
Executive Producer: Phil Edgar Jones

CONTENTS

ACKNOWLEDGEMENTS

The author would like to thank all the production team, the web team, the Outside Organisation and the Channel 4 Press Office for their help. Particular thanks to (in alphabetical order, like the nominations):

Julian Alexander, Julian Bellamy, Jessica Bendien, Markus Blee, Jonathan Braman, Melissa Brown, Sallie Clement, Peter Collett, Paul Coueslant, Phil Edgar Jones, Gigi Eligoloff, Nick Francis, Peter Grimsdale, Fran Goddard, Petrina Good, Cat Gros, Helen Hawken, Gavin Henderson, Walter Iuzzolino, Jonny Kinder, Sarah MacDonald, James Milnes, Sean Murphy, Claire O'Donohoe, Paul Osborne, Susy Price, Susan Quilliam, Wendy Rattray, Deborah Sargeant, Sandra Scott, Chris Short, Julian Stockton, Karl Warner, David Williams, Victoria Wood, Ruth Wrigley, Matilda Zoltowski.

Feng Shui expert and Chinese astrologer Paul Darby can be contacted at: www.fengshuidoctor.co.uk

Astrologer Alinda Bartlett, who did all the housemates' astrology, can be contacted at: www.alinda.co.uk

Doodle analyst and psychic Ronnie Buckingham can be contacted on 01376 349198

Palmist Robin Lown, who did the housemates' palm readings, can be contacted on 01424 731 895

Graphologist Emma Bache can be contacted on 07951 091 526, or at emma.bache@virgin.net

INTRODUCTION

As the heavy door closes behind him it is eerily quiet. The frenzied cheers of a 1,000-strong crowd and the famous frantic rush of the *Big Brother* theme music are shut out. He's hugged his mum and dad, been frisked by burly security guards, and now he is inside the house. Alone. Except, that is, for the 6.8 million television viewers who watch as he wanders around the airy, bright living room, still holding his metal suitcase and looking dazed by the madness of his final few moments in the real world.

The door swings open again and the tall young man in the red leather jacket is joined, in quick succession, by the five boys who will be his housemates for the weeks to come.

'What was that like?'

'Is that the best fu**ing thing ever?'

'Wow – scary!'

These are the first words we all hear from the *Big Brother* contestants 2003, as they share the heady realization that they have left their old lives behind.

For fifteen minutes it is a boys-only house. Names are exchanged and repeated, the house and garden are explored, football is discussed and the first practical joke of the series is planned as they decide to tell the girls that the nice bedroom is theirs, by order of *Big Brother*.

Then the electronic lock on the door clicks open, and a pretty black girl in white boots, a denim jacket and with braided hair appears at the top of the 18 wide steps that lead down from the door.

'Hi, boys,' she says.

'It's Girl One!' shouts one of the boys, and she is quickly followed by girls two, three, four, five and six. Handshaking gives way to kissing and hugging and a round of name-swapping: Jade, Katie, Jonny, Adele, Alex, Spencer, Alison, P.J., Sandy, Lynne, Sunita, Lee.

They will learn them quickly enough. And so will we. And in the not-too-distant future we will add two others, Sophie and Tim. They're our companions for the summer of 2003, and life is never going to be the same again for any of them. From now on, they know that every move they make, every breath they take, we'll be watching them.

CHAPTER ONE

HOUSE HUNTING

It was a dismal, wet day last November when Phil Edgar Jones stood in the middle of a sunken concrete slab at the back of Elstree Film Studios. The view looked bleak: rain splashing into deep puddles of dirty yellow water, a few scrawny weeds forcing their way up through the concrete, an empty black plastic rubbish sack tumbling along in the wind. The sides of the vast tank were slimy and stained, and topped by a galvanized spear-tipped fence which caught and held the wind-blown litter. Huge lumps of broken concrete were scattered along the sparse grass verge.

Looking around at the miserable scene, Phil felt a rush of excitement.

'We've got it,' he shouted into his mobile phone. 'I've found the place where we can build the house.'

Big Brother 3 was under way.

It was three days past the deadline for finding a site when Phil, the executive producer (boss man) on *Big Brother 3,* drove through the gates of Elstree Film Studios in Borehamwood, Hertfordshire. For six weeks he and the two series editors, Helen Hawken and Gigi Eligoloff, the top three who would be responsible for making the show, had been scouring London for a place to build the new house.

Location scouts, whose job is to find sites for films and TV programmes, had come up with lists of waste land dotted around the capital. Estate agents had chipped in with suggestions. But as the weather grew colder and the deadline loomed, finding a location was becoming urgent.

The first two series of *Big Brother* were filmed at Three Mills studio complex in Bow, East London. But planning permission for the house there had expired; and besides, the team felt it was time to move on, build a new home for the contestants, make *Big Brother 3* unique and different.

'We looked at sites all over London. You just don't realize how much derelict land there is,' says Phil.

The three, who were joined on many of their expeditions by Markus Blee, the man who would design the house, and Petrina Good, the production executive who would be in charge of all the costs and making sure everything happened on time, had drawn up a checklist of twenty things they were looking for in a site, and they travelled around ticking boxes to assess which locations came nearest to their ideal.

'There were three main things we needed,' says Gigi. 'First of all, the site had to be big enough – at least 500 square metres, to contain the house and garden. Secondly, it had to have electricity and water supplies to hand. And thirdly, in an ideal world it would be close to a studio. Otherwise, we'd have to build one, which would greatly increase the costs.'

They considered many options. They were impressed by sites in Battersea and Wandsworth, and they even looked at the ground in Islington earmarked for the new Arsenal stadium. They visited just about every studio within the radius of the M25, they looked at empty factories, derelict warehouses. They spent some time working

---

AIN'T GONNA NEED THIS HOUSE NO LONGER...

What happened to the old *Big Brother* house, in Bow, the place where television history was made? It's gone. There's no trace of it left, apart from a silver birch tree that was planted in the garden.

'We had to demolish it and return the land back to the state it was in before we arrived,' says Petrina Good, who was in charge of making sure the operation happened. 'We left the tree as a present to the environment where our housemates had lived so happily. But otherwise, you'd never know they'd been there.'

on plans to erect a three-storey building, with the 'house' on the top floor, offices beneath and a studio on the ground floor. The garden would have been on the roof. They examined the possibility of building the whole house inside a studio.

'But there was something wrong with everywhere we looked,' says Helen. 'Maybe there were houses too close, or there wasn't enough space for the Friday night audience, or something. Often it was too expensive. Estate agents initially became excited at the prospect of finding a home for the *Big Brother* house – I think they imagined they could sell it afterwards. But space in London is at such a premium that the property managers for most of these sites soon realized they could get more money than we could pay to lease

---

THE TOP TEAM

Phil Edgar Jones describes himself as 'the bloke with the best job in Britain'. As executive producer, he's been living the *Big Brother* experience for months – ever since the contestants vacated the last house.

'Imagine, I go to work every day and I immerse myself in *Big Brother*. It's great.' Phil wasn't around for BB1, but for BB2 he ran *Little Brother* and the Friday night live eviction shows. Before joining what he describes as 'the cult of *Big Brother*', he was executive producer of *The Priory*, and worked on the *Jack Docherty Show*, *The Word*, and the *Big Breakfast*.

Phil's sidekicks are Helen Hawken and Gigi Eligoloff, the two series editors. These are the people who make all the big *Big Brother* decisions.

'I make the jokes, Helen makes the programmes, and Phil separates us when we're fighting,' says Gigi.

Gigi and Helen are both veterans of all three series. Before entering the *Big Brother* world, Helen worked on *Pet Rescue* and factual programmes like *Watchdog* and *Food and Drink*. Gigi's background is youth entertainment: she's worked on *The Word*, *Big Breakfast*, *Live and Kicking* and *All Rise for Julian Clary*.

---

it. We also had to think about how everyone would get there – the staff, the audience, the press. We loved Pinewood Studios, but it was just too far out: one of our important checklist items was that it had to be within the M25.

'We also needed a site that we could use for three or four years, because *Big Brother* is here to stay for the next few years, and we didn't want to land anyone else with the problems we were going through.'

The list of possible locations was getting very short, and Petrina was getting edgy.

'I was very worried. I knew we'd have to finalize the design, get planning permission, build a house in record time, negotiate dates for the show with the studio, sort out offices for the production team... It was fast becoming a nightmare.'

Phil went on his own to look at Elstree Film Studios because he lives in North London and could drive there easily.

'The minute I looked at the site I thought, "Do you know what? I could stick a house there – and it would be great". It was the first place we'd seen that I felt really enthusiastic about. It's the perfect size, and right next door to a huge studio. It would be easy to keep it secure. Wow – we've got it!'

The first Helen knew about his success was when her phone rang. 'He literally shouted, "I've found it!"' she says.

The plot Phil had found was a 550-square-metre concrete reservoir. It had been specially constructed in the early 1950s for the filming of some of the scenes in *The Dam Busters*, the film about British pilots who dropped the famous bouncing bombs on German dams during the war.

The reservoir, which had since been used in other films, had been derelict for some years, drained of water. Not only was it roughly the right size for the construction of the house; it was built on proper foundations, which meant that there was no need to excavate and create a raft foundation – a saving of both time and money.

Only 100 metres away was the huge, new George Lucas stage, named after the director of *Star Wars* (which is filmed there) – a massive red and grey building housing an enormous studio and three floors of other facilities: dressing rooms, offices and storage space.

The next day, Helen and Petrina met Phil at the site.

'He stood in the middle of the tank, held his arms out and said, "Do you think it could work?"' says Petrina. 'We both said "Yes, yes, yes." It is such a good location. From my point of view it had everything we needed – a studio, and plenty of office space. Phil, Helen and Gigi were thinking about wonderful houses – I was worrying about practical things like whether there was a sufficient power supply, how much we would have to spend, or how many phones and computers I'd have to install.'

Helen was just as enthusiastic. 'It gave us the space we need to fit the house and garden inside the tank area; and there was a studio close by, but not too close. There's a 24-hour supermarket next door – Tesco's again, just as we had at the last house. And there are catering facilities on site, which is important when you've got a huge staff.'

Gigi, who didn't see the site until a few days later, was also very impressed.

'I think it was the cappuccino machine that did it for me – but there were a few other reasons.'

One of those other reasons was the fact that it is a studio complex, and the people who run it understand the problems that come with television programmes and films. What's more, they were endlessly helpful.

'It was great because they didn't look at all shocked when I said we needed to dig a huge trench for the cables, that sort of thing,' says Petrina, whose first job, having decided that everyone loved the site, was to negotiate a deal on it.

Helen agrees. 'We'd seen so many places that had no infrastructure, and here we had everything we needed, and people who understood and wanted to help. When we said we'd need to knock a hole in the studio wall they didn't say, "I don't know if you can do that." They understood, they spoke our language.'

Elstree Film Studios has a history dating back to 1926, and was central to the early days of the British film industry. The list of films made there is impressive: as well as all the *Star Wars* films there are classics like Stanley Kubrick's *The Shining*, which was shot

TALKING TOUGH

No more Mr Nice Guy. *Big Brother* has turned hard man: the rules of the game have been toughened up this year.

The contestants were told before they stepped over the threshold that this year they will be issued with official warnings if they break any of the serious rules of the game. And there's a 'three strikes and you're out' rule, which means that three official warnings result in instant eviction, with no appeal.

Another crime that will definitely result in an official warning is not giving a good reason for a nomination – and a good reason means not pulling any punches.

Bad reasons are the sort Darren gave in *BB1*: 'I think she would like to go home to see her family,' or the sort that Dean gave in *BB2*, which the other housemates picked up from him: 'I have lined the others up in my head in a queue, and I'm nominating the two who are at the end of the queue.'

'What we want are the real reasons why they want certain housemates out, not excuses that are engineered to prevent them having to say anything nasty or critical about anyone else,' says Phil.

Big Brother has also been meaner about what the housemates are allowed to take in with them. For the first time this year, no books and no musical instruments are allowed.

'You can hide behind a book or with a guitar,' says Phil. 'Housemates can bury themselves away for hours, not interacting with anyone else, lost in their own world. They won't be able to do that this year.'

Games are also banned, and the number of magazines is limited to one per housemate, and even these were confiscated after Lee and Adele used them to pass secret messages.

almost entirely at Elstree, *The Railway Children*, *Look Back in Anger*, *The Dam Busters*, and loads more. A chequered financial history in recent years means that in 1996 the studio complex was taken over by the local council, Hertsmere Borough Council – the only council in Britain that owns a film studio.

When Phil, Helen and Petrina made their first visits, the latest *Star Wars* epic, *Attack of the Clones*, was being finished.

'It was supposed to be a closed set but the big studio door was open, and we all poked our heads round to see what they were doing,' says Phil. 'When they spotted us the hydraulic door swung shut, but it was very exciting just to have a look. And there was a pod racer parked in the car park, just along from Del Boy's yellow three-wheeler, with Trotter's Independent Traders written on it.'

'We were like kids,' says Helen. 'We were peering round at the big blue screen they had up, with marks on it to show where the aliens were flying about. There's something terribly glamorous about film. And there was also this amazing sense of history, that we were going to work where so many great films had been made.'

The distance between the tank and the studio was crucial to the decision to build the house at Elstree. It's important that when the contestants are evicted, they have to walk past the cheering crowds and face the huge explosion of camera flashes before reaching the studio.

'We knew we couldn't replicate the bridge they had to cross at Three Mills. That scene became iconographic; it's the visual memory everyone carries with them of *Big Brother*,' says Gigi. 'But it couldn't be any old walk – we couldn't have the studio ten feet from the house. There has to be a sense of making a journey from the cloistered world of the *Big Brother* house back to their old life, with the audience throwing reality into their faces. There has to be the moment when they are caught like a startled deer in headlights as all the press photographers' flashes go off – a chance to be momentarily reunited with friends and family before being whisked into the studio by Davina.

'In a funny kind of way, that space they walk across is as important as the other two spaces, the studio and the house.'

Within a couple of days, Markus Blee, the house designer, had his first sight of the place where it would stand.

Designing the *Big Brother* house requires a particular combination of skills and talent; and Markus Blee, who came in fresh to create the brand-new house for *Big Brother 3*, has them all. On one level, he had to design a fully functional house to accommodate twelve people: a more demanding architectural challenge than coming up with a standard family home. On another level, what he was designing was a television set – a set that is in constant use for nine weeks and which can have very little maintenance work carried out on it in that time, and with a phenomenal number of camera angles to be taken into consideration. And on a third level, he was coming up with an aesthetically interesting and stimulating environment – one which will, he hopes, amuse, soothe and provoke the housemates throughout their stay.

Markus was the ideal choice. He has a background in conventional architecture, having worked on a diverse range of buildings from churches to golf clubs to housing estates; he has studied interior architecture; he's worked in television and film set design for the past twelve years; and is also an artist who has had his work exhibited in galleries around Britain and has two sculptures on permanent public display. *Big Brother* was a good choice for him, too – the *BB3* house is the only project he has ever worked on where all his skills and talents have been needed at the same time.

'That has made it fun, and challenging, ' says Markus, whose television credits include *The Priory*, the Johnny Vaughan shows and *TFI Friday*. 'I love being diverse, multi-faceted, and this project has incorporated architecture, set design, interior design and even, in my interpretation of the interior, my art work. I've always felt that design is a holistic thing, and extends from the shape of a room down to the smallest detail like the design of the door handles.

'This project is such a hybrid, bringing together all the fields I'm involved in, so I was keen to do it from the day I was approached. The whole concept of the show is so fascinating: my job has been to design a laboratory for the study of human beings.'

He wasn't daunted by the prospect of creating a house from scratch. Once he had a site for the building, Markus started pulling all his ideas into a coherent design. Looking across the abandoned water tank on a dreary November day was not, he says, dispiriting.

'I didn't feel fazed by it. I'm used to the immediacy of television, things having to happen quickly. A house this size should have taken ten to twelve months to build, but I knew we'd have to do it in two to three months. I knew there were bound to be problems, but there's always a way round them. It's no use panicking: it fetters progress. So from the first sight I had a positive outlook. It was, after all our searching, close to ideal.'

The next thing on Petrina's agenda was to get planning permission, which meant that Markus had to adapt and finalize his plans. Because this house is a more permanent structure than the first one, it has had to conform to building regulations.

'It's been a learning curve for me,' says Petrina. 'I know more about building regulations and fire regulations than you ever normally need to know working in fluffy television. I've learned about waterproofing roofs, the strength of foundations, and all about sewage, water and power supplies. The main effect of the building regulations is that we have to have air-conditioning in the bedrooms, as they don't have windows.

'The planning authority have been very helpful. There was only one objection to our plans, from a councillor who was naturally worried about the effect that our large Friday night audiences would have on the town. But we reassured her, and she withdrew her objection.'

The *Big Brother* team is aware of the impact of the 1,000-strong crowd who come to cheer and jeer at the evictions. But they are lucky: the people of Borehamwood, where the studios are located, are used to the eccentricities of film and television work. Just down the road from the *Big Brother* house are the BBC studios where *EastEnders* is made, and *Who Wants to be a Millionaire?* is in the adjacent studio to *BB3*. When *Star Wars* first came to town, the locals got used to seeing Wookies walking down the High Street to lunch; and until last year, *Top of the Pops* was made at Elstree, bringing with it an audience of excitable teenagers.

'The locals couldn't have been more welcoming,' says Helen. 'Lots of local people work in television or film, so they're sympathetic. And the town is proud of its history and its connections with the industry. But we still need to be sensitive, and that's why we have such good security arrangements on eviction nights.'

Residents and those who work at the studio site are being invited to the first few live evictions, and sixth formers from the local comprehensive were given an exclusive guided tour of the new house before the contestants moved in. Petrina has spent time in meetings with the local police and councillors, assuaging their worries.

The planning application went in on 17 December, and by mid-January, the team had permission to start work. The first thing for Petrina to organize was the digging of a £35,000 trench, which would house the 50-60 cables that supply power to the house and feed pictures from it.

'We had to bury them all, for health and safety reasons. If they were above ground it would be dangerous – especially on Friday nights, when the audience will be flooding into the yard next to the house.'

The massive rope of cables surfaces at the side of the studio, where it threads through a specially made hole.

While Petrina was organizing the trench, Markus was hard at work on the house itself.

'I realized immediately I saw the site that I could build the house on stilts, leaving space underneath it, in the cavity that was the water tank, for all the plumbing and cables to be fed through. You can actually crawl under the house – there's a space about three feet high – which means we can carry out essential maintenance and make changes.'

Sump pumps underneath have drained away all the accumulated rainwater, and are kept in place to make sure the cavity beneath the house stays dry. The whole structure is within the original water tank, which to some extent governed the size and shape of the building; but it was a big enough area for the design to be relatively unaffected.

The first major decision was what construction material to use. In order to get the building up rapidly, Markus opted for a pre-fabricated system called Sip panels, which consist of insulation sandwiched between two pieces of board, each panel strong enough to be load-bearing. It's a very flexible system, manufactured by Woodco, a company based in Inverness. But the panels didn't come from Scotland – they had to be shipped from Canada, and arrived on 17 January complete with a team of five Canadian construction

WICKED *LITTLE BROTHER*

This year, *Big Brother*'s naughty *Little Brother* sneaked in and got there first. The first sight viewers had of the new house came half an hour before Davina McCall launched *BB3* on Channel 4. It was on *Big Brother*'s *Little Brother*, the magazine programme that takes viewers behind the scenes in *Big Brother* land, and it gave E4 viewers a taste of what was to come over the following weeks.

BBLB, fronted again by Dermot O'Leary, is a cross between a news magazine programme and a fan club. Monday to Thursday, on E4, viewers can listen to experts, take part in discussions, meet the people who work behind the scenes, ask the evicted housemate questions, and catch up with the very latest action from the house. On Fridays and Sundays, Channel 4 viewers can join in the fun, with an early evening *BBLB* slot on Friday to kick off eviction night, and a special Sunday afternoon show where the evicted housemates give their first full televised interview to Dermot.

'*BBLB* is a mixture of things,' says Gavin Henderson, executive producer. 'Essentially we're a news programme, so if anything exciting breaks in the house we abandon all our plans and cover it. And like a news programme, we get experts in to comment on it and interpret it. The joy of the house is that there are always a multitude of stories going on, even on the days when it seems boring.

'But we're also a magazine show, with lots of interviews. We've got the most exclusive access to anyone on the *Big Brother* team. Want to know about the chickens? We know who to ask. Want to know about the body language? We know who to ask.'

There's an irreverence about the show – it really is like a naughty little brother trying to occasionally trip up his big brother.

'We're not frightened of poking fun at our *Big Brother*. We love him, but if he cocks something up we'll be laughing along with the viewers.'

The immediacy of the live show is a great plus – especially for viewers.

'They know that when we go over to see things happening in the house, it's happening now. With the Channel 4 programmes, they're a day behind. Viewers really love the rawness of live television, particularly the tele-literate viewers of *Big Brother*. They like to know it's happening right now – these are the people who would rather watch the housemates all asleep on E4 than watch a show they believe has been edited and refined. They know that the Channel 4 programme is half an hour out of 24 hours in the life of the house. So *Little Brother*, which pokes around behind the scenes, reacts to news live, and tells it like it is, is the sort of programme they love.'

Little Brother was such a success last year that this year the team is much bigger. The new live Sunday programme on Channel 4 will give viewers who don't have digital television their first chance to see how the housemates have reacted to the Saturday night task results, which can change the dynamics of the house so profoundly.

'Some of the things viewers loved from last year are back again,' says Sean Murphy, *BBLB* series producer. 'We've brought the housemate who was evicted back into the studio for a week, as a guest on the show. And we're getting even more phone calls, e-mails and text messages from viewers than last year. And we've expanded the bits where Dermot goes into the gallery to talk to the producers – viewers loved that glimpse of how a programme is made, and it's quite mind-blowing when you see that huge array of screens behind him. People want to know the mechanics of how a programme like *Big Brother* is made.

'New this year is a ticker tape rolling over the screen with news updates. And we've got lots of quizzes and competitions, with winners getting the chance to come to a live eviction. Celebrities are popping in to talk to Dermot – but they're coming because they are *Big Brother* fans, not because they are celebrities.'

Even no news from the house fascinates *Little Brother*.

WICKED *LITTLE BROTHER continued*

'Sometimes not a lot happens at all. But it's somehow totally fascinating, and little things like the bread getting burnt become so important. When it's boring, we aren't frightened to say so.

'And that's the big difference between us and the Channel 4 programmes. They don't comment on or interpret what's happening in the house. Only the psychologists are allowed to do that. The commentary is very straight and factual, so that the viewers make up their own minds about what's going on.

'But on *Little Brother* we can go "Ooooh, did you see what she just did..." Just like the viewers do at home.'

---

workers who looked exactly how you imagine lumberjacks to look. By the time they arrived, Markus and the three-strong design team had moved into offices on the second floor of the studio building.

'Everything was shipped from Lake Ontario,' says Petrina. 'It was only after we'd ordered it that Phil said to me "Do I have to worry about ships sinking in mid-Atlantic?" I'd been trying not to think of those sorts of risks, but I rang Woodco and they said, "We haven't lost one yet!" I'm glad to say it didn't happen – but we did have one disaster, when one of the three shipments was mistakenly sent back to Canada from the docks at Liverpool. Woodco had to fly it over to be with us in time, but the Canadian workforce were great and didn't let it hold things up.'

'They bashed it out in amazing time,' says Markus. 'They would work eighteen hours a day if necessary. Their job was to get it done by the middle of April, and they were determined to do it. A strong incentive was wanting to get back to their wives and children in Canada as soon as they could, and that suited us. They knew what they were working on, although Canada has not had its own *Big Brother*.

'What they created is a watertight envelope, which acts effectively as a studio. The roof is made of timber panels, and beneath it there is a loft space we can access to lower or adjust microphones and other technical equipment. When they left we had the framework of the house, but only the exterior: what happened inside was up to us. The walls were ready to be clad, but I had to decide what to clad them with.'

Working alongside the Canadians were plumbers and electricians, installing the services needed in the house and all the lights and cameras. Luckily, this year the house has mains sewage laid on; at the first house there was a cesspit because there was no provision for sewage.

Early in January, before work started on the house, Channel 4 screened a documentary about other *Big Brother* houses around the world. Davina presented it – and she was filmed standing on the empty site at Elstree.

'I was sitting at home watching it on a Saturday evening,' says Petrina. 'Davina was saying how hard it was to imagine that in five months' time there would be a house on this derelict land, and I shouted at the telly, "I know I've only got five months! You don't have to tell me!" Somehow, in the office with my schedule of dates in front of me, it all seemed doable. But seeing it on the screen in its untouched state – that was frightening.'

Every week, she and Markus would go through the schedule to make sure they were on track.

'There were no real panics, although there were occasional days when lots of little things went wrong. It was the kind of project where, if we'd had an extra couple of months, we'd have filled them. But because we didn't, everyone worked incredibly hard and got it done.'

The completed house cost between £400,000 and £500,000 – pretty much what a house of that size would cost in Hertfordshire.

As well as getting a house ready, Petrina had to mastermind the conversion of the huge George Lucas sound stage into the *Big Brother* studio.

'It was a vast empty shell to begin with. The first thing we did was move in some portable cabins to house some of the edit suites and the web team. Next came an edit truck, brought in by Resolution, the company that provides our edit facilities and editors. Then Roll to Record, who are responsible for supplying and manning the cameras and sound equipment, brought a truck in and started to build controls for all the cameras.'

They also built the gallery, where 50 monitors show the producers and directors every angle of life in the *Big Brother* goldfish bowl.

Finally, studio sets for the live Friday night shows and for *Big Brother's Little Brother* were built.

'That bit seems easy – it's normal, it's telly as we know it,' says Petrina. 'Everything else on *Big Brother* is unique.'

CHAPTER TWO

THE TAPE MOUNTAIN

Everyone expected a lot of tapes. Nobody expected the deluge that hit the *Big Brother* office in Shepherd's Bush during the second half of January and beginning of February. Nobody forecast mail vans pulling up outside the building three times a day, each one filled with 70 or more sacks. Nobody envisaged producers going square-eyed in front of screens, each of them racing to meet a target of viewing 70 tapes per day. And nobody, but nobody, could ever have predicted the bizarre, wonderful, clever, funny, disgusting, sickening, delightful, professional, amateurish, boring, riveting, elaborate, inventive, surreal content of so many of the tapes.

It all kicked off after the launch programme went out on Channel 4 on 4 January. Would-be contestants were told they could download an application form from the web, or phone a hotline to have one sent to them. A staggering 151,000 forms went out, which was the first inkling anyone had that *Big Brother 3* would be even bigger than in the past two years.

But it wasn't warning enough. After all, everyone was being asked to fill in a six-page form and send back a two-minute video tape of themselves. That's a lot to ask, and would weed out loads of them... And lots of them would have downloaded the form several times, wouldn't they? Last year, 5,000 videos were sent in. This year, maybe it would be a thousand or so more – a lot, but *Big Brother* could cope...

Well, that was the thinking at the time. And at first everything seemed on course. Sallie Clement, one of two senior producers on *Big Brother*, started work in January, and her first job was to devise a method of logging and viewing all the tapes that came in.

'It was calm and manageable in the early days. We were getting three sackfuls a day, each sack with about thirty tapes in it. We knew it would build up, but we felt we could handle it all without any problems.'

Sallie immediately set up a system for logging the tapes. The country was split into the seven regions where auditions would eventually be held, and a colour code was introduced – for instance, a red sticker on a tape meant it was a London-based contestant, a green sticker meant Manchester. Then, within the regional classification, every tape was given a number, preceded by a letter for the region: N for Newcastle, E for Edinburgh etc.

'Tapes always go missing, and find their way into the wrong boxes. The colour codes meant we could spot them easily,' says Sallie. 'It was a laborious job, putting a sticker on the tape, a sticker on the first page of the form, allocating a number and then inputting certain basic information about the applicant into the database: their name, contact phone numbers, region, whether they were married or divorced.'

Two production runners, Vickie Ager and Roman Green, worked full time on the database, logging the tapes as they arrived.

'At first it was going oh-so-smoothly. Every tape they logged went into the appropriate "to view" box, and two producers would work through them, reading the application forms and whacking the cassettes into the machines.

'We had one special box labelled "Vidiots" – this was for all the tapes that came in without any name or form attached to them. Some people sent us the form and a three-page letter explaining why they hadn't sent a video, but we couldn't consider them. If they didn't make a tape, they fell at the first hurdle. This box also contained all the tapes that were made on odd systems, not VHS. We'd clearly stated what we wanted, so if they didn't provide it, it was tough, but we had to reject them. Tape-viewing was a bit like a factory production line, and we couldn't cope with anything that didn't work on our system. There were also quite a few who hadn't checked the tape before sending it, and it was either a blank picture with sound, or just silent pictures,' says Sallie.

The producers who viewed the tapes graded them from A to D.

A meant the applicant looked outstanding. It was a very rare award – only a few videos out of the whole 10,000 which eventually flooded in received a straight A. B was for definitely worth seeing, and there were lots of those; C meant a distinct possibility; and D was for those who might be good in the mix, even if they weren't the most exciting applicants.

'The Ds were those who could possibly be good "glue" people, holding the group together, fundamental to the dynamics of the group, but not front runners.'

The rest went into a huge "No" box – or, to be accurate, many boxes, each containing fifty tapes. As these boxes filled they were moved out of the cramped office space, and, as Sallie puts it, 'condemned to outer darkness – or at least, to a cupboard down the corridor – never to be looked at again.'

The producers were able to refine their grades with pluses and minuses, to show just how borderline or how good someone was, and they also added one-line comments to jog their memories of what was on the tape – for example, 'girl wearing cowboy outfit from Stoke-on-Trent'. The team developed their own shorthand, using acronyms like 'B and B' for 'bright and bubbly'. They also added a little smiley face symbol to the forms of anyone who sent in a weird, funny, shocking or unbelievable video. (These were later compiled into fourteen hours of tape which was shown on E4 continually during the day in the two weeks before the start of *Big Brother*.)

'Obviously the grading was subjective – one person's D is another person's B. But it gave us a structure to work on when we started organizing the auditions. Everyone understood what we were looking for, although it's hard to put it into words: we wanted people who were engaging, watchable, with that X factor which makes you stay glued to the screen when they're on. There were no other rules. They could be any age, size, background. They could be comic or serious, academic or empty-headed. It's an elusive thing,' says Sallie.

Phil describes it as 'a popularity contest based on personality. It's not about being able to do anything. It's about who you are and what you are, a really indefinable thing.'

In the first few days, two producers viewing 50 tapes each per day could handle everything that came in. But within a week the number of tapes arriving was up to 300 a day, then 450, and eventually three lorryloads were arriving, bringing in over 1,000 tapes a day. Sallie began to worry.

'It suddenly looked like we just couldn't get through them. I'd made sure we kept up to speed, because I knew we would be hit by an avalanche – but I had no idea how big that avalanche would be. We'd got provisional dates for auditions, and I was afraid we'd only be through half the videos by then. The office was completely mad. Every time I looked around there were more sacks. We were tripping over sacks and boxes – the space just wasn't big enough. The logging system was getting unwieldy, and in the end we had to split it into three, with London having a database of its own, and two other regional ones each containing three regions.

'The producers were viewing way into the evenings, and their rate was up to 70 a day – but there was obviously no way they could do it all.'

Two more producers were drafted in to help, Helen and Gigi also spent any spare time they had viewing tapes, and eventually even more producers joined the team crammed into the small office, so that there were as many as ten people viewing tapes.

'Even then, I was just praying it was going to be all right,' says Sallie. 'Every time we seemed to be getting on top of it, another van would arrive full of sacks. And eventually we got to the stage where we had such a big team viewing them that we caught up with the logging system – there were loads of new tapes arriving, but we couldn't view them because they hadn't been logged. So there was one afternoon when at around 3.00pm the whole machine screeched to a halt and everyone was sitting around. So we brought in Jess Bendien and Susy Price to help with the logging, but it wasn't possible to have more than one person inputting into the database at any time.'

Despite the amount of work they had to get through, the logging had to be done very accurately.

'One wrong number, letter or sticker, one surname spelt wrongly, and we'd be stuffed. One incorrectly filed bit of paper and we'd be up the creek,' says Sallie. 'Some days it was really disheartening, arriving early at work and there were already new sacks sitting there.

MOST POPULAR FIRST NAMES FOR *BB* APPLICANTS	
Boys:	**Girls:**
1. David	Sarah
2. Mark	Emma
3. Steven	Claire
4. John	Michelle
5. Paul	Louise
6. James	Kelly
7. Andrew	Rebecca
8. Christopher	Samantha
9. Matthew	Amanda
10. Michael	Zoe

One morning I arrived just as they were being delivered, and for a second or two I was tempted to stick four sacks in the boot of my car, drive away and dump them. It occurred to me that nobody would know. But the winner could be in those sacks. However much work was involved, we all wanted it to be a really good show – we wanted to find the good videos.'

The pressure of work may have been frenetic, but the room was strangely quiet, with all the producers perched in front of monitors with headphones clamped over their ears, viewing their own pile of tapes. Occasional shouts of surprise and laughter would go up, and sometimes the producers would hand videos across to one another for a second opinion.

'I was sitting opposite Wendy Rattray,' says Sean Murphy. Both he and Wendy are senior producers. 'We'd show each other the ones we liked. And sometimes we'd show them just for a laugh, because they were so terrible or so weird. If you got a really good one, everybody would crowd round.'

At the end of each day, there would be a short viewing session attended by Phil, Helen and Gigi of all the really good ones. Even at this early stage, it was a team effort, and everybody's views were canvassed.

Paul Osborne's first day on viewing produced a great result.

'The first video I put forward to be viewed at the evening session was the best one I saw in all those weeks of viewing. It was Alison, who went on to be one of the contestants in the house,' he says. 'I never met her at any of the auditions or interviews, but it's nice to know that I was the very first person to spot her potential.'

For Sean, too, there are a couple who really stuck out in his memory. 'They didn't make it into the house, but they were into the final shortlist.'

The viewers nicknamed the room 'Mike Baldwin's factory' because 'it was like being in a sweatshop'. Sallie, with deadlines to meet, says she was 'the Sergeant Major from hell'. She would e-mail messages to everyone telling them how much work they had to get through:

'1,720 tapes viewed last week. The target was 1,650. We are down to 3,490 tapes – and more arriving by every post! We can do it! We have two weeks from today.'

'Still to process: estimated 80-100 sacks unopened, plus 27 opened, and 50 boxes full. That's 4,600-5,200 tapes still to view. This week really is crucial! If we continue at this pace by the end of Thursday next week all the tapes will have been graded and most will be up to date on the database. Yeeeees!'

'I turned into Miss Mathematician, always doing multiplication and division sums which involved the number of sacks multiplied by the number of tapes in a sack divided by the number of people viewing, divided by how many days we had left before auditions. I was running a mail office, and it was all so anal – the administration was so important. But even though I wasn't viewing tapes during the day, I always saw the selection made by the producers at the end of the day, and that reminded me what it was all about!'

Everyone, from the executive producer downwards, was lending a hand. 'If anyone had a spare twenty minutes they'd simply open the packages,' she says. 'In the end, we couldn't even cope with that, and I brought in relays of youngsters who'd written to us asking for work experience – what they got was experience opening sacks and envelopes!'

Twelve of them came in all, keen young graduates hoping to break into television.

'We were only able to offer one of them a job, but the others were rewarded with a trip round the house before the contestants went in.'

To keep her team hard at it, tallies of how many videos they'd viewed would be read out at the end of the day, and prizes given by Phil for the best scores.

'It was all very jokey. I was given a plastic hammer full of sweets, someone got a pineapple, once it was a coconut. And Sallie got a toy gun to fire at us when we weren't working fast enough,' says Sean. 'And we'd all get chocolate bars, just to keep us going. If we hadn't made our target of 70 we all came up with amazing elaborate excuses, which nobody believed.'

Other prizes included a Barbie doll, an Action Man, a plastic bracelet, and a bag full of lollipops.

'It was all a lot of fun, but naming and shaming the ones who simply weren't getting through the videos fast enough kept them hard at it. And they were so damned good, they put up with it all and they really shifted through those tapes,' says Sallie.

The videos were astonishing. Some people had gone to enormous lengths to make one: one announced that he had bought a £340 video camera specially to make the tape. But the prize for ingenuity had to go to a guy who whispered into the microphone because he was secretly filming the video at the home of a girl he was spending the night with, while she slept – and he was only there because he knew she had a video camera.

There was a great deal of nudity: people on the sofa nude, playing football nude, running down the street nude, one man naked except for an accordion in a field full of cows, a naked girl smearing mud over her body, lots of women with tassels on their breasts doing stripping routines, a man jumping about on a pogo stick without his clothes.

'Boobs and bottoms with PICK ME written on them in big letters were a constant theme,' says Sean. 'The first time you see it you smile, but when you're on your thirtieth set of boobs that day it all gets a bit stale.

'Some would start off naked, which meant you knew before you started that they were a no-no, but some would make a really good video and only at the last minute would they stand up and reveal they were naked or stripped down to a thong. You'd look at it and think, "Why did you do that? You've just blown your chances!"'

The favourite fashion item for the nearly-naked men was a posing pouch with an animal's head at the vital spot. There were lots of elephants, naturally, and an astonishing number of horses.

'I must have seen seven or eight different men running around wearing nothing but a horse thong that neighs!' says Deborah Sargeant.

There were lots of people sitting on the loo, a few who simulated sex, the occasional masturbation scene and one man who certainly got the attention of the producers (for the wrong reasons) when he pierced his own penis on camera.

The aren't-I-brave-I'm-being-filmed-on-the-loo scenes were a particular turn-off for the video viewers. 'Especially when there were realistic sound effects,' says Paul. 'At least one man took the loo to the top of a hill, which made it slightly more acceptable because it was surreal. But most of them were just filmed in their own loo at home. Gross. I guess they think they're proving to us that they don't mind being filmed in the loo – but the whole point is that we never screen pictures of people in the loo, we only have a camera in there to make sure they don't have secret meetings. And we really, really don't want to watch pictures of people on the loo.'

This year there were also a lot of people cooking, or pretending to cook. 'They'd be saying "Hey, Big Brother, I can cook!" So what? We're not running a cookery show,' says Sean.

The producers who viewed all the tapes have come up with a checklist of tips for making *Big Brother* videos. It is mainly a list of things NOT to do:

● DO NOT play music in the background while you're speaking – we won't be able to hear a word you're saying.
● DO NOT send in your own version of a TV show, or pictures of you reading the news. *Big Brother* isn't looking for newsreaders or presenters, but for real people.
● DO NOT record more than two minutes. It's no good doing twenty minutes of cabaret – there's only time to look at two minutes.

- DO NOT put special effects on. It may prove you're clever with the video camera (or you know a man who is) but if it doesn't give a clear picture of what you look like, it's no use.
- NO POEMS. Loads of applicants thought it was clever to write a rap about their *Big Brother* aspirations. One contestant intoned 'I'll do something wacky and sing you a rap, but it's only for fun and it's really quite crap'.
- NO SINGING
- DO NOT re-enact scenes from other *Big Brother* series – it's new ideas, new angles, a fresh approach that count. On the same theme, DO NOT do impersonations or remakes of famous scenes from films, because this isn't an audition for acting talent.
- DO NOT plaster your video with the *Big Brother* theme tune – it's a great tune, but everyone in the production team has heard it many, many times, and they want to hear what you've got to say.
- DO NOT stand 50 metres away from the camera.
- DO use either blue or black ink to fill in the form. It is hard to read photocopies of forms written in rainbow colours – and a form that can't be read gets an immediate NO.
- DO make sure the video shows you clearly. Chins, talking belly-buttons, and Blair Witch nostril shots don't work. 'Loads of people thought they'd do a Blair Witch type film – it got very boring, but it also usually meant we couldn't see them properly,' says Sallie.
- DO rewind your tape and label it clearly. 'You'd be amazed how many didn't bother to rewind. It sounds like a small thing, but when you are watching 70 tapes a day, it's really irritating to have to wait while it winds back,' says Sean.
- DO NOT film yourself on the loo.
- DO NOT run around naked.
- DO NOT scream 'Pick Me' at the camera, or write it anywhere on your body. We know that you want to be picked – you wouldn't be making the tape otherwise.
- DO NOT say 'I would have done a better video but I ran out of time/tape/props/money'. We really don't care what you would have done: we're judging you on what you have done.

But just in case this all sounds very negative, there is one DO on the list:

- DO be inventive. 'After watching literally thousands of tapes, we are really turned off by people who sit around looking bored – we like people who give us something different and clever,' says Sean. 'And don't be put off entering whatever you want to do on your video. If you look at the application videos of the housemates in *Big Brother 3*, you'll find that between them they broke at least half of these rules, and they still got in.'

The final number of videos viewed was 9,166. More were delivered for several days, even weeks, after the closing date, but they were not opened and viewed.

'That would have been unfair on all those who took the trouble to get theirs in on time,' says Sallie.

So that's another DO for the checklist: DO get your video in on time.

Out of the total, 5,621 were boys and 3,515 were girls. Of these, 4,274 were single, nearly 2,000 were in a relationship, over 1,000 were married or co-habiting, and a strange 452 said they were both single and in a relationship. A lot of the men were gay – thanks to the success of Brian in 2001, every would-be gay comedian in Britain seemed to apply.

Although *Big Brother* is not ageist, it's a young person's game. Only 51 people who applied were over the age of 45, and the majority of those came from London. The most popular age range was 18-24, and two-thirds of all applicants were under 30.

Almost half of all applications came from the London area, with Manchester next, and Birmingham third. Despite having a winner from Northern Ireland last year, Belfast had the smallest number of applicants by far – although the figures are not entirely representative, because the applicants were put into the regions where they are now living, not where they come from.

Overall, the standard was very high.

'It may sound as though we are being very picky with all our complaints,' says Sean. 'But it's easier to say what was wrong than it is to say what was right. There were loads of good ones, people who were engaging and watchable.'

After days of watching back-to-back tapes, the viewing team had square eyes and could not face watching television in their own time.

'The television did NOT go on,' says Sean. 'And if anyone suggested watching a video, I think I would have shot them. I was cross-eyed by the end of the day. I didn't want to look at anything.'

Paul says, 'I travelled home on the Tube with one of the others one evening and we tried to think what we could do without looking at anything square. We couldn't watch television or go to a film, but if we wanted to eliminate all square things then we had to rule out books, magazines, CD cases, and even the microwave. But, thankfully, bottles of wine are not square.'

They also started looking at people in the street or on the bus or train differently.

'I'd be weighing them up, thinking, "She'd be OK, she's very watchable",' says Sean.

For Paul, 'I'd put him/her in the house' has become a general-purpose phrase of approval. 'Sometimes when I'm out I see people and I look at them and think: "Have I seen you before, or have I just seen your video?" You look at so many faces a day that it becomes confusing.'

Every so often, about once a week, the producers had a half-hour break from viewing tapes – to play games. James Milnes, who joined the *Big Brother* team in January, is the Taskmaster for the house: his job is to come up with the tasks that the contestants do live every Saturday night, and the mini-tasks they are given during the week. He was drafted in to help view tapes, but at the same time he was coming up with the games that the producers would use when they went out on the road to audition the applicants.

'I had to compile the Games Audition Bible, which gave the producers a selection of different kinds of games they could use at the auditions. Some were ice-breakers, some were team games, some required physical skills, some got the applicants to reveal a great deal about themselves.

BIG BROTHER'S BROTHERS

They're all at it. – 21 countries, 448 contestants, five million Euros in prize money... The world is *Big Brother* mad.

And some of it is very mad. Much, much madder than our home-grown *Big Brother*. There are only two countries in the world where there has been no sex in the *Big Brother* house – that's us and America, although how close P.J. and Jade came we'll probably never know. But out of 10,000 hours of television, sex only accounts for about 30 minutes – and it's not the most exciting 30 minutes, either. Still, there have been some staggering records: Rodney and Annette, in Norway, managed it six times in one day; and Andres in Holland managed to seduce five of the six women in the house, including Kelly, who looked all woman but was born a boy. The Belgians had such a marathon drink-fuelled sex session one day that the TV company wouldn't broadcast it: they were at it in the pool, in bed, and one girl even managed it on her own. The producers had to ask them to sober up and quieten down. And viewers certainly aren't impressed by the sexual prowess of the contestants: out of the nearly 50 winners worldwide, only three have had sex in the house.

Ruth Wrigley, Head of Entertainment at Endemol, says:

'*Big Brother* isn't about sex. At least, it's not in Britain. It's about the soap opera of relationships. If sex happened, we would be allowed to show it, but where sex has happened in *Big Brother* in other countries, it has actually been rather dull. What we find is that people are true to their national characteristics. The Scandinavians have sex like rabbits, the Germans are efficient at the task, the French are romantic and the Spanish are fiery. But the Brits are very British, and sit around talking and drinking tea.'

The Brits have been pretty buttoned up, literally: there's been a lot more nudity in most of the other shows. In Portugal, there was a very provocative striptease, watched by 90 per cent of the total television audience. In Switzerland, a male stripper was brought in as a birthday present for one of the girls. And in loads of countries there have been naked bathing sessions and near-naked frolics.

And we're pretty cool, calm, and law-abiding, too. Housemates here do shout at each other now and then, but you should see what they get up to in other countries. They quarrel with each other – the Norwegians nearly came to blows over their shopping list, the Italians yelled at each other at full volume, and in Portugal one housemate had to be thrown out for attacking another. And they also quarrel with *Big Brother*, sulking and getting angry over rules they don't like. In Denmark they went on strike, and seven of them managed to escape. Five of them agreed to go back – but only on condition they were allowed weekly family visits.

Across the world, the *Big Brother* hothouse has allowed 53 relationships to blossom, there have been eight marriages and two babies, including one born to our own Claire and Tom from *BB1*. And contestants don't only marry each other: in Sweden one married the presenter of the show. Of course, Davina's already married, but there's always Dermot...

'Ideas for them came from everywhere – the producers came up with lots of them. They have to be different each year, because some applicants make it through to the auditions in successive years, so we don't want it to seem stale,' says James. 'My job was to collate them and make sure we had all the props we needed to send out with the audition teams. I needed to make sure we had enough games of each different type, so that the producers could have a choice. They all developed their favourites, but when you've been auditioning all week, sometimes it's just nice to change the games towards the end of the day.'

Everyone was roped in to test out the audition games.

'It was only half an hour a week, so it didn't borrow too much time from the tape viewing. I felt a bit daft at first, when there was so much hard work going on, asking them all to stop and play games. But it became a welcome break.'

'It was great to run off and do silly things for a while,' says Sean. 'It provided light relief we all needed. And it was very interesting. Even though we were all working together and knew each other, it's amazing what you learn in those team games. Some of the bizarre facts that came out...'

At the end of the mammoth viewing sessions, the team had reduced the number of videos down to 2,500, and these were the applicants who were invited to take part in an audition. Before the viewing was over, Sallie booked halls and rooms for the auditions, and then her team hit the phones, letting applicants know – often with only a day or two's notice – that they had been selected.

The venues had to be places with rooms big enough to hold 30 or so people, with space for them to play silly games. They also had to be private: no windows on to the street, no rooms on the ground floor, and close at hand there had to be another room that could be used for filming interviews. And, of course, they had to be reasonably close to public transport.

'Everyone was hitting the phones, making arrangements. We all had a stream of patter. We'd say, "I know it's really short notice but if you could get here..." and almost all of them did. It's amazing how many of them reorganized their lives around it: I think there were probably quite a lot who reported in sick to their jobs! Loads of them rang us back – they were all so excited when they took the call, and many of them realized when the phone went down that they'd not really listened to the directions or the address for the auditions. They were also told not to tell anyone except perhaps someone really close, who they could trust. This was probably the hardest thing they had to do: naturally, they wanted to share the news that they'd been selected. But we made it plain to them that everything had to remain secret.

'It was a mammoth organizational task, ringing 2,500 people and arranging times for them all to turn up. Last year we did two rounds of auditions on different days, but this year we decided to speed the process up by seeing lots of people – as many as a hundred – in the morning, in four-hour-long shifts, and then invite back for the afternoon the ones who had come through as interesting. It means we saw a lot more people, but for initially shorter auditions.'

Sallie also had to brief and equip the producers who were going out on the road. Each team had to be provided with the props needed for the games, the application forms of all the people they would be meeting, name labels to stick on everyone, and maps and directions to the audition venues. They also needed all the technical equipment for filming during the games, and for the one-to-one interview on camera that applicants who made it through to the afternoon session would face.

The auditions started on 3 March in Manchester for three days, followed by two days in Newcastle. In the same week, another team of producers was in Bristol for a day and a half, followed by three days in Birmingham. Edinburgh and Belfast were next. London was left until last, simply because of the weight of numbers – producers were still viewing London tapes while the auditions were going on around the country. Four days of auditions were planned for London, but in the end an extra two days were added on, which mopped up not just the rest of the London applicants but anyone who couldn't make a regional audition. There was a one-day rail strike right in the middle of the dates planned for the London auditions, which meant a frantic reshuffling of audition appointments.

'There was a really noticeable difference between the regional auditions and the London ones,' says Sallie. 'The regional applicants were refreshingly straightforward; the London ones tended to be much more media savvy.'

To the surprise of the production team, a number of candidates selected for auditions pulled out when they realized that if they were chosen to go into the house, their stay would conflict with England playing in the World Cup.

'At least we helped them sort out their priorities,' says Phil.

CHAPTER THREE

IT'S SHOWTIME

There's a babble of excited voices from the adjoining room, where coats are being left and names are being checked. Then the door opens and 25 young people, twice as many boys as girls, spill in and sit down in the horseshoe-shaped arrangement of chairs. It's a chilly Thursday in March, and we're in a bare room in the University of London Union building for one of the 19 days of *Big Brother* auditions. The atmosphere in the room is charged with nervous energy: everyone wants to do their best in this brief chance to shine in front of the *Big Brother* producers. Despite being complete strangers five minutes ago, they are laughing and introducing themselves: there's no shyness here. Combat trousers, cropped tops, sweatshirts and trainers are the standard uniform, but one or two of the guys wear suits, and there are some preposterously spiky heeled shoes, tiny skirts and shirts unbuttoned dangerously low among the girls.

Audition days are run on tight schedules: there's a lot to get through. Batches of 25 hopefuls arrive each hour for four sessions in the morning, starting at 9.00am. From each group a few lucky ones will be selected to come back for more fun and games in the afternoon. Each audition is run by two producers – in this case Deborah Sargeant, a willowy blonde, and David Williams, a slim, dark-haired young man, who stand at the top of the horseshoe.

'The first thing we want to say is: well done for getting this far,' says David, when everyone has found a seat. There are one or two late arrivals for this early session; they've travelled from all over the south of England to be here, and there are the usual problems with trains and tubes running late.

'We've been inundated since Christmas with videos, so I can't claim to have watched your tapes personally; but someone at *Big*

Brother has,' says David. 'You've done fantastically well to be selected to be here today.

'Were any of you at last year's auditions? No? Good-oh, we can tell the same jokes. For the next hour, what we want is to get to know you all better.'

The first getting-to-know-you routine is very simple. Two sticks, taped together, are laid out in the middle of the horseshoe of chairs. One by one the hopefuls come forward, jump over the sticks, and tell the group a fascinating fact about themselves. To demonstrate, David goes first.

'Hi, I'm David, I'm twenty something, and at weekends you can call me Shirley,' he says, getting the first of many laughs that the group will have in the next hour.

Then it's the turn of the would-be contestants, starting with Bill, an 18-year-old from Basildon, Essex, who tells the group he can't believe he's here, and that his Dad brought him. His really fascinating fact is that he supports Arsenal, which gets a round of cheers from some of the others. He's quieter, more reserved than most, and it's easy to see that he really can't believe this is happening.

Next is Ben, who has been up since 3.00am because he couldn't sleep. He wants to be a personal trainer and he gets an even bigger cheer, particularly from the girls, when he says he does not like football. Some of the group keep it to a couple of simple facts – 'I'm a teacher, I live in London and I write poetry,' 'I'm 27, I'm a surveyor,' 'I'm very nervous, not just about this but because I'll find out later today whether I've got the new job I've applied for,' – but others take the chance to give a sales pitch about why they should be in the house. Donna jumps enthusiastically over the sticks, and announces that at 44, she sees herself as 'the token oldie'. She says, 'I'm probably the most annoying person any of my friends know, so if I get into the house I'll be out of the door so fast you won't believe it. I'm opinionated, I'm rude, I'm a bit of a tease and if it's smutty jokes you want you can guarantee I'll have them.'

Ray, who is tall and blonde with floppy hair, tells a funny story about nearly running out of petrol and then getting stopped for speeding as his Mum drove him into London. He's a hairdresser, and he loves performing, acting, fashion and cars. He's not quite as fey as Jamie, another willowy blonde boy, who says he's always up for a laugh, loves 'going out for cocktails, dressing up and having a good time'.

Others come up with bizarre facts about themselves: there's one who says that he's got something important in common with Chandler from the TV series *Friends*: they've both got three nipples. Ewa, from Hertfordshire, tells us that her name is pronounced 'Ever', which means she gets lots of jokes about ever-ready, ever-always, ever-after, and her claim to fame is that as she was getting off the tube yesterday Eamonn Holmes trod on her foot.

Laura, who is 20, says she's looking forward to her twenty-first and wants to be a police officer. She says she's an Essex girl, 'as you can probably tell'. 'I'm funny, I'm a flirt, I like going out and getting drunk,' she says. Lots of the girls are anxious to let us know they are ladettes. 'I like pubs, nightclubs, anywhere you can buy booze,' 'I can drink as much as any man,' 'I love going out with my girlfriends and getting bladdered.'

Some own up to bunking off work for the day, especially the ones with respectable jobs in banks and building societies. There aren't too many of those around; there are lots of IT workers, personal trainers, teachers, students, hairdressers.

Some have very unusual jobs. One striking blonde, with her hair in pigtails, tells the group she was born and raised in Alaska. But that's not what causes the most interest; she also says she edits literary porn for a living, and she's had her own first novel published.

Some try hard to be different and get themselves noticed: one picks the stick up and passes it over his head instead of jumping over it – 'the stick jumped over me'.

After the stick-jumping introductions, the group is split into three. They stand in a circle facing inwards. Each of them has to hold out their left hand and grasp the left hand of another member of the group from the other side of the circle. They do the same with their right hands, making sure they join up to someone different.

'Believe it or not, from this position, you will be able to untangle yourselves so that you are back in a circle, without letting go,' David tells them. There's a great deal of noise, chatter, giggling, and pandemonium as they bend down to step over arms, stretch up in the air to make arches with them, yell orders and counter orders at each other. After only a minute or two a huge cheer goes up from one group: they've done it. The others struggle on and another group manages it, but the third are still in chaos when David tells them the game is over. There's a bit of good-natured banter about whose fault it is that they didn't untangle themselves, but they're quickly on to the next phase of the audition. For David and Deborah, the results are unimportant: what they have been taking note of is who led the group, who made the others laugh, who refused to obey orders.

Now it's more getting-to-know-you stuff. Sitting in the semi-circle again, they are allowed to ask each other, in turn, three questions. The questions are as illuminating as the answers, and range from boring ones (What's your favourite pop group? What would you do with the money if you won? What's your favourite food?) to the bizarre (Who's your favourite dictator? Do you wear underpants?).

One question comes up a lot: are you single? If the answer is yes, it's usually followed by: are you looking? There are some genuinely funny replies to some of the questions, and some replies where the would-be contestant is trying too hard to raise a smile.

'How long have you had a beard?' 'Since I could grow one – about an hour ago.'

'How long since you hit puberty?' 'About an hour ago.'

When one camp contestant asks another of the guys if he is single, the answer comes back, 'In your case, no.'

But when one fit guy admits he's single the girls rush in with, 'By choice? Why did you split with your last girlfriend?'

The girls are also keen to question Alison, who is wearing lethal-looking stilettos. 'Do your feet hurt? Did you have special training to walk in them?'

When Jamie says his perfect partner would be Brad Pitt, the girls all agree. Donna is asked to name her ideal threesome, and says it would be Bruce Willis, Cybill Shepherd and herself.

'When did you lose your virginity?' proves to be a duff question because it gets a short answer: 15, 16 and 17 are the most popular ages for the big adventure. One young man, whose sexuality appears to be ambiguous and who says 'No comment' when asked if he is gay, replies 'Animal' when one of the girls tries to pin him down by asking if he first had sex with a man or a woman.

'When did you last have sex?' draws a range of answers. 'I had a blow job last night,' says a youth with bright bleach-blonde hair. 'Not for six months,' says a pretty girl, to a chorus of offers from the lads.

'How do you chat someone up?' Billy is asked.

'I can't, I'm crap at it,' is the honest reply.

'Try "Get your coat, you've pulled" – it works for me,' says another of the lads. The girls pull faces and tell him it wouldn't work with them.

One youth's announcement that he hasn't had a bath for a year is greeted with horror by the group, until he adds that he has a shower every day.

There are more serious questions. A nurse is asked to give her opinion on what's wrong with the NHS. 'We're up shit creek without a paddle,' she answers succinctly. Someone else has to give their opinion on capital punishment. A diatribe against President Mugabe is delivered by a girl who grew up in Zimbabwe.

But nobody can stay serious for long. When Lynne is asked why her favourite country is Peru she says it's 'raw and hard'.

'Is that the men or the country?' one of the other girls asks.

Sometimes the questioning touches on real human heartache. 'Are you in a relationship?' one of the girls is asked.

'No, we broke up.'

'Why?'

'He went back to his wife.' she says, blushing deeply.

'Did he have kids?'

'Yes, but I never met them,' she says, looking down and shuffling her feet. They've had their three questions, and the interrogation shifts to someone else. Ewa, who says she can speak fluent Polish, is asked to prove it. 'What do you want me to say in Polish?' she asks. 'I love you,' says Mark.

Now it's decision time for Deborah and David. They have to choose who to ask back for the longer afternoon audition. They split the group into two, give them all straws and a Polo mint for each team to pass from one to another, using the straws in their mouths and without touching it with their hands. It's a race, and Deborah and

David leave them to get on with it, under the supervision of researcher Liz Milward.

The two producers retire to discuss the group. There's no spare room to use, so they huddle together at the top of a chilly stairwell, and compare notes.

'I quite like him. He's a bit media, but he's older, more savvy, still cool...'

'I really liked him until he said one thing...'

'No, he's definitely out. Wearing sandals in March – and really nasty trousers...'

'He's OK, but he sort of drifted in and out, as though he was only half with us...'

'I quite like her, but not enough...'

'I really like her. She's witty and bright.'

'She got asked duff questions, but she coped. She might be worth another look...'

Eventually, the list in hand, they agree who is to come back. There are no arguments over the choice: they are both looking for that indefinable something that makes a *Big Brother* contestant, and they both recognize it when they see it. Occasionally they call someone back who has not shone in the audition, simply because the notes they have tell them that this applicant made a really good video, and they therefore deserve a second look.

Back in the games room, the race with the Polo mints is reaching its conclusion. Everyone is laughing and fooling about, but there's tension in the air. They know that they are about to find out if they have made it through to the next round. Deborah asks them to go back to their seats, and David thanks them all for coming and tells them how much their contribution has been appreciated.

Then the smiles fade and the strain begins to show as David reads out the names of those who are invited back: Harvey, Anthony, Donna, Simon, Mark, Katie and Alison are the ones who've made it through this first round of the audition. Deborah tells them it's only a start: there are several more scary rounds to go. They're asked to come back in the afternoon, either at 1.30pm or 3.30pm, but not to spend the intervening hours together. For this group, who were here at 9.00am, there are three and half hours or more to kill in London. For those who audition between 12.00pm and 1.00pm, there will scarcely be time to grab a sandwich if they want to be in the first afternoon session.

Nobody shows their disappointment, and there's a bit of hand-shaking and wishing good luck to the chosen few; coats and bags are collected and the room clears rapidly – the next group are already waiting for their turn to shine.

'I'm gutted. I've really enjoyed the day, and I'll definitely be applying again,' says Ben, as he leaves.

'I'm very disappointed. I've travelled a long way to be here today. But I wouldn't have missed it. It's been fun,' says Richard.

'I'm chuffed to have got through,' says Donna, who teaches in a comprehensive school. 'I thought I had a chance, as long as I got an interview. I've wanted to be in the *Big Brother* house since it first came on, two years ago, and I'm fed up with other people saying to me "You should be in there". So this year I decided to give it a go.'

Simon is really surprised his name was on the list. 'They all seemed more outgoing than me. I've always been the quiet fellow at the back of the class. I want to do *Big Brother* because I'm bored with my life.'

The second group are already in the big room, sitting in the semi-circle of chairs. They're almost an identikit crowd to the last lot, although there are even more with multiple piercings (Lee owns up to eleven, 'including three you can't see'), and one would-be contestant arrives in shaggy boots with roller blades, and insists on wearing them for most of the audition. At the introduction stage, one of them walks over the stick on his hands, another does a somersault over it. A psychiatric nurse tells the others that he's here 'because I'm a bit mental myself'.

A fresh assortment of odd facts come tumbling out: Laura has 'a tattoo which looks like a dolphin jumping over a tomato'; Nikki hasn't told her kids she's come for the audition; Jim owns up to being a Kylie fan; Ian gets a round of applause when, asked who he would most like to sleep with, chooses 'my other half'. Stacey, on the other hand, draws gasps of horror from the others when she admits sticking a fork up her backside before giving it to a man to eat his dinner with. 'Would you do that in the house?' someone asks anxiously, obviously not keen to be incarcerated with Stacey.

RULES INSIDE THE BIG BROTHER HOUSE

There are ten basic rules regarding life inside the Big Brother house:

1 There is no contact with the outside world.

2 You are filmed 24 hours a day and must wear your personal microphones at all times.

3 The diary room is the only place in the house where Big Brother will acknowledge you. Visits to the diary room are a vital part of the *Big Brother* experience and are therefore compulsory.

4 Each week you will be required to go to the diary room and nominate two people; you must give frank and honest reasons for your nominations. Big Brother will deal firmly with housemates who try to give reasons which are deemed unacceptable.

5 You are not permitted to discuss your nominations, or try to influence anyone else's nominations.

6 If you decide to leave the house voluntarily you must give your reasons in the diary room and allow sufficient time for *Big Brother* to organise your departure.

7 If you break the rules you may be asked to leave the house.

8 You may not intimidate, threaten or act violently towards any other housemate.

9 All tasks, unless otherwise stated, are compulsory.

10 You may not discuss the previous series of *Big Brother* or your plans for the prize money.

By ten to eleven, Deborah and David have retired to the stairwell again.

'She's too like Anna from the first series.'

'He's terribly patronizing – but one of the best of a bad lot.'

'He's posh – but we've had an influx of posh, and he wasn't comedy posh.'

'I think he might be a journalist.'

They, and all the other producers, are on constant journalist alert: there have been many attempts to infiltrate the selection process, and weeding out spies is part of the process. Deborah and David agree that this is not an inspiring group, although they choose five for the afternoon session.

'At one audition in Newcastle we only asked two to come back – and one of those we put through because we didn't want there to be only one,' says Deborah.

Stacey, who told the terrible story about the fork, has travelled from the Isle of Wight to be here, and has not been selected for the afternoon session.

'I'm half-relieved and half-disappointed,' she says as she leaves. 'I only found out I was coming yesterday. It wasn't too difficult – I'm at university and I don't have any lectures on Thursdays. But I'd put all my clothes in the launderette, so there was a crisis over what to wear. I couldn't tell anyone I was coming – but now the first thing I'll do is ring my best mate.'

Every group is dominated by boys – there are roughly two boys to every girl. The third group has even fewer females: only seven out of 23. But it's the girls who make the most impact. Ann is covered in tattoos, and has a belly button piercing; 45-year-old Jayne is a rhinestone cowgirl with a deep tan, an even deeper cleavage, long blonde hair and sparkly jeans. She sits, by complete contrast, next to a girl with short spiky hair wearing army fatigues. When one of the guys, Richard, announces for no particular reason, 'I look good in a dress,' the spiky haired girl replies, 'So do I – sometimes.'

Jayne's cleavage features big in the question and answer session. 'What size are they?' is the first of her three questions. 'A double D' she replies proudly, adding that they cost £4,000 and she paid for them by cashing in her British Airways shares. 'Do they take off?' one of the boys asks her.

Deborah and David quickly whittle them down to the possibles. 'He's too much like your dad, isn't he?' 'He could be worth keeping as an older one,' 'He's a little ray of sunshine.'

Jayne, who comes from Windsor and says her friends call her 'Barbie' – it isn't hard to see why – is thrilled to be on the list. 'I'm overwhelmed, so excited. The whole day has been a fantastic experience. It's been great fun meeting everybody else. I don't mind that I'm older than most of them – that's part of the fun, and I don't look or act old.'

Kriss, who is 23 and comes from Ramsgate, is 'super-chuffed' to have made it through. 'I felt there were a lot of good characters there, so I'm flattered to have been chosen. I'm used to living with loads of people – it's a great crack. So I'll be fine if I get into the house.'

The final morning group are streaming into the room. It's a big group, 27 altogether, and almost equally divided between boys and girls. There's a professional rugby player from New Zealand, an unemployed comedy writer, a single parent, a girl from Wales who insists 'I'm not as thick as Helen'. There's an ex-Butlins redcoat, and a couple of holiday reps, as well as the usual teachers, IT workers and nurses. One guy tells everyone he wants to be the tallest person ever to go into the *Big Brother* house – he's six foot six inches.

One girl startles the group, and then gets a smattering of applause, when she admits, 'I'm still a virgin at 20.' Another pretty girl wears a T-shirt that says, 'I like to make boys cry,' which leads to some fierce questioning from the boys. The summit of one girl's ambition is to own a Yorkshire terrier; another says yes when asked if she would sleep with Peter Stringfellow for a million pounds. 'But I'd want to see the money up front.'

When the Polo mints and straws come out for the fourth and final time of the day, it's the cue for another session in the stairwell.

'He was painfully straight when he introduced himself,' 'She's a bit stagey, too dramatic,' 'She's posh totty,' 'She's very Page Three,' 'He had a really cool video, so he might be worth another look.' 'I love her – she's stunning, bright as a button, sassy,' 'He's a cool Scot,' 'She irritated the rest of the group.'

Then it's back to break the news, and there's just time for the four-strong production team – two producers, a researcher and a runner – to snatch a sandwich and chat about what they're looking for, before the afternoon session begins.

'It's really tricky,' says Deborah. 'It's a combination of things. It's nothing to do with whether you like them or not, it's a matter of searching for an indefinable quality that makes them good to watch on television.

'We rule out any possible journalists, and anyone with a television connection. One of them this morning announced that he's going to be a competitor on *Ready Steady Cook* – so that was him out, instantly. We're very selective with the under-21s. Although in theory we'll take anyone over 18, they have to be specially good to make it through if they are under 21. There's no upper age limit, but there just aren't that many older people coming forward.'

'This just hasn't been a great day,' says David. 'We haven't seen anyone we're really excited about. There's nobody I feel sure will make the shortlist for the house.'

At half-past one the first of the two afternoon auditions begins, with 12 would-be contestants. One girl admits she was far too nervous to eat anything – she's hoping her tummy won't rumble too much.

David kicks off the session with another talk, this one longer and more serious than the one that started the day.

'Thank you, you've all come back. It's nice to see that nobody has run away. You've done really well, all of you, but before we go

FAVOURITE FILMS
ADELE: *The Colour Purple*
ALEX: *Clockwork Orange*
ALISON: *Raging Bull*
JADE: *Rush Hour*
JONNY: *Airplane*
KATIE: *Pretty Woman*
LEE: *Karate Kid*
LYNNE: *Shawshank Redemption*
P.J.: *The Godfather*
SANDY: *Chariots of Fire*
SOPHIE: *Fight Club*
SPENCER: *Scarface*
SUNITA: *Pulp Fiction*
TIM: *Jerry Maguire*

any further I'd like to spend a couple of minutes talking you through some of the things you should think about now. Perhaps you have thought about some of them already, perhaps you think they're obvious, but it's worth thinking about them again. So take it all on board now while I'm speaking, and then when you leave this afternoon have a good hard think about whether or not you want to carry on.

'We've got another questionnaire to give you before you leave and – groan – it's much bigger than the last one. If you decide you want to carry on, we need to have it back within a week. But first, we want you to think about what you may be letting yourself in for. Coming on *Big Brother* may be the best thing you do with your life; it may also be the worst thing you ever do. We have to be honest. That's why we need to reiterate why we pick people for *Big Brother*.

'We are looking for an across-the-board range of people from every part of the country, every kind of background. We are looking for ordinary people, not people we think have any future in television. As it has to be such a diverse mix, it's more than likely there will be a couple of people you won't like – perhaps even half of them. That's bound to be the case.

'We don't want anyone to use the show as a showcase for any talents they think they have. So today is all about finding out more about you and how you would cope if you did come on to the programme.

'The first thing to think about, and it may sound like stating the obvious, is that you would be watched all the time in the house. That's what the show is all about. But people mistakenly think that they can present some kind of image of themselves, the image they would like to be seen by the people watching. The fact is, nobody can do it. The mask will always slip. You'll tie yourself in knots trying to do it. It's futile, and you'll give yourself a big headache along the way.

'We'll see you looking your absolute worst, you can guarantee it. Just when you wouldn't want to be seen, we'll be focussing on you. Every spot, every wrinkle, every roll of fat, when you are crying, when you are feeling really low, when you wake up in the morning and you've slept with your mouth open and there's dribble on the pillow: you can guarantee it will be seen.

'And when you come out of the house, my next guarantee is that you will hate the show. It won't be because of the way we have edited it, it will be because everybody has something at the back of their head that they don't really like about themselves, whether it's a physical thing or a personality thing or whatever. You will watch the show and you will see nothing but this flaw magnified a million times. You'll hate it and there won't be anything you can do about it.

'*Big Brother* can also be hugely, hugely boring: no newspapers, no music, no television, no idea what's going on in the outside world, no idea what your friends are up to or what your family thinks of you. For long periods you will be bored rigid. It's tough: it's an absolute test. And one of the few things I can tell you about *Big Brother 3* at this stage is that it is going to be tougher still this year.

'Another thing you know after watching the programme a few times is that *Big Brother* is fundamentally about rejection. Every week there is an eviction and for everybody, not just those who are nominated, it's an emotional roller coaster. You may be having a terribly tough time, you may be hating it, but of course there is nowhere to hide in the house. If you do fall out with someone there's nowhere you can go for a bit of peace and quiet on your own.

'So think about it for a few minutes. Imagine you've done brilliantly and gone into the house. Let's say two weeks have passed and it's the first nominations. You think you have got on well with everybody, and made a couple of good friends. Then you find yourself nominated, you find you are the least popular person in the house, and the people you thought were your friends actually dislike you most of all.

'And not only is it likely that at some point the people in the house won't like you, but remember that millions of viewers will spend their time, energy and cash voting to get you out because they don't like you. It may even happen – it already has a couple of times – that when you leave the house the crowd will boo you. For a lot of people this is far too much to cope with. So the final stages of this procedure involve you seeing a psychotherapist and possibly also a psychiatrist, who will decide whether in their opinion you can do it, and not do yourself any harm struggling with it.

'Another part of the procedure is police checks. If you have only a minor criminal record, going into the house might not be a complete no-no. But obviously we couldn't let in someone with a history of violence.

'Then you must think about fame, which people rightly or wrongly associate with *Big Brother*. At its best, fame is very fleeting. In a year or less it is more than likely that no one will want to know you or really care about you. It has happened that immediately after coming out, contestants get invited to a few swanky parties and get their pictures in the papers. But it may not happen. And it's not going to pay the bills.

'You probably think "OK, if something happens, that's brilliant; if it doesn't I'll go back to my normal life." Unfortunately, if you come on, whatever happens afterwards you will find yourself with a lot of baggage and notoriety, and it may not be easy or possible to slip back into your old life. Some of the previous contestants thought they would get jobs either in front of or behind the cameras, but they found it didn't work and then nobody wanted to know.'

When David tells them that they may end up famous but only 'for being a complete tosser', a giggle runs around the room. Not me, they are all thinking. But David continues to ram home the downside of *Big Brother*.

'Remember, it's not just you but your friends and family who will be dragged in. If you are in a relationship, the tabloids may dig around and find someone who will say they have had a passionate affair with you. If you are a parent you might find yourself dubbed the worst mother or father in Britain for abandoning your children in pursuit of fame and fortune. And the worse thing is, whether it's true or not, you are not there to present your side of the story.

'All of us have something that our friends and family don't know and that we'd rather they didn't know. So think how you'd feel if it came out. If you have some huge issue, secret or worry, and you would be devastated if it came out, have a good hard think about going in there. Journalists are good at finding these things out, and they don't care about hurting you.

'You obviously know that you have to stop your life for ten weeks or so, but what you may not realize is how much hard work you have to do before then. Not only more questionnaires, but long phone calls just when you're not feeling like it. From our point of view, we need to know everything about you, and if we discover anyone is hiding stuff from us, they'll be disqualified. Like I say, a minor criminal record doesn't rule you out, but lying about it does. Similarly, if you say you are single and you are not.

'Going forward from this stage is a huge, huge commitment from you guys, which is why we want you to think about it so carefully now. We'd be gutted if you got in there and then found after a couple of days that you had to come out. And you'd feel a terrible sense of failure. So really think hard.'

David hands over the baton to Deborah, who carries on with the doom-laden warnings, this time about the dangers of any news of the auditions or the selection process leaking.

'If any stories appear in the media involving anyone who has been to the auditions, that person will be disqualified. We're not being precious about it, but the fact of *Big Brother* is that it is a group of complete strangers who go into the house, strangers to each other and to the viewing public. It just wouldn't have much impact if the faces of the contestants had been seen beforehand.

'It won't be you who leaks the information to the newspapers, but you have to remember that in London – and probably any other big city – you are only three steps away from a journalist. You'll tell someone in confidence about getting through the auditions, they'll tell their mum, she'll say something at the hairdressers and before you know it, someone will have blown it for you.

'However excited you are when you go away today, you must curb it and say nothing. If you can't keep a secret now you will find it much harder later in the selection procedure. We don't want anyone to cock it up for you, and we don't want you to cock it up for yourselves.

'You must also go your separate ways after today – just as you had to at lunch time. If you keep in touch with each other by phone, text message or anything else, you will be disqualified. It is possible for two people who meet at the auditions to end up in the house together – it happened last year with Bubble and Brian. But they didn't see each other again until they were in the house.'

David takes over to lighten the atmosphere. 'That's just a worst-case scenario we have painted for you, to get you thinking. It's also possible that by going into the *Big Brother* house, you could have the best time of your life.

'So, let's get on with having some fun this afternoon.'

In the first game, everyone is given a piece of paper with the name of a household object on it – vacuum cleaner, food mixer, television, microwave etc. Without speaking, they have to act out their object, moving around the room until they tie up with another person who is impersonating the same thing.

There's a lot of laughter and the ice is broken. Next, they form a circle and someone has to point at another person across the group, who in turn points to someone else until they are all linked. Then they have to impersonate and exaggerate the mannerisms and speech of the person they are pointing at, which means that ripples of speech pass round the group like echoes, coming back to where they started and then going on with a life of their own. The producers watch as some of the group wildly over-dramatize the actions, while others are more restrained.

Then it's game three, and this one takes their breath away. Paper and pencils are handed round, and they are told to write down the name of one person they would like to leave the audition. They must not show it to anyone. They can write down a reason if they want, but they don't have to.

David collects the slips of paper and one by one reads them out. They all manage a smile when their names come up for eviction, but they're the same strained smiles masking anxiety that are seen in the *Big Brother* house on nomination days. A quick tot up of the scores shows that Jayne, the 45-year-old from Windsor, has the most nominations.

'Right, it's time for you to go,' says David, looking at her. Gamely, Jayne gets up and begins to gather her belongings when David says, 'But you are only going as far as the next room, where we are going to do an interview with you.' She looks enormously relieved, and so do the others, who give her a round of applause. They have all just experienced the complex pain of rejection, either by feeling it when their names were read out or by inflicting it, and the group has momentarily lost its buoyancy.

The interviews are an essential part of this second round. One by one the would-be contestants are taken away to be interviewed on camera by either Deborah or David, while the others are given more games to play.

'It's vital to see how they are on camera,' says David. 'Some people go all shy, some act up to the camera. The best are the ones who stay natural.'

The next game is called Truths, and involves the group splitting into two teams. Each player writes down one bizarre fact about themselves on a piece of paper, then the papers are collected and shuffled and exchanged with the papers from the other team. Each group then has to decide which of the strange facts belongs to which member of the other team. When they've made up their minds they hand out the slips of paper to those they think they belong to, announcing loudly the name of the contestant and the fact.

Some weird secrets are revealed: 'My first boyfriend turned out to be gay,' 'I went to school with one of S Club 7,' 'I dressed up men as women for a living.' Some of them turned out to be beautiful – but not many, 'I collect bus tickets for a hobby.' They manage to correctly identify about half of the facts at their first go.

In the meantime, Jayne is being interviewed on camera in the next room by David. Liz Milward, one of the researchers for the programme, is behind the camera. Jayne tells David she works as a personal trainer, and specializes in exercises to firm the boobs, belly and bust, but still works part time as cabin crew for British Airways.

'Million dollar question – why do you want to do *Big Brother*?' asks David.

'It would be the experience of a lifetime, fantastic, I'd have a jolly good time and I'd make it good for other people, too. I'm strong, confident, loyal, trustworthy and I know I'd bring a lot of inspiration to the house. I feel my experiences with British Airways and with running my own company and my fitness would help. I'm flexible and can deal with almost anything.'

David asks how she felt being nominated to leave the group, and she remains resolutely upbeat. 'I took that, I don't think of that as being a negative. Good luck to them all, they have their reasons, but you just have to carry on, don't you?'

She tells David she's a girlie girl – but then covers her options by adding she loves football and 'going out for a beer with the guys'.

David comments on her looks: 'You look fantastic, you obviously turn heads.'

Jayne, astonishingly, describes herself as 'a very natural person', and says she doesn't seek attention for the way she looks. 'I'd like to share the true me with the nation. They'd see me wake up without my makeup on, then put it on and make myself all girlie, and if they see me shaving my body in the shower, well, that's just me.'

Next in the hot seat is 25-year-old Jascha, who admits that 'some people could misconstrue my confidence and think I'm an arrogant twat, but it's not true, I'm a nice person'. He says he's 'fairly opinionated, but rational. I think I'm diplomatic'. He's working for himself, designing and making glass furniture, which he assumes 'the world will bite my arm off for' and he's looking forward to 'speaking to obscenely rich people who I hope will buy it'.

He says he wants to take part in *Big Brother* because 'it's a fascinating social experiment. I like the voyeurism of reality TV'.

He's followed by Alyson, 27, a retail manager, who doesn't have any such high-blown opinions about why she wants to be on the programme. 'I've been a dedicated *BB* watcher from day one, and other people would say I'm an exhibitionist. I have life, a bit of flavour, constant energy. I'd be able to keep myself occupied. I'm always the first on the dance floor and the last to come off.'

Like most of them, Alyson points out there are two sides to her personality – she's deeper than she appears, 'a real thinker'. It's a pattern that emerges in all the interviews: they're all anxious to stress their well-rounded personalities. Many of them also emphasize that they're the sort of people others 'pour their hearts out to'. They're keen to let *Big Brother* know that, given half a chance, they'd be wheedling the darkest secrets out of their fellow housemates.

Glen, a 30-year-old carpenter from Maidstone, says he's spent the last twelve years enjoying himself, and he wants to carry on doing just that. While friends get married and have babies, he's still partying. 'Fuck it, you should just enjoy it,' he says. 'You've got to do some stuff in your life, and not take it seriously. Chill out, have fun, make people laugh.'

His philosophy is shared by 26-year-old Debbie from Hemel

BIG BROTHER TASKMASTER

When James Milnes and Liz Milward walked into the London Toy Fair with *Big Brother* badges pinned to their lapels, there was a small stampede of toy manufacturers towards them. Everyone wants to get their latest game into the *Big Brother* house, and James and Liz were inundated with offers to supply everything from small plastic toys to complicated electronic gadgetry.

James is the *Big Brother* taskmaster, the person whose voice can be heard explaining the rules of the tasks and chivvying along the contestants during the live show on Saturdays.

'When I was given the job, I started to amass ideas for the kind of tasks that we saw in the first two series of *Big Brother*; but Phil, Helen and Gigi quickly told me it was going to be very different this year,' says James, who is assisted by researcher Liz.

It was decided that the tasks would be more varied, ranging across mental, physical and strategy games. Some would be individual, others would involve teamwork. Saturday was the perfect day to stage the live task show, 'because we know from previous years that the natural rhythm of the house makes Saturday a down day – the day after an eviction when everyone feels a bit flat,' says Helen.

Gigi and Helen run the Saturday night task show, and they, with Phil, have the ultimate say on which tasks to use. But it was down to James to come up with the shortlist.

'All my original ideas were wrong, and so were most of those suggested by others on the team. It took a little while to get the hang of what would work in a half-hour slot. We couldn't have anything involving complicated gadgetry, and we had to have games where the instructions are very straightforward and simple. We didn't want the whole half hour taken up with them going back and forth to the Diary Room asking for clarification on the instructions. There were some wonderfully creative ideas, but we just couldn't strip them down to fit the slot.

'They needed to have impact, maintain tension, hopefully reveal a lot about the housemates, and give the psychologists on the Sunday show lots to talk about. We also needed games where it is very clear whether someone has won or lost. We can't call in panels of experts, or view the tapes later before we make a decision, or have a complicated points system: it has to happen straightaway. Sometimes the contestants themselves will instantly know whether they have passed without being told, but other times we will announce it. Either way, it will be clear to them by the end of the show. And with so much riding on it, it's a big dramatic moment.'

The more traditional task ideas have not been completely discarded: they're being used for mini-tasks during the week. And the task team know they have to be flexible with their plans.

'We tested the tasks on the guinea pigs, the volunteers who were in the house for a fortnight before the show started, and they all worked well – but the group dynamics of the real contestants are different, and who knows whether the tasks that looked great in the rehearsal will work as well every Saturday night?'

For James and Liz, finding the tasks has been a licence to become kids again. 'We had a great time going round Hamleys, the famous toy shop. And I bought lots of gadget magazines, to see what is on the market.'

As soon as *Big Brother 3* was announced to the press at the beginning of May, James also found himself targeted by phone calls from firms with games ideas to push.

'They ranged from really high-tech electronic gadgets to Interflora wanting us to run a flower-arranging task. They come at the rate of a couple a day, and we log them all – although we're honest with those whose ideas just aren't right for us. But we've certainly lined up a couple of mini-tasks from the calls. We've also been given lots of ideas for treats and rewards for the housemates.

BIG BROTHER TASKMASTER continued

'It's amazing how keen people are to get involved with the show. It's hard to tell whether they are trying to promote their products or whether they are just *Big Brother* fans.'

Although the contestants know they will have a regular Saturday night task, the mini-tasks are decided on by Phil, Helen and Gigi, according to the needs of the house and the programme.

'The mini-tasks are dictated by how things are going in the house, so I have to be ready with a whole bank of different ideas,' says James. 'Many of them will never be used, but we have to be prepared for any of them to go in at short notice.'

James reckons he started out 'with no more interest in games and gadgets than the average bloke', but now he's an authority.

He's also an authority on management training manuals, having scoured the Internet and bought piles of books looking for revealing games to include at auditions. 'One game, which involved an imaginary bush fire scenario, was one of ten drawn up by a company that specializes in providing games to sort out job applications. But some of the games just came out of party games books.'

Hempstead, who says she still feels 18 and she's not ready to settle down, like her mates, and have babies. She reckons she may be too loud, too honest, but she's not frightened of showing her emotions. She got this far through the auditions last year, but she says she feels more confident this time round. And besides, she thinks it's time a girl won.

The games are progressing in the big room. Split into three groups of four, the contestants are told to make themselves into living sculptures of different objects: one group is a corkscrew, another a bookcase, the third a hostess trolley. Deborah watches and takes notes about who dominates each group, who is argumentative, who says nothing and simply does what they are told, who makes everyone laugh.

The next game reveals even more about who are the natural leaders and who find it hard to work within a group. Again, the contestants work in two teams, and they are given a detailed 600-word written account of an imaginary situation – they are stuck in the Australian bush with certain pieces of equipment while a bush fire is raging through the land. They are asked to rank the equipment, which includes a map, a fire extinguisher, a ladder and snorkels and flippers, in order of importance for their survival. They all get it hopelessly wrong, but that's not what Deborah is watching for: she's much more interested in how they interact with each other than how high a score they get.

Meanwhile, Katie, a 26-year-old wedding photographer with a degree in Russian, is telling David that she really wants to work in Africa with HIV victims. She says that if she was in the house she'd be able to calm down difficult situations. 'I'd be neutral, like Switzerland.' She says it articulately, but it's an echo of what many of them say: they cast themselves in the role of peacemaker, never the one likely to be breaking the peace. She, too, sees herself as someone the others would all open up to.

When all the interviews are over, the group are issued with another form, even longer than the one they filled in when they sent in their home videos. David tells them, 'It's a "Don't call us, we'll call you" situation now.' He explains that when the forms are returned, a shortlist will be drawn up, and the lucky ones will be hearing again from *Big Brother*. 'If you don't hear, we've still appreciated everything you've given to us today, and you've all done fantastically well to get through this far.'

Then they're off, collecting their coats and bags and heading for the door. Katie, the wedding photographer, explains how she feels.

'It's been a fun day. I always enjoy meeting new people, and I've had a good time, so even if I don't hear any more I won't feel too disappointed, although there will be a slight sense of rejection. Luckily, I didn't have much time to think about this audition, so I wasn't nervous. It's interesting being with people in a completely new situation, having to bond with a group of strangers, yet at the same time being told not to develop any real friendships today. Now I'm going away to get on with my normal life, and I'll try hard not to get too keen to have the next phone call from *Big Brother*, in case it never comes.'

The second afternoon group have arrived, ten of them. They hear the same talk about the negative aspects of the programme, this time delivered by Deborah. Then it's that tricky nominations game again, only this time they are also asked to vote for who they most like in the room. Nina and Adam share top place in the popularity poll, but Kriss gets five nominations to leave, making him first in front of the camera.

He's a psychiatric nurse who's into 'break-dancing, hip-hop, etc, etc, etc'. He says, sarcastically, that he thought it was great to be nominated. He adds, seriously, that the people in the other room had only known him for a couple of minutes, so he doesn't think their opinion of him was based on any real knowledge.

'Why do you think they might not like you?' Deborah asks.

'Because I'm always talking, always messing about, acting the goat, enjoying a joke. Maybe my breath stinks!'

He wants to do *Big Brother* 'For the crack, for the experience, for a good laugh'.

The others are playing a game where one person is blindfolded and guided verbally through an obstacle course by another member of his or her team, collecting ping-pong balls on the way. They take it in turns to be the one in the dark and the one giving instructions. There's quite a lot of confusion about left and right, and there's the problem of making the instructions clear from those being yelled by the other team. Nina turns out to be particularly good at giving clear orders to Harvey.

Then it's time for the amazing facts game. 'I've eaten shark fin, frog and toad,' 'My chest hair is in the shape of the Batman symbol,' 'I shared a pint of milk with Donovan on the Isle of Skye,' 'I was thrown out of a Japanese hot spring for not having a modesty towel,' 'I shagged a bird in a showroom cupboard in Texas when I was 12.' This last fact is pinned on to Kriss, but it's only when the others question him about the heat that he realises that they are thinking of Texas, USA. 'It was Texas the shop, which sells furniture,' he said. 'This girl, she was 14, just dragged me into a cupboard, in the bedroom section.'

Donna the schoolteacher is being interviewed. She describes herself as 'a pain in the arse, middle-aged, eccentric, annoying, rude, earthy. Everyone remembers me, they either love me or absolutely hate me, there are no in betweens. I'm strong, I speak my mind a bit too much, I call a spade a spade.'

She says her husband thinks she'd be the first out if she got into the house, and Donna thinks he's probably right.

'I'm very relaxed, I'd walk around without my clothes on. People in this country are so hung up about nudity. I don't care. I've got hairy armpits – so what? I'd be a catalyst. I'm obviously not one of the young, sexy, gorgeous ones, although I do look good naked.'

She says she's happily married, but she's a tease. 'I get on fine with people of all ages,' she says, but admits that Kriss 'is getting on my tits, and I'm not very good at hiding my feelings'.

Nina, 21, is next in, a beautiful Chinese girl who was born in Bournemouth and calls herself 'a BBC – British-born Chinese. I'm like a banana – yellow on the outside, white inside'. She thinks 'people like me because I smile a lot'.

Rebecca, who is coming up for 21, is the one who has caused eyes to widen by announcing that she's still a virgin. She's a Sociology student who wants to go into PR or marketing. She says holding on to her virginity is not a religious stand. 'I don't think there are enough people like me around. There's so much peer pressure to have sex with boyfriends. I just don't like the thought of sleeping around, one night stands.' What she wants from the house is to meet a whole range of people of different ages and backgrounds and 'to come away with a group of good friends, and have a laugh'.

When everyone has been interviewed and the forms handed out, it's time to clear the room. As he leaves, Mark says, 'I'm really happy to have got this far. I came along for a laugh, but having got through to the afternoon I feel I'm getting close and I really want to go into the house more than ever. It's been a great day – I wouldn't change one minute of it.'

For Deborah and David, it's time to pack all the games equipment back into boxes, put the empty Coke tins and sandwich packets into the bin, stack the chairs and move out. Tomorrow they'll be back in the office with all the video tapes: they've been on the road for two weeks doing auditions around the country, and another team will be taking over here.

'It's not been our best day, but it's very difficult this year: there are so many good people to choose from,' says David. 'Some of them think they haven't had a fair crack of the whip, after the morning sessions. They say, "I didn't say much." But it's tough – and if they can't handle this amount of rejection they wouldn't cope in the house anyway.'

The next day, producers Paul Osborne, a spiky-haired Scot, and Claire O'Donohoe, a pretty dark-haired girl, are running the London audition, and they are happier with their quota: they reckon they've got a really good selection of possible contestants at their audition. A total of 32 are invited back for the afternoon session, fifteen in the first group and seventeen in the second.

Predictably, they don't like the nominations game at all. 'This is horrible, isn't it?' one of them says, as Paul makes them write down the name of the person they most want to leave. The unlucky nominee is Rachel, who is a transsexual, although it's hard to tell. She's tall, elegant, and speaks softly. But one of the others has written 'I think there's something she's not telling us' as his reason for nominating her, so perhaps he's sussed it.

Rachel herself is open about it.

'Being nominated made me realize how quickly people make assumptions. It's very superficial: I was brought up to believe you shouldn't judge a book by its cover. But I wasn't shocked. I want to go into the house to find out about myself, and how other people react to me. I want to see how I am as a person after the show, if I do get in. I want to find out about myself in depth.

'I know that people will find out about me. It's challenging: if I can make people think a bit more about judging me straightaway, that will be good. At the end of the day, it does hurt if people say nasty things, but I'm hardened to it, and so are my family. If I went in, I'd expect the press to be cruel. But I want to put across that being a transsexual is only a small part of me. I'm a real person. I'm a student, I've got a life, I've got a great family. But it is different, and it does intrigue people, and I just want to put it across in a positive way, and make it easier for the next person who has to go through what I've been through.'

Richard, who is training to be a barrister, says he's intrigued as to what it will be like in the house. 'I think I've got a lot to offer. I'm a good cook, I'm used to living with other people. I think anyone who says they're not worried about going into the house is probably a liar.' He says he's been involved in student politics, and would like to go into national politics – and that being on *Big Brother* would raise his profile.

In the other room, the Truth game is under way, and everyone is writing down their bizarre facts. 'I almost fell off a waterfall in Central America,' 'I bungee jumped five times in one day because I fancied the instructor,' 'I was National Young Cartoonist of the Year at the age of eight,' 'Michael Crawford told me he loved me,' 'Davy Jones from the Monkees gave me a pound when I was busking on the streets of Wolverhampton.'

Amelie, a pretty Swedish girl, is doing her five minutes in front of the camera. She speaks fluent English, and has the advantage of having seen *Big Brother* in Sweden as well as in Britain. 'I think it would be fun to have some international input. I'm not doing it for a life-changing experience, just for some fun.'

The Australian bush fire game is overheating with Tara rowing volubly with Sheldon. Neither of them is going to give way. Tara, who is wearing tiny denim shorts, fishnet tights and a low-cut top, stands out among all the sweatshirts, jeans and trainers.

The final game of the session is Jenga, the wooden block game in which everyone removes a block in turn and then carries out the forfeit written on it. One of the guys has to answer, 'What was the most daring thing you ever did?' He replies, 'When I was a kid we chucked bangers into a nudist colony.'

The second session of the afternoon underlines the imbalance between boys and girls in *Big Brother* applications: there are 13 guys and only four girls. They reveal another collection of bizarre facts about themselves: 'I have an extra testicle,' 'I once ate a can of dogfood for a £10 bet,' 'I was in an Oasis tribute band,' 'I've got 14 pairs of underpants all the same,' 'I beat Tim Henman at tennis.'

When they are asked to nominate someone for eviction, it is one of the girls, Josie, who collects the most votes. Being interviewed on camera by Paul she says the nomination experience 'has made me come to terms with it being real'. Josie has been a self-employed mural artist for the past 15 years, and has lived and worked in the Caribbean. Paul asks her to name the five best things about herself and she says they are 'my inner self, which is warm and nice; my love of natural things; I'm very talented; I love to think a lot; and I'm very active, dynamic, outward-going, daring, adventurous'. She says people find her odd because 'I've seen some amazing things and dreamt some amazing dreams'.

Leon, a 28-year-old quantity surveyor, was at the auditions last year, and wasn't fazed to find he'd had a few votes in the nomination procedure. 'You have to make an impact for people to react to you in such a short amount of time.' He says he wants to have a break from his structured professional life. 'It's an opportunity to do something different, out of the routine. I get on with people and I'm mentally strong. I'm a sound geezer.'

Lee is a devastatingly good-looking 21-year-old who loves going out socializing, going to the gym, and spending time with his girlfriend. He mentions his girlfriend a lot, and says he loves her a great deal. 'And she's right behind me doing this,' he adds. He says he's

FAVOURITE SONG OR ARTIST

ADELE: 'Finally' by Kings of Tomorrow and Julie McKnight
ALEX: 'Your Song' by Elton John
ALISON: Paul Weller
JADE: 'Heart Breaker' by Mariah Carey
JONNY: 'Let Me Entertain You' by Robbie Williams
KATIE: 'Music' by Madonna
LEE: 'Another Chance' by Roger Sanchez
LYNNE: Zero 7
P.J.: 'Let's Get it On' by Marvin Gaye ('it guarantees sex')
SANDY: 'I Still Haven't Found What I'm Looking For' by U2
      ('it will be played at my funeral')
SOPHIE: 'Fallin'' by Alicia Keys
SPENCER: 'Man in the Mirror' by Michael Jackson
SUNITA: 'Lazy' by X-Press 2
TIM: 'Man in the Mirror' by Michael Jackson

funny when he's drunk and he tries to get on with everybody. He's had a happy life, and he wants to go into *Big Brother* to entertain the nation. He admits he's got a bad shopping habit, and probably cares too much about the way he looks.

Alan has lived in London for the past three years, but was born and bred in Scotland. He was a hit at the morning audition, reducing everyone to laughter. 'I can be a joker, but not always,' he says. He wants to go into the house to get out of a rut: he works in computer programming but would like a change.

David, a 34-year-old advertising and marketing account executive, is planning another big event in his life as well as *Big Brother*: he's getting married in September to the girl he has been with for the last five years. He says she's pushing him to change his life, give up his job and go full time into his passionate hobby, which is photography. He says he will bring 'brutal honesty' into the house. His worst point is that he's a perfectionist. 'When I'm washing up I have a pile of forks all pointing the same way, when I chop vegetables I keep them in neat piles, my desk at work is always tidy. That's the thing about me which would wind people up the most.'

Amanda, 36, is about as unconventional as they come. She shares her home with her 15-year-old son, a snake, two tarantulas and a cat, but it's not this menagerie that makes Paul's eyes widen in surprise. It's her job. 'The official name for what I do is an angle grinder. There are four of us in Europe. We strap sheets of metal to our bodies, and then attack it with a power tool. It gives off lots of bright sparks. I do it in nightclubs, to entertain people.' She also does circus tricks – 'the harder the better'. She wants to do *Big Brother* for 'the challenge, and to show I've got the strength you need. I think it's probably a harsh test of personality. It's so scary, that's what's appealing'. She says the things that make her angry are 'lies and deceit, automated telephone services, wallpaper that looks like wood, and coat hangers that get tangled up together'. She says, as so many of them do, that she's a good listener who will bring out the thoughts and fears of the others in the house.

Claire takes over the interviews from Paul halfway through the session. There are a lot of people to get through, and the room has been booked for use by an evening class at 6.00pm, so it's becoming a race against the clock to fit in all the interviews.

There are certain stock words and phrases that come up all the time. 'Mad' and 'zany' are favourite words to describe themselves, and 'my friends all tell me I should be in the house' is a familiar refrain.

Jason, who has been one of the star entertainers at the day's auditions, has a variation on it: he says he should go into the house 'because I'm told I'm amusing'. He says the energy he's been displaying all day is natural, and permanent. He says people often describe him as arrogant, although among his real friends he's well liked. He wouldn't worry about press intrusion into his private life because his family and friends would love to tell terrible stories to journalists about him – 'Like the time I slept with seven men.' 'Tell me about the time you slept with seven men,' says Claire. Jason laughs. 'Oh, I was joking. It was only six.' He says he loves climbing, abseiling, extreme sports, and says his main worry about the house would be the boredom. 'I'd have to give myself challenges, whether it was just making bizarre sculptures out of pots and pans, or gardening, or anything.'

One of the last interviews of the day is with Lisa, a lively 22-year-old student who wants to be a fashion journalist. When Claire asks why she would enjoy the house she says, 'I talk a lot, I could make it into an Olympic sport. I'm known as little Miss Chatterbox. I'm always the last person to bed – late night chats are my thing. If I like people I really like them, but if I don't I find it hard to pretend. I'm not bitchy, because I'd rather say it to someone's face, but that might not go down too well in the house.' She says her bad habits include farting and burping, 'but only when I'm comfortable around people', and that she is, in general, 'very well-liked'.

Paul sympathizes with the applicants, having to face the camera in a difficult situation. 'It's not easy. They're plucked from the room, where they're surrounded and supported by a network of their peers, and they're completely on their own in front of the camera. It's a test of their character, but it's also an invaluable opportunity for us to get to know them better. Some people freeze up, some open up.'

Before they all head off home they are given forms to fill in, and are reminded that if they want to pull out, this is the time to do it. None of them will: they are all thrilled to have made it through both rounds on a long day, and they're all going away to wait for the phone call which will tell them they are through to the shortlist of 80.

The producers have come up with another checklist of things NOT to do if you want to survive the audition round of *Big Brother*:

- DO NOT say you want to go in for the money.
- DO NOT think you have to impress by being an all-singing, all-dancing performer – you'll get turned down for being too desperate.
- DO NOT ham up to the cameras. There's a video camera recording the games at the auditions, and some contestants are very conscious of it, winking and waving and performing for its benefit. Similarly, when you're doing the one-to-one interviews, look at the producer who is intervewing you and don't keep giving camera checks. 'That's a definite no-no,' says Paul.
- DO NOT beg or plead during your interview. It smacks of being desperate.
- DO NOT slag off the contestants on the past series of *Big Brother*. The producers probably worked on those shows – and even if they didn't, they know how amazingly successful they were. Telling them that you could do better is not a good idea.
- DO NOT talk to the press. Only talk to the people you really trust, because if your name leaks out in print as a possible *Big Brother* contestant, you're off the list.
- DO NOT impersonate last year's contestants – the team are not looking for another Brian, Helen or Bubble, they are looking for original and interesting personalities.

CHAPTER FOUR

THE FINAL ROUNDS

After the auditions, everything went quiet for the applicants. They'd been warned they might never hear from *Big Brother* again, and for most of the 650 who were screened at the afternoon auditions, that's what happened. They could console themselves that out of 10,000 applicants, they made it through much further than most. But even for those who went on into the final rounds, there was an ominous silence for a couple of weeks.

Not that it was quiet at the *Big Brother* headquarters. As each team of producers returned to the office they put their stash of taped interviews into three folders: Yes, Maybe, No. The Nos were ruled out straightaway, which reduced the number of interview tapes to nearly 400. Sallie Clement and Wendy Rattray, the two senior producers, then sat down to another marathon viewing session, watching every single taped interview between them. For Wendy, who was part of the massive viewing team of the original tapes, it was a pleasant change: all these would-be contestants had now been screened three times, and the ones left in the race were all good. The toilet scenes and the simulated sickness and all those acres of naked flesh had gone. She watched all the tapes from the London auditions. Sallie, who had organized all the viewing but had not spent hours in front of a monitor, enjoyed the chance to see the people it had all been about.

They created another database and they pruned down the list of potential candidates to 120. They were working against the clock, as usual. The final audition was held on Friday 22 March, and only four days later they needed the pruned list.

'We were viewing like crazy. We both worked all weekend, and in terms of sheer pressure, I don't think anything will ever be as bad as that. The Easter weekend was coming up, and I was determined everybody on the team would have a four-day break, because they'd all worked so hard, so it was vital to move on to the next phase.

'Cutting the list to 120 wasn't too difficult. We cross-referred to each other so that we knew we were getting a good mix of different types, and we used the notes the producers had provided. Then we created a tape of them all, which we showed to Phil, Helen and Gigi. They simply would not have had time to view all 400.'

The next event was a mass meeting in the biggest room available at the Shepherds Bush offices on Tuesday 26 March. Everyone who was involved in the programme at this stage was there, from the runners through to the top trio – 35 people altogether.

'We didn't quite lock everybody in, but it was almost like that,' says Sallie. 'Sandwiches, tea and coffee were laid on, and we had a huge brainstorming session. Everyone in the room had the application forms and producers' comments on the 120, and a two-minute sample of their interview tapes was shown on a large screen.'

After each applicant's film was shown, the tape was stopped and the whole room discussed them.

'Everyone's opinion counted. Phil was very good at making sure that even the youngest and shyest of the runners expressed their feelings about them. After all, we're not making a television programme designed to appeal to television executives – we're making it for a huge cross-section of people, and we needed to hear every possible reaction to the people on the screen. He took time and trouble to make sure he heard all our thoughts about them.'

The session lasted from 9.00am to 8.30pm.

'Everyone was knackered, but quite excited by the end. We all had our favourites. The producers were interested to see the ones chosen by other teams. Some of the applicants provoked strong reactions, either of liking or not liking. Others, you could look round the room and see that people were talking among themselves, doodling, not watching the screen. If that was happening after thirty seconds, it said a lot, and the decision was quite easy,' says Sallie.

The following day, armed with all these reactions and

comments, Phil, Helen, Gigi, Sallie and Wendy went through the shortlist again. They were joined by two producers, one male and one female, for balance. Between them, they whittled the list fairly easily down to 84.

'We knew we had to get it down to 80, and the final four to be removed were very, very difficult. We argued and discussed for hours, went through all the notes again, reminding each other of who they were: "You know, that bloke with the funny hair from Manchester" etc. Opinions could change during the course of the day: someone you said no to first thing in the morning might be back in the mix by the afternoon. When at last we agreed on who was in and who was out it was with a feeling of relief, but also a bit of sadness that we had to lose some good people. But you never completely lose them: they're always at the back of your mind as possibles. In the end, we decided to call 82 in for interview,' says Sallie.

Phil had already sampled the quality of candidates coming through, both by looking at videos and by attending one day of auditions.

'From a very early stage I knew we had a very strong field this year. We felt in general that we wanted a younger, funkier mix, but there were so many good people cropping up across all age ranges,' he says. 'What is really special about *Big Brother* is the passion it generates among the people working on it. We all had really strong opinions. We are hooked on *Big Brother* three months in advance of the viewers, as soon as the selection process starts. Because it's all about the people. Finding the site and building the house are important, but it's when you start meeting the people that it becomes really special. And now we were down to the final shortlist and I was going to start meeting them, it was exciting.'

Next came another round of phone bashing: the final group had to be summoned to London for interviews with Phil, Helen and Gigi. For most of them, there would also be an interview with Brett Kahr, the psychotherapist whose expertise and advice has underpinned the success of *Big Brother* from the first series. Another intricate timetable had to be composed, and it was Jess Bendien and Susy Price who made most of the calls. Again, soon after putting down the phone having told the contestants the details, they would take return calls from them: they'd been too excited at the news to take note of the directions for meeting, or they simply wanted to check it was a genuine call, not a hoax call from one of their mates.

'Lots of them thought it was a wind-up when we called them. They were really excited – but underneath the excitement was this fear that it was all a big leg-pull,' says Paul Osborne. 'We tried to fix the times to suit them, within the very limited window we had. If someone had a really good excuse for not coming on the day we wanted, that was OK. But if they were just not sure if they could reorganize their lives around our schedule, we had to ask ourselves if this person really wanted to go into the *Big Brother* house.'

It was all very secretive. Hotel rooms were booked; the team needed three or four in the same hotel, one for the interviews, one for the psychotherapist, one to act as a reception room, one where photographs and details could be checked – and where contestants could be kept apart from each other. They masqueraded as a market research company, so that nobody on the hotel staff would know *Big Brother* auditions were taking place – the nearer the selection process got to its final stages, the more the team knew there would be journalists on the look-out for them. A tip-off about a location would mean a photographer with a long lens parked outside.

There were some comic moments. Booking the rooms under the company name of EUP – for Endemol UK Productions – one member of the team was asked by the hotel clerk what the initials stood for. On the spur of the moment he made up a suitable market research-sounding name: Enterprise Unions Performance. Remembering the false company name was tricky – at one hotel, Phil arrived first and requested the keys to the rooms, only to be asked what company he was representing. Unable to remember the phoney name, he had to wait until someone else from the team arrived.

There were ten days of London interviews, with an average of eight contestants a day. It was vital that they didn't overlap and meet each other: the essence of *Big Brother* is that the contestants are strangers when they meet inside the house. So a clandestine operation that would do credit to MI6 was put into operation. Each contestant was told to wait at a place a couple of hundred yards away from the hotel. The producers had scouted out suitable meeting places, usually outside a well-known takeaway chain.

Each contestant had a producer assigned to look after them for the whole of their interview day, and it was this contact who would meet them in the street. The producers would always wait until the contestants were there first, before crossing the road or emerging from around the corner to join them. Luckily, the weather was mostly fine: nobody had to hang about in the rain for too long. The main thing they were checking was whether the contestant had really arrived on their own, or whether there was possibly a press photographer lurking somewhere in the background.

'We had contingency plans – we would have left them standing there in the street without any qualms if we genuinely thought they were being shadowed, or were in league with the press,' says Sallie.

Walking routes to the hotel were closely worked out so that incoming applicants would not meet those already leaving.

'We looked after people we hadn't already met at the auditions. That was deliberate – it gave us the chance to meet new faces and form an opinion of them,' says Paul, 'We'd know what they looked like, because we had seen the video of them and looked at their photograph. You could always spot them, trying to look nonchalant and inconspicuous – and usually looking very conspicuous. From a distance, as you walked up, you could see them looking at everyone, wondering who it would be.'

All the contestants had been briefed not to mention the words 'Big Brother' when they met their minder, or when they were escorted through the hotel. The secret words could only be uttered inside the safety of the hotel room.

'So it was all very small-talky, asking about their journey and whether they'd had time for breakfast and that kind of thing,' says Paul. 'They were invariably a bit tense and nervous, so we had to try to help them relax.'

Before coming to the interview, every potential housemate was asked to go to their local police station and order a criminal record check to be done on themselves. They had to pay £10, and this was reimbursed to them at the interviews. As soon as the criminal record details arrived, they had to send them on to *Big Brother*. They also

---

FAVOURITE BOOKS OF ALL TIME

ADELE: *Wuthering Heights*
ALEX: *Oliver Twist*
ALISON: *Harry Potter*
JADE: *A Child Called It*
JONNY: *The Twits*
KATE: *Bridget Jones's Diary*
LEE: *David Ginola, Le Magnifique*
LYNNE: *Papillon*
P.J.: *The Godfather*
SANDY: I've never finished a book
SOPHIE: *A Time to Kill*
SPENCER: *Where's Wally?*
SUNITA: *Memoirs of a Geisha*
TIM: *The Downing Street Years*

---

had to bring with them to the interview two documents proving their address was correct – a passport or birth certificate, a bank statement, and a payslip.

'So they had quite a lot to organize before they came, especially as some of them had to collect documents that were maybe at their parents' house or whatever. But it was another way of measuring their commitment,' says Paul.

A Polaroid picture was taken of them, and then they were whisked in to meet Phil, Helen and Gigi.

'We know it was very difficult for them,' says Phil. 'They were facing three people they'd never met before who, in their minds, could affect their lives in a dramatic way. Some of them were actually shaking when they came in. I was trying to put them at their ease, but generally the effect I have when I do that is make them really scared, which doesn't help. Plus towards the end of the interview sessions I did my back in – I think it was a combination of having spent hours in hotel chairs and terrible posture – and I had to be almost carried to an osteopath by one poor producer, and given all kinds of powerful drugs. It meant we had to reorganize one day of auditions. And it must have been even more scary for the candidates, because I was walking around bent double, a bit like Julie Walters' character Mrs Overall from *Acorn Antiques*, which must have been unnerving.'

At first, most of the candidates would say what they thought the top team wanted to hear.

'A lot of them would come in with a plan of how to impress us. We had to get beyond that, and try to work out whether we really wanted to know them better. Do I want to keep on talking to this person? Can I relate to them on some level? I'm no more able than anyone else on the team to say what it is we are looking for, but there's something about some people that leaps out and grabs you, you want to see and know more of them.

'But it wasn't just a question of whether they were right for us. We'd try to explore their motives. People come to *Big Brother* with lots of different expectations, and it's important for us to suss out what they are. Some have done it for a laugh, and maybe haven't thought through the consequences, despite the talk of doom they've already heard. Others are trying to escape from their lives: perhaps they don't like their job, or their wife. Some want to be famous, and however well they try to disguise it, that's their prime motivation. We've done a lot of sifting out of motives at the audition stage, but we're aware that we may be seeing the people who were too clever to give away their true motives.

'So a large part of the interview is spent managing their expectations. We give them an absolutely realistic appreciation of what *Big Brother* can do for them, and how it could adversely affect their lives.

'We talk about the press and they ask questions. "Will the tabloids really find out about that affair I had?" Yes, they will. "Will they bother my mother and father about the drug habit I had years ago?" Yes, they will.

'We tell them to think about the effect all the publicity will have on their girlfriends, boyfriends or anyone else they've left behind – the people who will be hassled all the time. Do they want to feel responsible for that?

'We explain to them that it's not fashionable to be an ex-house-mate: it doesn't lead to a celebrity career. Brian, Craig, Helen, Anna and Mel are the exceptions to the rule. We want them to know that it could have a very negative effect on their lives. It was the talk of doom all over again, but this time being delivered straight at them, not at a room full of other hopefuls. I felt like a dour, Scottish miserable git who is going to mess up their lives, by the time we finished. But at every stage of the selection process, including this, people decided to pull out – which shows that it is important to help them think through what they're getting into.'

After twenty minutes, the producer/minder would knock on the door, and if things weren't going too well in the room, the top trio would use it as an excuse to wind up the interview and say goodbye.

'With some of them, we'd lost the will to live after five minutes. When you've run out of questions you want to ask them after twenty minutes, you know you aren't going to want to watch them in the house for nine weeks,' says Phil. 'But if it was going well, we just said we wanted a few more minutes, and generally they stayed for between 45 minutes and an hour. There were only three or four out of the whole list who went after twenty minutes. We had to wind up after an hour, but with some of the good ones we were still asking them questions as they went out of the door.'

The producers who were waiting to whisk them away would be getting tense if the interview lasted a full hour.

'It was a bit like a production line, and the longer they stayed the more risk there was of them bumping into another contestant,' says Paul. 'But on the other hand, we knew it meant that Phil, Helen and Gigi really liked them, and if we liked them, too, it was good news.'

In the minutes snatched between seeing candidates, Phil, Helen and Gigi argued about the ones they had already talked to. 'We are different people coming from different backgrounds, and a lot of it is down to personal taste. But interestingly, the really good ones appealed to all of us. It was on the borderlines that we had differences of opinion.'

After seeing the top team, most would-be contestants were taken to another floor in the hotel to meet Brett, again travelling by devious routes to avoid other candidates.

'We spent a lot of time on our mobile phones, talking to each other about which staircase or lift we were using. The phone would ring and it would be another producer saying, "Where are you? We're coming through," and you had to dodge round a different way with your contestant. At one stage there were three of us juggling five people who were all in the hotel at the same time, and astonishingly their paths never crossed. But it was a bit fraught,' says Paul.

The team were still on constant alert to weed out any journalists who might have got this far through the selection procedure. There was one false alarm for Paul. 'This girl was so inquisitive about the logistics of producing *Big Brother*,' he explains. 'She was throwing questions at me. Maybe she was just bright and curious, and maybe asking questions to cover her nervousness, but I felt a bit suspicious. I left her with Roman Green, one of the runners, while I went away and used a computer system check to see if there was any record of her working as a journalist. She would have been checked before, but the advantage of seeing all the documents was that we knew if anyone had ever used any other names, and we could check those out, too. She came back clear.'

Each contestant spent at least an hour, usually quite a lot longer, with Brett, which meant that there simply wasn't time to do them all on the same day that they saw Phil, Helen and Gigi, and more arrangements had to be made to bring some of them back at another time.

'We sent everyone we were really interested in to see Brett. It wasn't because we thought they were nuts. It is simply that he can find issues in their lives that we have missed, or he can explore them in more depth, in a safe, confidential space. And we always followed his advice. If Brett said someone was not right for the house, however sad we were to lose them, we dropped them. There was never any question about that,' says Phil. 'Sometimes, with his help, we would realize that going into the house could be the worst decision this person has ever taken. Maybe some people would say that's not for us to decide, it's up to them. But you have to take a responsible attitude. Some people are perhaps too fragile, some have more to lose than others. With two years of feedback to go on, we know how it changes people's lives.

'We're making a game show, and at the end of being addicted to these people for nine weeks, we'll all go on holiday and get on with the rest of our lives. But they will go back to lives that have changed, and the effects of *Big Brother* will be with them for a long time, although not necessarily in the way they want. We're not showbiz agents – our commitment to them starts and ends with the programme, which probably sounds awful. But we want to be sure that they are the sort of people who can cope with the rejection they may experience in the house, and the rejection they may experience afterwards.

'We don't want to damage people. We want to enjoy them, we want the viewers to enjoy them, and we want them to enjoy themselves.'

At the end of each exhausting day, Phil would call the whole production team together and they would all chat through their opinions of the people they had met that day. Brett would listen to their views, but say nothing: his vital opinions would be delivered privately, to Phil, Helen and Gigi. The whole team worked very long days. Although in theory the interview sessions were due to start at 10.00am and last until 7.00pm, they always went on longer.

At the end of the ten days, the triumvirate were able to get the list down by half, to the last 40. That's when the serious arguments began. Channel 4, who commissioned the programme, got involved, looking at the videoed interviews of the shortlist, and other senior executives from Endemol also gave their opinions. Ruth Wrigley, Head of Entertainment at Endemol, has been closely involved in both the previous *Big Brothers*, pioneering the first one as Executive Producer. Her views were very important, and tapes of this selection were taken to her home by taxi.

But again, it wasn't entirely left to the top team. Everyone who had at any stage met any of the contestants could still contribute to the discussions.

'One day Helen walked into the producers' room and asked us all who we would most fight for if we had to keep one person in the house,' says Paul. 'It was an interesting exercise. It made us all think very hard about who we most wanted in there.'

'It was still the only topic of discussion,' says Sallie. 'We went over every aspect of every one of them so many times, and tried to push our personal preferences to one side. We'd try to think of everything: "Have we got anyone like him? I don't like him, but he'd be good for the mix." It was good fun: my work in the early days had

GETTING YOUR *BIG BROTHER* FIX

You can watch it live on telly, you can see it on big screens in stations and shopping centres, you can get news updates on your phone, you can go on-line and see live pictures from the house, you can play interactive games, join other addicts in a chat forum, have e-mail bulletins of the latest news... You can be *Big Brothered* 24/7. Shame it only lasts nine weeks.

This year, the show is even more interactive than ever. Could be that the only technology you can get to grips with is your telly remote: that's OK, you can watch the daily programme on Channel 4, and if you've got digital TV you can tune in for the twenty hours of live-from-the house coverage on E4. Sky Digital viewers can choose from two different video views of what's going on in the house, and then watch compilation highlights; they can even place their bets on who's going to be evicted from their television screens.

But if you want to be more adventurous, there are lots of other ways you can join in the *Big Brother* bonanza. The website is bigger and better than ever this year, and the team of 30 web journalists will be pumping out news stories around the clock. If you log on, you can watch the contestants live, go on a virtual tour of the house, play games, test your trivia knowledge, win prizes, and suggest questions for Davina to ask the housemates when she meets them on eviction nights. You can meet the celebs who share your *BB* passion. You can also pick up all the latest news and gossip from the house, updated the minute something fascinating happens in there.

If you can't bear the thought of missing the action when you're away from your telly and your computer, don't worry. Mobile phone company O$_2$, sponsors of this year's show, have teamed up with the web team to put out text messages and spoken news bulletins on any phone system. You can also, for the time ever this year, vote via text, as well as by phone or through interactive television. And if you've got a WAP phone you can visit the *BB* WAP site for news and games.

If you're a real *Big Brother* anorak, you can have the *Big Brother* music as your mobile ring tone, and you can have a personalized *Big Brother* voice greeting for your callers. You can even play a virtual *Big Brother* game, where you move into the house and try not to get yourself evicted.

'We want people to feel that they can join in, and make a difference,' says Chris Short, the guy responsible for the web. His title is Director of New Media for Endemol. 'We've got three times as many people working on the web this year, and the news service is a lot slicker and a lot faster. We're putting out stories whenever they happen, and that includes right through the night. After all, *Big Brother* is a 24-hour programme so we need to provide a 24-hour news service. And every story we put out will be illustrated with a still picture or with a video clip of the house.

'We've also improved our mobile phone message services – we want fans to be able to stay in touch even when they haven't got access to a computer or a television. You can have messages silently texted to your phone, so that if you're at a wedding or out on a romantic date, you can keep in touch without anyone realizing.

'You can even listen to the housemates live down your phone, or you can get an audio update of what's happened in the house – you can choose whether you want an update for the last 24 hours or for a week.'

Chris constantly liaises with the other *Big Brother* teams across the world, sharing info about phones, interactive TV, websites, and so on. Mostly, it's a matter of them coming to him for advice.

'We've got the largest interactive TV audience in the world, and with Germany we have the largest Internet audience in Europe. We're pretty sophisticated in terms of technology, so we're in a high profile test tube as far as the *Big Brother* experiment goes. Every time *BB* comes around, we have new developments to add. It keeps it very fresh and exciting.'

been so anal, running the tape viewing, and it was wonderful to feel more creative, to feel we were actually dealing with the people who would make it into the house.'

There was another hurdle for the candidates: another interview with Brett. He saw the final 30 for another in-depth chat.

Three weeks before the programme began, after a great deal of heartache, the list was down to 24; and all of these were put under contract. They signed legal agreements that bound them to secrecy. But it was still too many, and the arguments and discussions continued.

'We pretty much agreed on who our 12 would be,' says Helen. 'But at all sorts of odd times of the day or night you'd find yourself thinking about them, wondering if this particular combination would be better, or whatever.

'We'd look at them and think we'd got it, and then someone would say "Wait a minute, what about so-and-so?" and we'd be off again, worrying away at it. It's not as if we are simply picking a group of individuals; we have to think very hard about how they will interact with each other, and whether there is a sufficient mix to keep a cross-section of viewers interested. It has to work well on a lot of different levels over a long time – nine weeks. We were not only trying to choose twelve strong individuals, but we also had to look at how they would work together.'

For Phil, it was like a re-run of *Big Brother*. 'We were playing the game before it started on television – we were nominating and evicting people from our list.'

The next stage was a couple of meetings with the commissioning editors from Channel 4, who ultimately were paying for and putting out the show. Mark Rubens, Julian Bellamy and Katie Brosnan were sent the two-minute videos of the final 24, and then there followed two long meetings with Phil, Helen and Gigi. Polaroids of all the candidates were strewn across a huge desk, and the arguments began again.

'We had our 12 in mind, but they gave us their input, coming at it from their viewpoint. There were fierce rows about a couple of them – we were so passionate about them we felt they were non-negotiable, and any mention of them not being in produced storm clouds,' says Phil. 'We did change two people from our original line-up, because there were elements of the mix that weren't quite right.'

One of the elements was a preponderance of young men in the original twelve.

'Five of our six men were in their very early twenties,' says Helen, 'whereas the women were across a much broader age span. Although we loved all of those men, they didn't have the breadth and depth of experience we wanted, and we wondered how much they would have in common with the older housemates. Of course you can never know until you put people together how they will get on, because people are endlessly fascinating and surprising; but we try to give them some common ground.

'So we had to lose a couple of our favourites. On the whole, though, the Channel 4 executives knew that we'd met and chatted to these people, and we'd had feedback from the rest of the team; so we were in a better position to judge than they were from seeing videotapes and pictures. They were never categorical about rejecting any of the candidates.'

The decisions made, it was time to hold your breath and wait – while the 24 final candidates lived their lives on tenterhooks. They were not told until the last possible minute who was going in, to minimize the risk of leaks to the press.

'I personally phoned all of the 24,' says Phil. 'Some got about two weeks' notice, because they had to give up their jobs or whatever. Others who weren't in regular employment, who tended to be the younger ones, got ten days. We had to keep it as tight as possible, because the tabloid frenzy had erupted, with newspapers appealing for readers to phone in the identities of any of the housemates.

'The phone calls to the ones who hadn't quite made it were the worst. They were horrible calls to make. They had got so close, and they were falling at the final hurdle – I think it's much easier to be dropped when there are 2,500 contenders than when you are down to the last two dozen. Some of them were really disappointed. But they are all stand-bys, ready and prepared to go in if someone in the house chooses to leave or if we have to take someone out. And because the house is so much tougher, we're expecting that to happen.

'The 12 who made it were very, very excited when I rang them. I thought Jade was going to collapse – she was hyper-ventilating. I had to tell her to sit down and take a few deep breaths. P.J. politely said, "Do you mind if I swear?" I said, "Of course not." He held the phone away and let out a really loud "Fu**ing hell!" Spencer sounded very cool and said casually "Who are you again?" I said, "If you don't want to take part, that's fine…" He burst out, "No, I do, I do." Lee said "Oh man, that's the best thing that's ever happened to me." I told him it could be the worst. Kate was driving her car and she had to pull over to take my call. She went so quiet I thought the phone had gone dead. Jonny said "Oh man, that's great."' Then he told me that I didn't need to worry about any news leaking from his friends and family as he'd made them all sign a contract and he said he would sue thm if they talked to anyone. I pointed out that it was a really nice thought, but his contract probably wouldn't stand up in court. Sandy was riding his bike when I rang him, and had to get off it to talk to me. He said "I'm quite excited in my own quiet, wee way." Even then, he wasn't giving much away. Alison was a surprise – she was strangely subdued when I told her. She said "I haven't been allowing myself to get excited about this. I need time to let it sink in."

'I think most of them had not allowed themselves to think it would actually happen. They were all jubilant, which is strange considering how many times they had been told it might be the worst thing that could happen to them. I think the phone call was a very big moment for them, and they will all remember where they were when they took it.'

Phil talked them all through the arrangements they had to make: about their jobs, about getting their bills paid while they are away, about having a place to stay at short notice in case they found them-selves door-stepped by reporters. Most of all, he reinforced the message about telling as few people as possible.

Then it was just a matter of everyone on the production team crossing their fingers, their toes, touching wood, offering up a few prayers and hoping for the best; hoping that the final fraught days before Friday 24 May 2002 would pass without any major dramas that might result in changes to the top 12.

CHAPTER FIVE
THE SHRINK

For the contestants as well as for the producers, Brett Kahr is one of the most vital people in the *Big Brother* team. But he's a secret that isn't shared with the viewing public. As soon as the housemates go into the house, they lose all contact with the outside world, and the only link they have is Big Brother, a disembodied voice that is sometimes male, sometimes female, has a variety of different accents and never, but never, is called anything but Big Brother. The presiding spirit of the BB house is faceless, nameless and often non-committal, answering questions with 'Big Brother will get back to you,' throwing the contestants even more on to their own resources and increasing the surreal isolation of the experience.

There is, though, one exception to this fundamental rule of the house: Brett, the *Big Brother* psychotherapist. While they are in the house, Brett is the only person from the outside world they can talk to privately, and who they call by name. He won't, of course, tell them the football results, but he will be available at any time, day or night, to talk them through any crises and unhappiness they face. They are able to ask to see him whenever they want, he can be summoned by the production team if they are concerned about any of the housemates, or he may spot signs himself from the television that make him want to check on one of them. And sometimes he'll be there to talk to every one of them in turn, for no particular reason other than to touch base with them and run through any worries they have.

Brett is no stranger to them. Every housemate has met Brett for two long interviews before they go into the house, and he's been involved at every stage of the selection process. He has a distinguished title: he's the Winnicott Clinic Senior Research Fellow in Psychotherapy at the School of Psychotherapy and Counselling at

Regent's College, London. But he's just Brett to everyone inside and outside the house.

Brett's involvement with *Big Brother* goes back to the first series. It was only a couple of months after the end of *Big Brother 2* that Helen Hawken, with whom he has worked for three years, rang to ask if he would do the third series. His response was unequivocal: 'If you are working on it, Helen, I'd be only too glad.'

Brett knows from experience, not just of Helen but of many of the other members of the production team, that his role at *Big Brother* is taken exceptionally seriously.

'I expect that many of my colleagues and fellow mental health care professionals would imagine that a shrink working for a TV programme is just a bit of window dressing,' he says. 'But they would be completely wrong. I have nothing but praise for the extraordinary probity and integrity of the team. Never have I been taken more seriously over diagnostic assessments than I am when I am working on *Big Brother*. All hats off to the television company, Endemol: *Big Brother* must be the flagship of all reality television programmes, an example of how well it can work if great care and attention are given to details, and if the needs of the contestants are seen as important in their own right, and not just to make good, compulsive television.'

He also likes the production team as individuals. 'They're a fantastic lot of people. I've known Gigi and Paul Osborne for three years, and I got to know Phil last year working on the second series, when I was helping on Friday nights preparing questions for Davina to ask the contestants. I feel I'm now one of the *Big Brother* old-timers, but I find the programme endlessly fascinating; and the people who are attracted to taking part as housemates are intriguing. If I'd been told before the first series that I would still be wanting to work on the show in series three, I would have found it hard to believe, but each series is completely different to the ones before, simply because the people are different.'

Brett was involved in preparing the questionnaires that the contestants fill in.

'They are very similar to the ones we used for the second series – just a few tweaks. One important thing is that they have been

WHAT CAN'T BE TAKEN INTO THE HOUSE?

Items not allowed in:

- drugs and narcotics
- personal medication, except in consultation with Big Brother
- weapons
- watches
- money, cheque books or credit/debit cards
- mobile phones
- palm pilots or electronic organisers
- agendas or diaries
- books
- pen or any similar writing implement
- paper/writing pad
- musical instruments
- playing cards or games of any description
- any item requiring electrical or battery power (even if they are powered by solar energy or other sources)
- exercise equipment or weights

reformatted, so that there is more space for the candidates to draw a picture of themselves.

'We didn't ask for this in the first series, but I thought some psychological drawing would be useful, so we made room for it in the second year. It has proved to be very, very revealing, and that's why we've given it more space this time. It's what we call in psychology "projective testing" because when you draw a picture of yourself you can project aspects of your personality that are important to you. So it is a great addition, very helpful to me in making assessments.'

Brett first became involved meeting would-be contestants when Phil, Helen and Gigi were down to the final 82.

'I kept in touch with the team during the earlier rounds of video-viewing and auditions, and I knew from the reports I was getting that it was a very good choice coming through. In the first year, I suggested some of the games for the auditions, but they've grown organically since then and the producers put a lot of their own creativity into it. But they might consult me if they wonder whether a game will be useful and revealing.

'My real work began in April, with the psychotherapeutic assessments. I saw the vast majority of the 82 who made it to this round, and every one of them got at least an hour with me, many of them far longer. The very last question I asked them, and I've asked it for all three series, was about their reaction to being interviewed by me. I partly ask it out of curiosity and partly to help them make sense of the experience. I say, 'We're about to finish. What was it like talking to me?' Then I ask if they'd ever met a mental health care professional before – a counsellor, a psychotherapist, a psychologist or a psychiatrist.

'This year, as in previous years, 99 per cent of them have never met a shrink before, either socially or professionally. I find that extraordinary, and it shows how little mental health ideas have actually penetrated the inner recesses of Great Britain. These young people have been encouraged to fend for themselves for their emotional needs, and meeting me can often be quite impactful for many of them.

'Many of them are very nervous when they come to me, and they have some odd ideas about what I am going to do. They assume I am going to ask them to lie on a couch and close their eyes. Many of them think I am going to hypnotise them – they say, 'Are you going to put me in a trance or something?' And lots of them think I will give them the Rorschach inkblot test, where they are asked to say what they see in the shape of an inkblot. Their ideas appear to be based on old Hollywood movies from the 1940s and 50s. Very few thought I would do what I actually did, which was have a conversation with them.

'Many of them said they found it very helpful talking to me, and lots of them said it made them realize what a responsible television company Endemol is, to be taking this much care of them. For me, professionally, it is fascinating to meet people who would not normally be referred to me, or choose to see me or any other shrink.'

Interestingly, as soon as Brett introduced himself as the *Big Brother* psychotherapist, many of the contestants remarked that they remembered seeing him on the psychology programmes last year and the year before. But Brett never appears in front of the camera for *Big Brother* – his work is always behind the scenes, and it is academic psychologists who give their views on air.

'It's fascinating that they think they've seen me – talk about false memory syndrome. But it's also important to stress to them that their dealings with me are totally confidential, and that I would never talk about them or the other contestants on air.'

After each day of interviews, Brett would listen to the views of all the production team, and then talk privately to Phil, Helen and Gigi about his thoughts and opinions.

'We had some disputes, especially when I raised serious objections to a handful that they had earmarked as having really great potential. But to their great credit they never overruled me; they always took on board my recommendations. I'd say, 'Listen, at the end of the day the decision is yours, and I'm here in an advisory capacity. If you want to put X in the house I'll do everything I can to support him, but my professional opinion is that it could be dangerous for him and potentially for others in the house.'

'Sometimes I'd have to justify my reservations, but once I did, they could see what I was talking about straightaway. What people will tell a producer and what they will tell a psychotherapist can be two different things. Also, I have licence to ask very intimate psychological questions which might not occur to the producers to ask, or which they may not feel they are allowed to ask. It was good seeing them on the same day; it meant we all met them within hours of each other and we could compare notes while they were fresh in our minds.

'They'd say things like, "We all really loved Y," and I'd say, "I can see why, she's very beautiful and very funny, but do you realize she has a history of suicide attempts?" or "She's currently using heroin?" or whatever I had unearthed.

'It would be wrong to be too specific about what I'm looking for as exclusion criteria, but the big things are a history of psychological disturbance and a history of injuriousness to themselves or to others. These are the real warning signs.'

Brett has found that the groups of contestants he has interviewed each year have been of a rising standard in terms of their mental robustness.

FAVOURITE DAY OR NIGHT OUT

ADELE: Shopping in the morning, a picnic on Camden Canal in the afternoon, and a Lauryn Hill concert at Brixton Academy in the evening.

ALEX: Saturday night in a non-commercial London club with a large dance floor, funky house music, with all my friends there, dancing till my feet give way.

JADE: Shopping, grab a coffee and a bite to eat, then go out at night with the girls and have a good drink and a dance, then go home to my boyfriend.

ALISON: Alton Towers with all my best mates, then on to the cinema with lots of popcorn, then a Chinese meal and round the evening off with salsa dancing.

JONNY: A day on my favourite beach in Corfu, a nudist beach. The sun blazing and an endless supply of ice-cold juice, ice lollies, and menthol cigarettes.

KATE: Wake up early, do a big workout, have a sauna, jacuzzi, sunbed. Then get dressed up and go to the West End with my two sexy sisters and shop till we drop. In the afternoon, go-karting and a football match followed by a champagne dinner with a lovely man, or a girls' night out, all having the giggles and getting up to mischief.

LEE: A night out on the quayside in Newcastle, at the Baja Beach Club. It's awesome, with the sexiest ladies in the country.

LYNNE: Champagne breakfast in a five star hotel, aromatherapy massage from a tall, muscular black man wearing a gold loin cloth, a Lear jet trip to Rodeo Drive in Los Angeles for lunch with girlfriends, followed by some serious shopping, then fly on to Rio for partying, clubbing, fireworks and more champagne.

P.J.: A good day with the lads would be footie, copious amounts of beer, followed by copious amounts of beer and women at night. With a girl my great day would be shopping for lingerie, followed by the pictures, a meal and a bottle of red wine.

SANDY: A spontaneous collision of good food, good wine or beer and whisky, great company and an awesome collection of CDs to play in the very small hours of the morning.

SOPHIE: Spending the day with my closest friends at an amusement park, then on to a club, staggering home in the early hours. Waking up and laughing together about the night's activities.

SPENCER: Being with the right person or people, then doing anything can be fun.

SUNITA: A Friday in summer, after work when you feel you deserve to party. Start in Soho, sitting outside Latino's Bar with my friends. Then off to a club, usually Fabric, to dance our socks off. A saucy snog, if I'm lucky.

TIM: Going shopping, having a great meal, playing rugby or tennis, or watching Arsenal play. Then, in the evening, going out with my group of friends, all of us single, and getting VIP treatment eveywhere. Getting noticed.

'In year one I saw anybody and everybody, because the team did not really know who they were sending through to me. In the second year they themselves were much better at diagnosing problems, and they had a much more developed sense of how stressful the programme can be. Also, I think stronger people applied, and of course there were more to choose from.

'This year we have gone forward again, and the people I saw were an even more rigorous selection. Helen has worked so closely with me, and she has a really good native psychological feel for who may work and who may not, and that has percolated down through the team to the producers who carry out the auditions. Everything has been improved and refined, and we now have a great system in operation. We also all have a much clearer idea of who can manage *Big Brother* and who can't.'

But Brett's interviews don't simply help the producers with their choice of contestants. They also help the contestants face the reality of nine weeks in the *Big Brother* house, and the aftermath. No matter how many times they have heard the talk of doom about the negative aspects of the house, many of them have not, in their excitement at getting through the auditions process, really taken it in.

'Even if they sent me fully psychoanalysed people who didn't need to be screened, the meetings with the shrink serve another valuable function in terms of preparing them. My job is twofold: I'm not just screening them for the television company, working out if they can manage it on psychological grounds, I'm also preparing them for the possibility of being selected to go into the house.

'In this second function I help those with ambivalences and doubts to air their feelings, and explore whether it is the healthy part of their mind that is driving them into *Big Brother* or whether something unhealthy and self-destructive is pushing them forward.'

A disproportionate number of applicants come from large families, with lots of brothers and sisters, or have lived in boarding schools – both situations that prepare them for the experience of communal living. There are, Brett has observed, relatively few applicants who are only children.

'One of the questions I have to ask those who come from large families or from boarding school backgrounds is this – are they trying to recreate a family or childhood experience and do it better? Is it a creative way of working through difficult early experiences? Is it a way of replicating early family experiences that might have been pathogenic and not in their best interests?

'The trick is not just to establish their baseline suitability, but to explore their unconscious motivations for wanting to be in it. Most often, when you ask them why they are doing it, they say, "Because it will be fun." I don't consider that to be a substantial reason. Fun is going out for a night with your mates; it is not giving up nine weeks of your life in such an all-embracing way. They all have another agenda, which may not be conscious even to themselves. Ultimately, they may not be the best judges of why they want to go into the house, because they have never explored their own motivation at any deep level.

'After talking to me and looking at some of these issues, some of them do decide to drop out. Others have cold feet, but decide to go ahead – but they go ahead with much more realistic expectations.

'This year, nobody has gone into the house in a starry-eyed state. Experience of two previous sets of housemates has allowed me to be much clearer with them about the financial benefits of *Big Brother*. I make them do research – I tell them to read the books that give a clear picture of what it is like in the house on a day-to-day basis, and watch the videos.

'I also found it very useful to show them all a supplement from *OK!* magazine, which included a photo gallery of the 22 housemates from the first two years, with a star guide out of five for their media career potential. The majority only got one star. I say to them, "Let's not preclude any possibilities; you may end up with a modelling or television career. But it is actually most unlikely. You should use your time in the house as an experience to learn something, particularly about yourselves."

'I believe the unconscious reason why most of them go into the house is that they want feedback as to what they are really like. And, boy, do they get it!'

Brett has on call a team of some of the country's most experienced mental health professionals, from whom he could ask for second opinions whenever he felt it was necessary.

In May he saw the final 30 would-be contestants for a second time.

'It's very useful seeing them twice. Even Freud couldn't get the full measure of a person in one encounter. I want to see how people evolve over time, to see if they have the potential to change or whether they are going to show a rigid, obsessional personality that has no alterations.' We have seen at least two examples in previous series of how personalities blossom: Craig, the winner of the first series, was known as the incredible sleeping man until the confrontation with Nick, when his true strength and integrity emerge. And Helen, the runner-up in the second series, was quiet at first and was one of the two first nominees, and then opened up. It is this ability to grow that Brett looks for.

In the final run-up weeks, Brett has another vital role to play: he holds a training session for all the producers who will be on duty round the clock watching the housemates.

'Some of the producers are new, and even those who have been involved in previous years appreciate the session. Training them is important: they need to feel they have access to me at any time, because they are the people who are going to have to make decisions at 3.00am when one of the housemates is crying. Do we call them to the Diary Room and chat with them? Do we leave them alone? Do we call Brett? I stress to them that I am available 24 hours a day to be summoned, and that I'd rather be called than not if they have any anxiety about one of the housemates. But I also give them a few pointers to help them with Diary Room chats when contestants are feeling sad, or missing home, or there is friction between housemates.'

Once the contestants are in the house, Brett does not see them face to face until the night of their eviction, when he has an extended opportunity to talk to them after they have been filmed live leaving the house, reuniting with their friends and family, and chatting to Davina. They are naturally on a high. He sees them again for a much longer, more detailed session after they have been out for two or three days.

'This is a very productive session, when I help them to come to terms with leaving the house, and I go through the stories that have appeared in the press about them.'

In previous years, this interview took place on the Saturday morning after the eviction, but this year it has been moved back. Feedback from the first two series suggested that this was too soon, coming when excited housemates, who have barely slept all night, are still buzzing with the madness of the night before. A couple of days later, after they have seen the newspaper fever surrounding their evictions, they can appreciate and make use of their time with Brett better.

Brett's involvement with them is open-ended: he has follow-up meetings with them for months after they have left the house. Judging by the experience of the first two series, some will want to see him more than others, but all will need him in different ways. Brett's name is part of the mythology of *Big Brother*; it's a name that comes up whenever two or more housemates meet up in the outside world, when their *Big Brother* days are over.

CHAPTER SIX

COUNTDOWN TO THE HOUSE

It was on Friday 12 April, six weeks before the off, that the production team upped sticks and left their cramped offices in Shepherds Bush for Elstree, the place that would become a second home to them for the following four months. Everything they needed was packed into boxes and ferried up there in vans.

'Everything except the application forms and videos of the final contenders,' says Sallie. 'I was completely paranoid about them. I took them to Elstree in a taxi on Monday morning, physically escorting them to make sure they didn't go astray. We'd worked so hard getting the list down, I didn't want to run any risks.'

On the following Monday, loads of new faces flooded the *Big Brother* team. Over the next couple of weeks, the headcount of people working on the show rose to 300.

'It's not like running a television programme, it's more like running a village. Or a cult, because we all share the same obsession,' says Phil. 'But sometimes I walk around wondering what everyone does.'

Several of the producers were already in place: Sallie and Wendy, of course, the two senior producers, and Paul, Deborah, David, and Claire. Another seven joined, to bring the team of day producers up to strength.

'Choosing the producers was almost as difficult as choosing the housemates,' says Phil. 'We were looking for a group who would get on well together, as they have to support each other and work together, but everyone brings slightly different things to the *Big Brother* experience, everyone watches the people in the house in slightly different ways, and we wanted to reflect that in the programmes. Some will be looking harder for humorous elements, some will be more sensitive to the mood in the house. We think it's a plus: we don't want all the programmes to feel seamlessly the same.'

Melissa Brown and Walter Iuzzolino were two of the new bunch, and as neither of them had worked on previous *Big Brothers*, there was a mysterious induction into Phil's cult ahead of them.

'For the first week we sat around getting to know each other and watching tapes of the *BB* programmes from the first two years,' says Melissa. 'There wasn't a lot to do except steep ourselves in the atmosphere of *BB*. I think it was deliberate, to help us bond as a team.

'At first we were not part of the secret language everyone was using – all of those who had met the contestants and been involved in the selection process used to talk about the shortlist, only using initials; they were always chatting about TD, MB, or whatever, and we had no idea who everyone was until later, when we viewed the tapes,' says Walter.

In the second week, their training started properly. For two weeks Sallie and Wendy took them through their roles. In television terms, it's a unique job; it involves complicated shifts that cover 24 hours seven days a week, and alternates between the role of gallery producer, who monitors what's happening in the house, and story producer, who puts together the programme that will go out on Channel 4 the following evening – a job that can involve working 30 hours non-stop.

As gallery producers, one of their jobs is to be the voice of Big Brother. Whenever one of the housemates goes into the Diary Room, the producer has to go into the sound booth and talk to them.

'We needed training in how to do it, because there has to be some consistency in how we deal with the housemates,' says Walter.

'The training sessions were vital,' says Helen. 'Working on *Big Brother* is different from anything I have ever done, and I am sure it is different for everyone else. Normally, you plan a great deal of what you are going to shoot, and then adjust and edit when you need to. But with *Big Brother* we want to be as open and honest as possible. Even if we make a mistake, we don't hide it – which is a completely different rule from that of most other programmes. Also, the pace and content of the programmes are dictated by the housemates, not us, and we don't want to interfere with that. It's difficult to grasp when you're new to it, but if it's a boring day in the house that's just as relevant as a day when passions are running high.'

The producers were also sent out to meet a couple of applicants on the final short-list. They went to visit them in their own homes, met their families and went out with them.

'We'd book into a hotel near where they lived, so we could spend a whole evening with them,' says Melissa. 'I had to travel up north to see one of mine. He was great – he picked me up from the station, took me home to meet his mum and dad and girlfriend, and we all went out for a meal, and his best friend joined us. I was lucky, because all the people I met knew about his application. But some of the producers had to go under cover, pretending to be friends from London, or vaguely saying they were interviewing for a pilot for a new television programme, so that they could ask friends how they felt the applicant would be on TV.'

WHAT MAKES YOU LAUGH?

ADELE: Johnny Vegas, Ricky Gervais and Eddie Izzard.

ALEX: Lots and lots of red wine; *Monty Python's Flying Circus*.

ALISON: Anything and everything.

JADE: People with a good sense of humour. Graham Norton.

JONNY: Farting, I totally appreciate a good fart whether it's mine or someone else's.

KATE: *Trigger Happy TV*, *Friends*, *Dumb and Dumber*, my twin sister, being tickled.

LYNNE: Laurel and Hardy, Paul Calf, Wile E. Coyote, *The Simpsons*, my boyfriend, my mum, my friends.

LEE: Old comedy films, especially the *Carry Ons*.

P.J.: Rubbish jokes and rubbish wigs.

SANDY: Slapstick and people who are up their own arses.

SOPHIE: Someone with a great personality who is not afraid to make a fool of themselves. Billy Connolly, Eddie Murphy, Richard Blackwood.

SPENCER: Other people.

SUNITA: I laugh when other people laugh. I like practical jokes. *The Simpsons*.

TIM: Dry humour, Graham Norton, *Trigger Happy TV*, *Friends*.

'It was entirely up to them what they wanted to do. It wasn't part of the formal selection process, just a chance to get to know them on their own ground,' says Walter.

Two of the producers ended up in Birmingham on the same night, seeing different potential contestants (Alison and P.J.), so there was a lot of texting and phoning to make sure they didn't end up going to the same pubs, clubs or restaurants.

Afterwards, they wrote reports on the people they had met, their personalities, their families and their lifestyles.

'It was great for us to get feedback about what the contestants are like on their own territory,' says Helen. 'After all, coming to the auditions and then for interviews was a bit like a heavy duty job application, even though we tried to put them at their ease. They were on their best behaviour for us. But with the visits, the producers didn't have cameras with them, there was no pressure, everyone had time to relax. As a result, a couple of the people we'd liked but not felt entirely sure about went right to the top of our list because they revealed more layers to their personalities.'

While the producers were being trained, the top trio – Phil, Helen and Gigi – were spending hours inside the house, which was very nearly finished.

'You can love something when you see it on plans and in model form, but it's only when it's built that you can get a feel of what it would be like to live in,' says Helen.

'We kept popping in, at all sorts of odd times, to see how we felt about it, and to make changes. For instance, we soon realized there was too much furniture in the garden: it was very nice for the contestants, but it appeared very cluttered on camera.'

Then, after the training sessions, it was time for the 'guinea pigs' to go into the house. Three weeks before the launch, six young people went into the house for four days, followed the next week by eleven different youngsters. They were all people who had made it into the last 100 applicants, and most of them had been among the 82 interviewed. Jess Bendien and Suzy Price hit the phones again, recruiting them for their brief stays in the BB house.

'They were all such fans of the show they were thrilled to get the chance. They had to be available to come at short notice. They

First greetings.

Going down in to the house.

BIG BROTHE

The infamous diary room chair.

Cooking's tricky when it's raining and the poor house has to do it outside.

BIG BROTHER

Friendship across the divide.

'Keep the ball in the air, Adele, the longer you do it, the more football we get to watch!'

The divide hurts – P.J. and Jonny watch enviously as Jade tucks in to a huge steak.

Chill out time on the orange sofas.

The big fight – Alex tries to referee Jade and Adele.

Alex wins the right to be in the rich house.

Big ones and little ones – Alison and Kate compare cup sizes.

ALEX

Alex the baby boy.

Alex's parents.

Alex's love of cars started at an early age.

Alex with a couple of beach beauties.

Alex surrounded by friends and family.

Alex bares all.

Alex makes the best of a bad job, having a shower on the poor side.

Alex wins the task, again.

A top moment for Alex – sharing a bath with three house lovelies.

Alex keeps his feet verruca-free in the shower.

SANDY

As junior leader, age 17.

Sandy waves to the crowd as he enters the house.

Sandy, age 18, and his brother, Melville, just before Sandy went on his first tour of Northern Ireland.

Training recruits in Scotland as a Sergeant Instructor.

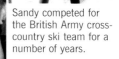

Sandy competed for the British Army cross-country ski team for a number of years.

Sandy and his wife, Claire, on the day they met.

The Tartan Army – celebrating Sandy's 40th birthday.

I'm Going For Everest

Climbing the height of Everest.

Exploring the Zambezi in a canoe.

Sandy and Claire.

Sergeant Instructor in the Black Watch, Berlin.

Up the ladder

over the roof

on the roof

bye!

Adele gathers her thoughts before a body building competition.

Adele as a little girl.

A tender moment in the pool for Adele and Alex.

Alex takes a chunk out of Adele's bum.

ADELE

Adele goes in.

Adele the body builder.

Adele and her mum.

Protecting the bits that don't normally see much sun.

Adele with one of her siblings.

LYNNE

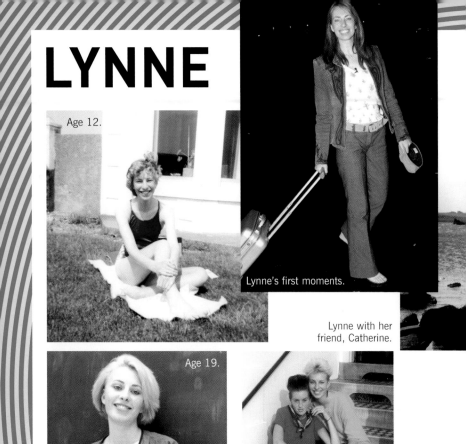

Age 12.

Lynne's first moments.

Lynne with her friend, Catherine.

Age 19.

Age 16.

Age 26.

Age 25.

Age 30.

Davina greets Lynne as she leaves the house.

Drink turns Lynne into Mrs Angry.

It's P.J.'s turn to catch the rough edge of Lynne's tongue.

NEXT

Lynne's Davina moment.

JONNY

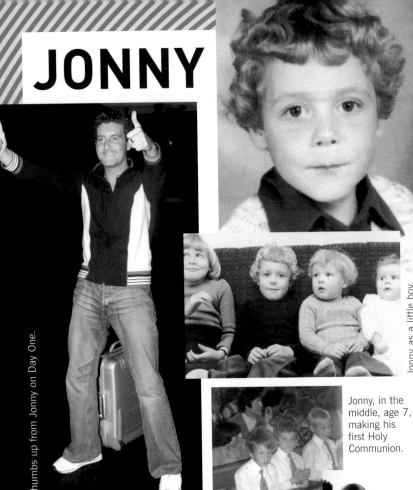

Thumbs up from Jonny on Day One.

Jonny as a little boy.

Jonny, in the middle, age 7, making his first Holy Communion.

Age 6 months old.

Jonny's parents.

Jonny, age 9, with elder sister Beverley and younger sister Joanne.

Jonny, age 10, on Christmas morning, playing with his Lego.

A touching moment when Jonny gives Alison a present before she leaves.

Jonny the stripper…

… takes the plunge.

KATE

Newborn baby, Kate.

Kate, age 1.

Kate as she goes in.

May queens for Beckenham – Kate and her sister, age 10.

Kate and her twin sister, Karen.

Kate, age 18, playing the part of MC in *Cabaret*.

Age 14, after running for her school.

Running the mini-marathon in London, age 15.

Disco dancers, age 9.

Kate on holiday with her ex-boyfriend.

Kate with her brother Robert and her sister Karen.

With her school class.

Just before entering the house – Kate and Karen's 22nd birthday, with older sister Kelly.

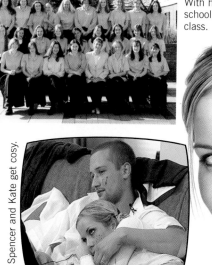

Spencer and Kate get cosy.

Kate's missing Spencer, and it shows.

'I've got to look my best.'

COAST
...AL SURF
...SSICS

SUNITA

Sunita makes her entrance.

Sunita shares her
worries with
Big Brother.

Free at last – Sunita
leaves the *Big
Brother* house.

already knew they weren't in the final line-up, so they all jumped at this. And they are now all on the stand-by list. We obviously couldn't put any of them in on the first day, as they already knew the environment, but we know from past years how hard it is going into the house later and joining an established group, so we certainly wouldn't rule out putting them in at that stage, if someone walks out. After all, we've seen them coping in the pretty intense atmosphere that there is in there,' says Helen. 'When they came out we had to tell them not to talk about what they'd seen, or the surprises would be spoiled for the viewers and the real housemates. But the great thing about them all is that they felt we had entrusted something really special to them. And they will all be given videos and photographs of themselves in the house, souvenirs to prove they lived the *Big Brother* life.'

'The guinea pigs tended to be very young,' says Phil, 'Probably because they found it easier to drop everything and come along for a week. Although they were good, seeing them made us realize why we needed a balance of older people in the show. They had fun – a couple of holiday romances sprang up while they were in there. I've no idea whether they survived back in the normal world.'

The first group were left to their own devices most of the time, as the crew tested camera angles, but the second batch had a far more structured time, following the route of the show, including an eviction show with Davina.

'One lucky guinea pig got a Davina moment,' says Phil. 'Being interviewed by her in the studio, just as if it was the real thing.'

'For us, it was a chance to have a real test run,' says Walter. 'We worked exactly as if we were making the programmes for real. It is more complicated than any other gallery job, because normally you can relax and just call the shots. But the Diary Room changes everything, because you are no longer just watching what happens, you are part of the narrative, as Big Brother. You have to forget what you were doing and concentrate hard on what the housemate is saying to you, because basically you could screw the whole show up if you don't act properly as Big Brother.'

For Melissa, when the little light flashes in front of her in the gallery to signal that someone in the house has rung the doorbell to go into the Diary Room, her stomach lurches.

PRESSING PROBLEMS

An urgent rush of *Big Brother*'s signature house tune cut through the babble of voices, and 90 journalists broke off their conversations and turned to watch a montage of clips from the first two series on a large screen, with the familiar Geordie voiceover from Marcus Bentley. For the hacks, just as for the production team, *Big Brother* started early. It was 3 May, three weeks before the housemates stepped inside for the first time, that *Big Brother* burst back into the headlines. Aerial photographs of the new house dominated *The Sun* and the *Daily Star*; colour pictures of the garden, the kitchen and one of the bedrooms were plastered all over the rest of the national press.

The day before, at the press conference for newspaper, magazine and radio journalists, the new house was officially unveiled. A marquee was erected at the entrance to Elstree Film Studios, and visitors were channelled through into a large restaurant room where the screen and a small platform had been erected.

There was a short speech of welcome by Peter Grimsdale, who is in charge of developing programmes for Channel 4 – in normal-speak, he's in charge of programmes that have more than just a slot in a traditional TV schedule, programmes that include interactive elements and which have link-ups with other media like the web. You don't get much more Cross Platform than *Big Brother*.

'It's clear that *Big Brother* is as much part of the British summer as Wimbledon,' he said, and the assembled journos agreed. But they weren't there for the speeches: what everyone wanted was a chance to get inside the house.

Escorted in groups of up to 15, they were taken along the road to the still incomplete house, where they were each issued with blue plastic overshoes to prevent damage to the floors and carpets. Helen and Gigi supervised the tours round the building.

'My God, it's claustrophobic,' 'I'd last two days, max,' 'It would feel like living in an IKEA showroom,' 'It's so exciting, actually seeing it,' were some of the comments.

Back in the press room, they had the chance to question executives from the show and from Channel 4. The launch successfully splashed the new series across the papers – but it also allowed the journalists to declare open season on *Big Brother*, and for the final three frantic weeks of preparation there was an equally frantic search by the red top tabloids for any clues as to who the final line-up of contestants might be. As usual, there was a degree of plea bargaining: if any newspaper got a sniff of who might be going in, they knew that by publishing anything they'd be scuppering that contestant's chances – and ruining their own story. Just as in year two, when several of the names were blown at the last minute but never published, the press held back. They were certainly geared up to swing into action as soon as the game kicked off: for days beforehand, they were running appeals for anyone who recognized a contestant to ring in with information about them.

It made for tense times in the production offices. Would they get through to launch day without a leak? They did by

'They may just want to ask for hot water, which is easy. But you never know – they may want to tell you that they are walking out of the house.'

The most surprising thing for two newcomers like Melissa and Walter was how quickly the guinea pigs – and the real contestants – forget that there are cameras on them, and that Big Brother is watching their every move and listening to their every conversation.

'They completely forget we are there, within a matter of hours. We listened to a group of the guinea pigs hatching a plot to go and hide under the beds in the girls' room, and they were wondering how long it would take Big Brother to notice. They completely forgot that we could hear everything they said! And when they do want to tell you something they pick up the mike and bring it close to their lips and say, "Hello Big Brother," as if we can't hear them the rest of the time!'

For Helen, too, despite being on her third series of *Big Brother*, the guinea pigs made fascinating watching.

'Seeing them in there confirmed to all of us just how compulsive it is, watching the house. Even though we're old hands, they're not – and that's what makes it unmissable. As soon as the guinea pigs were in and we found all the production staff standing around watching the monitors, we knew it was all going to work again.

'And you realize how difficult it is to really judge people until you see them in there. With some of them, as we were watching, we were thinking: why aren't they among the contestants?'

During the first guinea pig week, one of the girl housemates 'walked out'. The top team knew before she went in that she couldn't stay for the full four days, and that helped them stage a walk-out to give the producers a dry run of what it could be like.

'It was amazing for us – we didn't know till afterwards that it was planned,' says Melissa.

Helen says, 'It was really valuable to be able to throw in little tests like this. We were testing all the technical problems as well as testing the producers; after all, even those who had worked on it in the past had never worked on this new house, and we've never, ever had a walk-out before this series, so it was just as well we rehearsed it.'

The guinea pigs were also vital for testing the tasks, not just to make sure they could happen within the half-hour timeslot, but also to adjust any technical problems on the live Saturday night task show.

'We are using a large Outside Broadcast scanner truck, and we had a few technical hiccups,' says Helen. 'We didn't want to just follow the task, but also watch how it affected the rest of the group, so we were scanning different camera feeds from the house.'

The guinea pig runs also helped smooth out all the small but vital routines of the house, like the twice-daily change of microphone batteries. Despite the minor hitches, both Melissa and Walter felt they were joining a very well-oiled machine. 'So many lessons must have been learned in the first two years; the system works very well by the third year, and it hasn't been difficult to slot in,' says Walter.

Following their gruelling marathon shift, the producers get two days off.

'But we can't wait to get back in, and we all come in early, just to catch up on what's been happening. We're all watching it on E4 even when we're on our days off – we're as addicted as everyone else,' says Melissa. 'It's the first show I've worked on where all my friends and family want to talk to me about it. Before it started, they'd ring me up to ask questions, and I'd have to say firmly, "I can't tell you anything." Normally, nobody is much interested in my job, but a couple of weekends before it started I went to a wedding. It was as if someone had pinned up a notice saying, "The girl in the pink dress works on *Big Brother*," because everyone wanted to ask me questions. Even when we went out to meet the contestants and their family and friends, they all wanted to know things like, "Is there a hot tub this year?" and we had to say nothing. *Big Brother* is so much more inclusive than just a television show – in fact, the only thing that reminds me it is a show is when I go into the gallery.'

Walter describes it as more like a family than a job. Even when they are working through the night, with nothing more exciting to watch than a couple of bedrooms full of sleeping contestants, it feels special.

'Being on duty after 3.00am is a bit like sitting in an airport departure lounge,' says Melissa. 'It's timeless, and you're just sitting there with your headphones on, waiting for someone to wake up, something to happen.'

The producers have a room with a sofa where they can rest during their long shift as story producer, and there's an *en suite* shower room. They are not the only ones who work round the clock: even between 3.00am and 8.30am, the quietest time in the *Big Brother* house, there is one cameraman and one sound man on duty, one director and one logger. Loggers are young would-be journalists or television researchers who are employed to constantly type up everything that is said in the house. During the day there are two of them working, splitting all the conversations between them. Their record is fed into a computer, which can then retrieve any bit of dialogue, complete with a date and time of when it happened.

When the guinea pigs came out there was a large de-briefing meeting for them with the production team.

'Mostly, they reinforced things we were already wondering about. We made some changes to the building – we moved some interior walls at the bottom of the staircase that leads down into the living space,' says Helen. 'We thought when we were watching it on camera that it went back too far. The changes have made the living space feel more unified, and it's better for camera coverage.'

They also did a lot of work soundproofing the Diary Room. 'It's really important that the housemates feel confident they can't be heard, or they won't open up in there,' she says.

The camera runs, too, were noisy: in the middle of the night the guinea pigs reported being able to hear the cameras trundling around the run. Carpet was laid to muffle the sound. The garden needed extra screening, and more vegetables were planted when it became clear there probably would not be enough to last the whole run of the show.

'When the housemates are in there, it is important that they leave the outside world behind,' says Helen. 'It's not just a matter of having no newspapers, television, radio or phones. We want them to feel isolated, and if they can hear cameras and see buildings over the wall, they won't immerse themselves in the experience quite as much.'

The sofas that were originally installed have been replaced with feather-filled ones, in a slightly less vibrant orange.

'They looked wonderful, but they just weren't very comfortable, according to the guinea pigs,' says Phil. 'So they were changed in the final week.'

'We listen carefully to everything they tell us, because every little thing can impact on the way the contestants feel about living in there. Tiny things, like getting the exact level of oats or dried pasta right,' says Helen. 'We had to spend ages working out the height of the screen for the shower in the garden: we wanted the girls to feel comfortably covered, but at the same time we needed their heads to show, which meant a balance between the heights of the tallest and the smallest.

'However many times we, as the production team, went into the house, we always had too much knowledge beforehand, too many expectations: we couldn't view it through the surprised eyes of the guinea pigs, and we weren't spending 24 hours in there.'

BAD HABITS

ADELE: Causing arguments and behaving like a brat.

ALEX: Biting my fingernails.

ALISON: Picking my nose, plucking my facial hair.

JADE: When I brush my teeth I also brush my tongue and make dirty noises.

JONNY: Farting, picking my nose, squeezing blackheads, plucking nasal hair, biting nails – toes as well as fingers, using nail clippings as a toothpick, humming and rocking backwards and forwards while I eat, tugging at my privates when I'm talking to people.

KATE: I swear too much, bite my nails, whine about my bum, leave hairs in the bath after shaving my legs.

LEE: Farting.

LYNNE: Picking my flaky ear and flicking it, sighing, sneezing loudly, laughing loudly, feeling a bit of special material, like Linus in *Peanuts*.

P.J. Thinking I'm right all the time. Snoring.

SANDY: Snoring when I lie on my back.

SOPHIE: Talking too much; being stubborn.

SPENCER: Smoking, picking my feet – although what's the problem? They're my feet!

SUNITA: Eating junk food, playing practical jokes.

TIM: Picking my nose, spending 30 minutes doing my hair.

Another result of the de-briefing was an extra session with the producers to talk about how they handled their Big Brother role.

'The guinea pigs all said that they felt happier and more relaxed when they felt that Big Brother was actually listening to them, not just asking them a string of rehearsed questions. We went back to the producers and said that although Big Brother has to be impersonal, he does not have to be inhuman. Obviously, they all get nervous when they first do it, and tend to become a bit robotic and just follow the rules. We told them not to be too formal,' says Phil.

The final week before the housemates arrived was spent in an atmosphere of rising tension at Elstree. For the producers, there were last-minute training sessions: they had to meet the Channel 4 lawyers to be briefed on what could be screened; they had a training session with Brett; they had to immerse themselves in the ten pages of rules which govern life in the house, and which they are expected to know when they play their Big Brother role. By this time, both Melissa and Walter admitted they were dreaming about the house, the diary room, and being Big Brother.

Davina, also, was busy getting ready for Friday night. Although she did not meet the contestants before they went in, she was doing her homework on them: reading profiles and getting to know their photographs, so she would be able to identify them by name as soon as they climbed the metal staircase to the door of the house.

For the contestants, too, these were anxious times. They knew they were scheduled to go in, but they had to keep acting as normally as possible so as not to alert any media interest. They were told not to accept any phone calls from people claiming to work for *Big Brother* – a trick that journalists have tried in the past – but only to talk to the contestant care team: Susy Price, Jess Bendien and Karl Warner. These three made sure they all got their criminal record checks in, had their medicals, and knew exactly what to do in the event of being door-stepped by the press. One of the team is waiting for every contestant who leaves the house on eviction nights, and spends the whole of the next day helping them re-enter the real world. Two of them, Susy and Karl, also had to move into hotels with the two substitues, Sophie and Tim, before they went in, Even when the contestants' time in the house is over, Susy will be at the end of a phone for several weeks, to help them if they need to make contact with Brett or have any other problems.

'We know from previous years that some contestants are very happy to make full use of Brett's services, while others feel they can't ask for it, even though we bend over backwards to let them know it is on offer,' says Helen. 'Perhaps they feel it is displaying a weakness, rather than seeing it as something that can make them stronger and help them come to terms with the extraordinary experience they have been through. Whatever their response, his services are on offer again to all of them.'

Susy, Jess and Karl also went through with them all on the phone

---

TECHIE TRIVIA

- Five manned cameras trundle around the run that surrounds the house, peering in through the two-way mirrors at the contestants. Even in the dead of night, one cameraman is on duty.
- Producers in the control room operate another 15 remote-controlled cameras.
- A further 13 fixed cameras keep every area of the house and garden under surveillance.
- Over 40 microphones pick up the sounds of the house.
- And that doesn't include the individual radio microphones that the contestants must wear at all times.
- The voice of Big Brother is relayed through the house on a tannoy system.
- 50 kilometres of cable have been used to link the house with the studio.
- In the gallery, 50 monitors show the producers everything that is happening – or not happening – in the house.
- Over the whole nine weeks, 2,000 radio microphone batteries are used, the contestants having to replace them twice a day.
- 9,000 hours of tape will be recorded over the whole series.
- 150 production staff work on the show, with another 150 ancillary staff.

---

what they were allowed to take with them into the house, and made sure they knew the rules of life in the *Big Brother* compound.

For the top team there were numerous last-minute things to arrange. Helen had to talk to a local doctor who was willing to be on 24-hour call, a vet and a dentist. There was a meeting with Julian Stockton, who runs The Outside Organisation, a PR agency that looks after the contestants for two weeks when they come out of the house.

'We're here to take care of them in an impartial way,' says Julian. 'We advise them on any offers they may get from the media, and if it's appropriate we will help them find a showbusiness agent. Not all of them will want to, and not all of them will be taken up by agents. Our job is to try to return them to their normal lives. They will spend two nights in a hotel, and then go home, if that's where they want to go. We'll be giving them help in how to cope with public reactions, as well as the press.

'For some of them, offers from the media will be coming in while they are in the house, and we'll handle those and put them to the contestants when they come out. I saw them and talked to them before they went in – and like everyone else on the team, I've really stressed to them that they must not expect an amazing celebrity career afterwards.'

'We wouldn't dream of leaving them on their own when they come out – there is so much media attention and they need expert help coping with it,' says Phil.

The plan was for the producers to swing into action as chaperones on Thursday. But at the last minute it all had to be brought forward by a day – there were too many journalists sniffing around, and it appeared that some of the names may have leaked. So, on Wednesday the contestants travelled to London where they were each assigned a producer to look after them. It was another complicated secret manoeuvre, with the twelve booked into different hotels across the capital. They were allowed to bring partners and close family with them, but the chaperones stuck to their sides.

'We had to calm them down, check their luggage, try to encourage them to sleep, which wasn't easy as they were so excited,' says Walter. The production staff also had to keep their eyes open for any possible reporters or photographers lying in wait for them, as even at this late stage, if any of the contestants had been identified in the press, a stand-by would enter the house in their place.

Phil, Gigi and Helen visited them all on Thursday at their different hotels for a final chat. One of the topics they discussed is the exit plan: they made sure the contestants know what will happen to them after they are evicted.

'At that stage they have already entered the *Big Brother* world,' says Phil. 'Then on Friday there were things to do – checking their bags, having their photographs taken, briefings from Julian Stockton about how everything will be handled when they leave the house. And a lot of time spent waiting nervously for the big moment.'

CHAPTER SEVEN
THE BOYS

Here they are, the *BB* boys. They're in your living room every night – but how much do you really know about them? Which two house-mates both claim to be champion farters? Who was worried about the camera homing in on his hairy toes? Which three boys would like to be reincarnated as women? And isn't it interesting that all the boys, with the exception of Sandy, went into the house thinking they would win? Here's everything you'll ever need to know about *BB3*'s housemates, starting with the boys...

ALEX

Full name: Alexander William Hans Sibley
Nicknames: Al, Alex, Sibz
Age: 23
Marital status: Single
Star sign: Aries
Height: 6 feet
Weight: 11 stone 7 pounds
Tattoos and piercings: None.
Favourite food: Pasta, wild mushrooms,
kangaroo, sausages (German style).
Ambition: To make enough money to enable my dad to retire.
What's in his suitcase? 6 bottles of beer; container of sugar;
1 photo clip holder; 1 picture frame with two photos; 1 'No
Smoking' sign; 3 packs of joss sticks; 4 packs Tchai tea; 1 small
stuffed monkey; 1 eyepatch; 1 silver amulet; 21 pairs white
underpants; 1 pair union jack underpants; 1 food magazine.

Alex has drop-dead gorgeous looks, so it's no wonder he was
snapped up by a top modelling agency. But even lookers like Alex
have to work hard to get work – he goes to up to seven castings a
day, and reckons he only gets booked for one in ten of the jobs he
goes for. His big break was being chosen by Armani for their
campaign last Autumn, but the tragedy of September 11 dominated
everything and his new-found stardom went unnoticed.

Modelling isn't all glamorous. 'When I did my first catwalk
show I had to get changed in front of loads of women, and I was
in such a rush to put my trousers on that I fell over. They were
really tight and I couldn't stand up, and there were about 30
people watching me.'

He's also had a shoot for the Chinese Playboy Catalogue (a cloth-
ing catalogue). The pictures were taken in China when the temper-
ature was 35°C with 90 per cent humidity – and he was wearing
winter clothes.

He keeps in shape for his job by doing 200 sit-ups every morning, and some arm exercises.

Alex hopes that in ten years time he'll be settled down with a wife and children. He's very into family life: he's an only child and very close to his mum and dad.

'My Mum's German, and looks amazing for her age; she's loving, kind, a fantastic cook, always willing to help me. A friend and a mum, one in a million. Dad's an extremely hard worker, always willing to help someone in need. If I could be half the man my dad is I would be very happy. He's a good man and a great friend.'

He describes them as Superman and Superwoman: his mum Hannelore measures up to the tag by being brilliant at sport, good enough to be in the opening ceremony of the 1972 Munich Olympics with the German gymnastics team. And his dad Richard runs his own successful business.

'I think they're proud of me. They know I'm a good man and would never hurt anyone, and they know that at times I'm no angel.'

They're a sporty bunch. The craziest thing Alex has ever done is jump out of a plane at 14,000 feet, and mum and dad did it with him. He spent a year in Australia and his parents flew out to visit him.

'My mum is always telling me to wax my chest because I'm a bit of a hairy bugger, so I did. It hurt so much that I wanted to treat myself to a skydive, but instead my dad treated me – and he and mum did it too. So for one day we were The Flying Sibleys – and we've got the video to remind us that we were brave enough to do it.'

And his most embarrassing moment ever came after an early morning scuba dive with his parents, when they swam with about fifty white tip reef sharks, each about two metres long. It was a long boat trip out to the dive and a long boat trip back, and by the time they touched land again Alex was desperate to go to the loo, and only just about made it back to the hut where they were staying.

In Alex's list of the five things that most make him happy, his mum and dad come top, his friends are second, work is third, playing is next and fifth is his VW Beetle. He loves his car. 'It's not just a car to me. Even when I am stuck in traffic my little world is not affected. I know a bit about cars – it's the Essex boy in me!' He also goes go-karting with friends, which he reckons is another Essex boy pastime.

His Beetle figures in the list of things he's most going to miss in the house, along with the radio, his bed, and his home. He'll miss his parents more than anything, because they call him on the phone every day. If he had to choose a famous person to be one of his parents, it would be Nelson Mandela because 'he's a top man, he never let prejudice get in the way of freedom, he's an icon for peace'.

Working as a model takes him all over the world, which means he reckons he is well suited to the *Big Brother* experience. He's used to packing, 'and there is nothing I couldn't live without because I am used to living out of a suitcase'. He's proud of the fact that he's been to so many different countries; he can cope with the travel and never gets into trouble.

For Alex, the worst thing anyone could do to him is to steal from him. 'Anything, no matter how small. I don't like it when people take advantage of my trust. It's happened before – people have borrowed or stolen things and I haven't had them back.'

He gets angry with 'people who try to wash my car windscreen when I've told them not to. They put paint stripper in the water to get the windows clean'. He had a recent angry confrontation in Hamburg with an unwelcome windscreen washer, which ended up with him getting out of the car and confronting the guy. But when the man's friends rallied around him, Alex didn't hang around – he jumped back in the car and made a run for it.

Things he can't stand include skat music and the film star Jean Claude van Damme – well, he won't need to worry about either of those in the house.

He reckons he's tough enough for the house: nothing that could happen in there would reduce him to tears, and the only thing outside the house that could make him cry would be a death in the family. What's more, if he was upset about something, he'd be able to hide his emotions.

He would hate to be alone forever – no chance of that in *Big Brother*. But he doesn't mind his own company for short stretches of time, and enjoys travelling alone.

Looking like he does, it's no surprise to find that Alex is success-ful with girls. He has a girlfriend, but they've not been together for long. It's a good relationship because 'we don't argue, we have fun and we really like each other'.

He's a true romantic: he daydreams about having someone

ALEX	♈	ARIES

With so much fire in his chart, Alex will burn his way to the top of this world! In doing so, there will be some casualties. He is brave, outspoken and determined. Once he has made his mind up about something, hell on earth won't change his mind. This kind of make-up will cause some clashes of opinions. Lesson in *Big Brother*: to learn to adapt, and listen to other opinions.

special to come home to, and waiting for them to come home. He dreams of fun times together, and the thrill of being in love. He had his first girlfriend when he was 15, and there have only been three real relationships since then, the longest lasting for a year.

He may be half German but he's no fan of Michael Schumacher: if he could be reincarnated, he'd come back as the driver's left foot, 'so I could put my foot on the brake if he was winning'.

His dream job would be to be a long-distance jet pilot, 'but I'm not smart enough'. Despite what he says, Alex has seven GCSEs and A levels in German, sport and business.

He's not a big drinker. His favourite drink is a red wine from Australia, Penfolds bin 468, but he only averages a couple of glasses a week. And he reckons he only smokes ten cigarettes a week – but *Big Brother* has a funny habit of pushing up the house-mates' puffing rate.

The only thing he'd refuse to do in the house is eat liver and onions, because it would make him throw up, he thinks.

He reckons the other housemates will like him for his sense of humour, his good stories and his good breakfasts. He's also trust-worthy, and his criticism is always constructive. 'People get on with me because I'm a lover not a fighter. I'm never aggressive.'

But he reckons the others might want to nominate him for his smelly feet, or because they see him as competition – or just because he's from Essex! He's also a stickler about clean toilets and bathrooms, 'and if people don't keep them clean, I bite!'

The oddest fact about Alex is that he plays the didgeridoo. The other housemates are probably grateful for the new *Big Brother* rule: no musical instruments to be taken into the house.

JONNY

Full name: Jonathan Paul Regan
Nickname: Jonny
Age: 29
Marital status: Single
Star sign: Libra
Height: 5 feet 11 inches
Weight: 12 stone
Tattoos and piercings: None.
Favourite foods: Sunday lunch with roast beef and
Yorkshire pudding, fried egg and bacon sandwiches, chicken
and mushroom pie, chips, takeaways, chocolate fudge
cake, flapjack, custard.
Ambition: To hear the words: 'This is Big Brother,
will Jonny please come to the Diary Room.'
What's in his suitcase? 2 bottles white wine; 2 cards;
1 good luck charm; 300 cigarettes; 11 packets chewing gum;
2 cardigans; 6 pairs clamdiggers; 11 pairs underpants;
4 chocolate bars; *Viz* magazine.

Jonny's the Geordie fire-fighter who fronts his own band when he's not on Blue Watch – and says that if he had his life again, he'd have gone to drama college and taken to the stage.

Most of the funny stories in Jonny's life seem to involve the consumption of large amounts of alcohol. He likes a drink or three, and his family and friends know that as soon as he reaches the silly stage, he's likely to start stripping off.

'I don't have many inhibitions anyway, but [when I] drink I haven't got any. When I've had a drink I love people to bits, I'm dead tactile, I tell people I love them and I tend to strip off and do stupid things. It all started at a mate's stag night a few years ago. They couldn't get the stag to strip off, so I got everybody else on the minibus to strip, and we got his kit off him, too. Then I told the driver to drop us half a mile from home so we ran naked through the streets in the early hours. We saw a garage and we got the stag to go in, stripped off, and buy crisps and Coke. But while he was in there we all ran off, like naughty little schoolboys. He didn't know his way round the area because he lived twenty miles away, and he couldn't find his way back to where he was staying. In the end the police wrapped him in a bin liner and took him to the cells for the night.

'Ever since then, whenever we have a good night out with the lads, I try to get everybody to strip off and jog home.'

He's even done a bungee jump wearing nothing but his underpants. He was on holiday, it was the middle of the night, he'd had a skinful – and, well, the only surprise is that he kept his pants on.

Surprisingly, he was sober when he had his most embarrassing moment. He and his mates from the fire station were dressed in their uniform, collecting money in the centre of the town for the New York fire-fighters who perished on September 11. Most people were throwing money into their buckets, but one woman said she'd put a pound in if Jonny gave her a fireman's lift. She had visions of a big strong fireman hoisting her on to his shoulder.

'She was quite big, but not massive, so I said yes. Now there are two ways to do a fireman's lift, the male way and the female way. The male way, you put your arm between their legs; the female way, to be polite you put your arm around their legs. But she was wearing trousers, and I thought she might be heavier than she looked, so I decided to do it the male way. I told her I was going to put my arm between her legs, grab her arm, and that she should just relax on to my shoulders and I'd pick her up. By now there was a circle of people gathered round, all the shoppers and some of the market stallholders, and my mates.

'I started to get into position and she relaxed – a bit too much. She fell on us, and I fell over with her on top of us. I was lying on the deck on my back with her looking down at us. She says, "You shithead, you did that on purpose." Well, I didn't – but I thought to save face I'd say I did, so I apologized and said I was just playing a little joke. The lads were laughing so much they had to turn their backs and cover their faces.

'She dusted herself down and I said I'd have another go. By now the crowd was even bigger and it all goes quiet when I try to lift her. But I can't. I can only get her a couple of inches off the ground. She was hitting my bum and saying, "Come on, lift me!" but I had to admit defeat. So she says, "Are you saying I'm fat?" I had to say something, so I said, "No, but you're heavier than you look." She asked what I'd do if I was rescuing her from a fire and I said I'd just have to drag her out by her feet. The crowd was falling about laughing.

'None of the other lads would have a go, and some of them are a lot bigger than me. All day long, the woman kept walking past with her mates, saying, "That's the one who couldn't lift me." So now it's a bit of a joke – whenever we go into a new pub, one of the lads will go to the bar and when he comes back he'll say, "The barmaid's just said there's the one who couldn't lift that woman." It's a standing joke now.'

It's the sort of thing that always happens to Jonny. He once asked a stunning girl for directions and she said she would walk with him to show him the way. He was trying to impress her, then slipped and fell, and as he hit the deck he farted loudly.

'Just when I thought it couldn't get any worse I realized we were right next to a bench where a gang of schoolboys, about 15 years old, were eating their sandwiches. They roared with laughter, the girl politely kept her laughter in check. Then as we walked along I saw someone I knew and shouted "Wha-hey!" Then we got nearer and it wasn't my friend at all, just someone who looked like her. I knew I'd made a tit of myself so I dived into the nearest shop to get away from the girl – and guess what, it was a shop selling ladies underwear and other bits and pieces. I bought a hairband and fled back to the car.'

But for all his joking, there's a dark side to Jonny; the last book he read was an encyclopaedia of serial killers.

He's proudest of what he's achieved with the band. 'We put it together from scratch. We'd never done anything like that before, we were as green as grass.'

He's always popular, and he's not used to people not liking him. So the worst thing for him is when people sometimes take an irrational dislike to him. 'The most hurtful thing that could happen would be if someone hated me or thought I was an idiot when I'd been trying my best to get on with them.'

The one luxury he doesn't want to go without is cigarettes, which should make life interesting. 'I'm not a heavy smoker, but cigarettes are like sweets to me. I love them, especially when I'm out. But I know I've got to stop, so maybe the house will sort that out for me.'

He thinks we may see him cry while he's in the house. 'Emotions-

JONNY ♎ LIBRA

Jonny is young at heart and loves to fool around playing practical jokes. There is a quiet side to him emotionally, which he keeps in check. He will find it hard to discuss his emotions easily. Jonny will join in with anything, as long as it's a good laugh – sometimes at the expense of others. He will probably be the most faithful one in *Big Brother*. Lesson in *Big Brother*: to try to be brave enough to emote.

wise, there's nothing any of the other housemates could do that would reduce me to tears. But I'm not frightened to cry, and if I was missing people really badly and I'd had a drink, I might go and have a blabber in the Diary Room.'

He reckons he can conceal his emotions and put on a brave face when he has to.

'I did it when my dad had an accident and was in a coma for a week. I had to become the man of the house and stay strong for me mam and me younger brothers and sisters. I would go off and have a secret cry, but I didn't do it in front of them.'

Jonny's happy with his life; he doesn't want it to change much. In ten years' time he sees himself as married and with some children, still surrounded by his family and friends and 'just a bit older'. He wants to still be in England; he can't imagine living abroad. And although he may no longer be a fireman, he hopes he'll still be with his band.

He lives with his mum, dad and brother, and a Springer spaniel called Lucy. He's a real animal lover, and gets very angry when he hears of animals being mistreated. The death of his previous pet, another Springer called Sherry, was the saddest thing in his childhood.

His heroes are his parents. His dad is a really great role model for him: 'He's had so much thrown at him over his life, bad things. There have been plenty of good things, but lots of bad ones. I've watched him over the years and whatever happens he just deals with it. When he gets knocked over he just gets back on his feet, smiles and tries harder. I'd love to be exactly like him.

'My parents are like my bestest mates, in old bodies. When they see me in the house they'll realize that I do actually swear, I do talk about shagging. But I don't think they'll be shocked. My mum and dad are really hard-working people but they're always up for a laugh. I had the happiest childhood ever. We got loads of love; we had holidays every year, magical Christmases whether our parents could afford it or not. We had rules to obey and we were brought up to respect ourselves and each other. Our parents tried to keep us as innocent as possible for as long as possible – I believed in Santa until I was 11!'

He says he was shy and unsure of himself when he was a small boy, but after he left school and joined the fire brigade he found plenty of confidence.

He's a happy-go-lucky person, and he doesn't ask for much. 'I never mope about, and I try to live life to the full. The things that make me happy are my family and friends, my girlfriend, relaxing in the sauna, and making people laugh.'

The biggest love affair of his life is Joanne, the girl he has been with for the past eight years. 'Before that I always looked on it as a recreational thing: go out, meet a girl, see her for a few weeks and then dump her when I got bored or when I thought she was getting heavy. It sounds horrible, I guess, but I liked being single, going out with the lads, having a laugh. I had this thing in my mind that once you met a girl, your social life ended and you had to be with this girl all the time. But then I met Joanne, and she changed us. It's the best love affair, no doubt.

'She's my best friend, so supportive of me, no matter how crazy I am. She may be worried about me flirting with other girls in the house, but she really is my ideal partner. We love each other to bits and back.'

He had his first girl friend when he was 13, which was 'just holding hands, cuddling and kissing'. His first sexual relationship was when he was 17, 'but it only lasted a couple of weeks'.

He's interested in the way women think; if he could be reincarnated he'd come back as a woman, 'so I could see whether us men really are a pain in the arse like women always say we are'.

Going into the *Big Brother* house was so much on his mind in the weeks before he was finally chosen that he started dreaming about it. 'I was standing in a street in London and there were four lads and four lasses with suitcases and a man with a clipboard and he said "What are you doing here Jonny? You're not supposed to be here," and I walked away, gutted. Then I woke up and thought Thank God, it's only a dream. And that same morning I got the phone call to say I was in the team.'

He thinks he may irritate the others by being outspoken. 'When I've got a bee in my bonnet I have to voice my opinions. I'm not frightened of saying what I think.'

There's also the small matter of his farting: he claims he's the champion farter. 'I know it's disgusting and can upset people but when someone lets off a right rasper, I think it's hilarious. I won't just come out and do it in front of people at first, but when I know them, and if they're all doing it, I'll blow them away.'

And his energy levels: he reckons others can get irritated by the fact that he's constantly on the go, especially when they want to go to bed. Not that he's always full of boundless energy: 'I can sleep for Britain when I do go to bed, it's just I don't like to go to bed early. They might get annoyed with me in the morning because they'll have a job getting me up. I turn into half-man, half-mattress.'

On the plus side, he reckons he'll bring a lot of fun to the house; he's good at teamwork, and he can be sensitive and provide a good shoulder to cry on. He's also a good cook, a good mimic, and he'll fit in with all the other keep-fit fanatics in there because he likes to exercise. He's also a talented artist, with a qualification in graphic design.

He wants to be in the house because he believes he is an natural entertainer, but he also wants to meet people in the unusual circumstances of the house. 'Money, cars, clothes, mobile phones – all these things help form our opinions of people, and they're taken into consideration when people are getting to know you. But in the house there is nothing but personality to determine survival, and I want to put my personality to the test – in every extreme.'

He says he only smokes five to ten cigarettes a day. And yes, he likes a drink.

LEE

Full Name: Lee Peter Davey
Nicknames: Big Sexy, Lee-ski
Age: 22 six days after going into the house
Marital status: Single
Star sign: Gemini
Height: 5 feet 9 inches
Weight: 15 stone
Tattoos and piercings: Three tattoos, one on each
arm and one on right leg. Both ears pierced.
Favourite food: Pasta, tuna, jacket potatoes, tomatoes, pizza.
Ambition: To be on *Big Brother*.
What's in his suitcase? 7 photos of family; 1 cuddly toy;
7 packets of sweets; 8 packets of chewing gum; 9 pairs boxer
shorts; 7 pairs white socks; 3 pairs blue socks; 1 bandanna;
muscle fitness magazine.

He's one formidable fella. He gets his nickname from his size – and from all the attention he gets from females at the gym where he works as a manager and personal fitness trainer. His incredible physique is the result of dedication and hard work, but because he can combine it with his job it doesn't take over his whole life.

He lives at home with his dad, his younger brother Pete, and a 12-year-old cat called Tammy. His dad, he reckons, is the person who has most influenced his life, by making sure he didn't quit football when he wanted to, as a kid. 'He kept me going, and eventually I started playing for the county.'

Later on he joined a local team. He was playing for them when they got through to the local cup final, which was a big occasion: it was held at Leicester City stadium. But it turned out to be a disappointing day for Lee. He was nervous, and when someone winded him, he had to rush off the pitch to be sick. 'I was gutted – and I got subbed.'

Football even dominates his dreams: in the last dream he can remember, he was playing soccer in the back garden with an amazing line-up of big names: Henry, Figo, Rivaldo and Carlos. 'It was wicked, ridiculous.' He says if he had to choose a specialist subject for Mastermind, it would be football statistics. 'Sad, isn't it?' His hero, surprise, surprise, is David Beckham. 'He is so good at what he does, and he has had to deal with so much rubbish from fans, the press and a lot of jealous people. I really admire the way he has handled everything.'

The only regret Lee has in life is that he didn't take his football seriously enough and train harder at it when he was a kid.

He's pretty happy with his body, which he keeps in shape with five sessions of weight training a week. Anyone who saw his application video was treated to a very good sample of it, censored only by a discreetly positioned hat. But anyone who was in the street near his home on a recent Sunday night would have seen even more: as his girlfriend Carmen was going home, Lee was jumping about naked outside 'for a joke, because I felt like doing something stupid'.

He's proud of himself for getting the job he has: he was only 20 when he became a manager at the gym. He is the leader of a team of eight people, whose job is to make sure that members work out safely and effectively. He also runs weight management classes, a circuit class, resistance training class, spinning class and body combat class. And he has seven clients who he sees two or three times a week each, in his own time, as their personal trainer. He really loves his job, and he's taken lots of courses and has lots of qualifications. He doesn't think he'll ever want to change the type of work he does, but he'd love to one day own his own gym in Gran Canaria or the South of France.

He gets Fridays and Sundays off each week, 'and on Sundays I just don't leave my bedroom!' That's usually because he's recovering from a wild night of clubbing.

He's also proud of staying in a relationship for a long time. He's been with his girlfriend Carmen for three and half years, since he was 18. They met in a club on Boxing Day. 'I saw her mate first and thought she looked quite nice, and then she came over and said her mate fancied me, so I looked round and thought, "Yeah, she's nice as well". And we're still going!'

Lee can even remember what he was wearing when he first chatted up Carmen. 'I was wearing a Ralph Lauren zip-up top, trousers and my D and G shoes. She was wearing a trouser suit.'

LEE | PALM READING

The overall impression of Lee's hand is full and earthy but with sensitive fingers. The positions of his fingers and the slight jutting out of the little finger denote a person who is good at expressing his own wants and needs. He likes to get an idea of an overall situation before he shows his true self. He will get bored easily if not physically challenged in some way. His clearly defined lines show a naturally warm and loving person. In everyday life, he would choose his friends (and girlfriend) very carefully and stick by them like super-glue if they showed the same commitment.

The full characteristics of the lower quarter of the hand, and slant towards the index finger, show him to be a sensuous guy who would like to create the good life, with a beauty on his arm, an up-market car and a cool pad to hang out in. He is also a bit of a homebody underneath, who likes to be close to his family. He will certainly want to hang on to his present girlfriend and would like to have his own family. He is fiercely protective of those he says he loves.

The worst thing you could say to a man like this is an open 'no'. He likes to be centre stage and in control. This shows in his strong and resolute thumbs and thumb-ball area. His destiny or career line is clearly defined and deep, showing that he will take a keen interest in the visual arts and in clubs, pubs, the visual music scene, fitness and health.

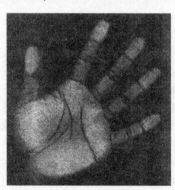 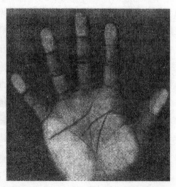

He says telling Carmen he loves her is the nicest thing he's ever said, and making her cry when he swore at her once is the worst thing he's ever said. But they soon made up: 'I bought her flowers and chocolates – works every time.'

Although he first kissed a girl when he was 10, he hadn't had a serious relationship before Carmen.

He thinks his time in the house will give him the chance to learn a lot, about himself and about other people, and although there is a downside – missing his family and friends – the pluses outweigh the minuses. It won't change his life radically, he doesn't think: he'll be raring to get back in the gym afterwards and spend time with his mates and family, then it will be business as usual.

Lee reckons he'll be able to mask his emotions in the *Big Brother* house. Nothing that happens will reduce him to tears – unless he has to peel onions. And he has learned to control and hide his emotions. 'At work, when I was going through a bad phase with the boss, I could have gone off on one, but I thought the best thing was to hide it. I talked to my dad and one of the older instructors, and my emotions came out when I spoke to them; but at work I hid my feelings. If you are having a bad day, you have to hide it. If something's on your mind, you can't show it: it's the sort of job where you have to put things to the back of your head and get on with things, walking around with a smile on your face.'

Before he went in, he said he hoped there wouldn't be arguments and disputes, 'because I hate arguing, it just makes everything so hard for everyone. I hope there won't be any.' Sorry, Lee, not much chance of that.

For him, the one thing that would tip him over into anger is racism or discrimination of any type. 'It is totally out of order, and it should not occur in this day and age. I feel very strongly about it.'

The last time he can remember losing his temper was with Carmen, when they were lying in bed watching wrestling on television. Lee was falling asleep, and didn't realize that there were two women wrestlers in bikinis on screen, but his girlfriend accused him of perving at them. They had a big row.

The saddest thing that has happened in his own life was the death of his Nan two years ago. He was also knocked sideways by

LEE	♊	GEMINI

Lee is an inquisitive, independent and warm person with a lot of restless energy in both mind and spirit. He is the eternal student with a love of travel and adventure. The need to communicate is important to him. When he has chosen his woman (after much flirting and gallivanting!) Lee will want to protect and take care of her. Lesson in *Big Brother*: to control his restless energy.

the September 11 terrorist attacks. 'That was the sickest thing I've ever seen in my life.'

Happiness, for Lee, is simple: the health and well-being of those closest to him; sunshine; going on holidays; seeing the results of his personal training on clients; and praise. Oh, and he's pretty happy when he gets paid and finds he has money left over to spend on anything he wants.

The craziest thing Lee has ever done was soon after he qualified as a driver, when he was driving through the village where he lives. Some of his mates were following in another car, and he was so busy looking in the mirror at them that he missed a bend, careered on to the wrong side of the road, mounted the pavement for fifty yards and then rejoined the road. His mates were crying with laughter – and Lee was just grateful that it was a quiet road with nothing coming in the opposite direction.

He thinks the other housemates will like him because he makes jokes, enjoys a laugh and he is good at working in teams. The five words he uses to describe himself best are 'busy, fun, exciting, intriguing and sexual', which he reckons is a recipe for doing well in the house. Also, with so many of the others sharing his passion for fitness, he reckons he'll find a role putting them through their paces.

'I can get on with anyone. I love pranks, talking stupid, making people laugh, ripping the piss out of people. I love doing it. I'm daring, and I've got a dirty mind.' But he admits the same traits may drive the housemates to exasperation with him, especially if he carries out a prank when someone is not in the mood. 'I think people are more likely to like me, but they may possibly dislike me.'

Other reasons for not liking him, he reckons, could include his vanity, as he spends a lot of time in front of a mirror flexing his fantastic pecs and biceps, his snoring (although he's got competition there), and the facts that he can't cook and he's a bad flirt.

'Also, I constantly have my hands down my pants which may irritate them. I don't know why I do it, it just feels comfortable.'

His brother Pete may be glad of the break while Lee in the *Big Brother* house: some of his disgusting habits won't be missed at home. 'I've farted on Pete's head a few times. I don't fart when Carmen's in my bed so I get up, go to Pete's room, do it in there and hold the door closed so he has to sniff it.' Charming.

But Lee will miss 16-year-old Pete loads: 'He is the funniest person I know. He has me in tears sometimes, and we get on really well. I take him everywhere. I will miss playing on the Playstation and playing football with him.'

He's also got an older brother who is married. He gets on with him really well, and he loves being an uncle to two youngsters.

Missing the World Cup is a tough call for a football fanatic like Lee. Asked what luxury he would most miss in the house he said, 'It has to be television, because of the football. But my mobile phone comes a close second.'

Although he may seem like a real man's man, there's a sensitive side to Lee, and he says that if he could be reincarnated he would come back as a woman, to see what it is like.

As you might expect from a fitness fanatic, Lee doesn't smoke or drink. The no-alcohol rule isn't a point of principle – it's because it doesn't agree with him, and he's sick every time he touches it.

P.J.

Full name: Peter James Ellis
Nickname: P.J.
Age: 22
Marital status: Single
Star sign: Leo
Height: 5 feet 10 inches
Weight: 13 stone 7 pounds
Tattoos and piercings: Celtic band tattooed around right bicep.
Favourite food: Chicken chow mein with spring rolls;
steak and chips; pasta; pizza.
Ambition: To *earn* one million pounds.
What's in his suitcase? 6 cans lager; 1 England flag;
7 family photos; 5 pairs of boxer shorts; 1 tie;
prescription glasses; 1 *FHM* magazine.

P.J. may not be as full-on as some of the others, but he's up for fun and he fancies himself with the girls.

He's one of the brainy ones in the house. Later this year, he'll be starting a career as a lawyer – he's just finished law school and he's aiming to be a solicitor. In ten years' time he'd like to be a successful legal eagle, a partner in his own firm, earning loads of money and, hopefully, in a relationship and thinking about having children: 'I'll be 32, a mature adult, so I hope I'll be behaving like one.'

He's very close to him mum and dad, and they've both inspired him in different ways. 'My dad instilled into me that although education may seem crap and boring, it pays off eventually. My mum keeps me level-headed and financially aware. My family is fantastic, they are always there for me when I need them. My parents are very liberal and generous. My brother is one of my best mates and my little sister is a pure gem – she's got the Ellis charm, so watch out, lads!'

Asked to describe P.J., his mother and sister came up with: 'Confident, funny, bigheaded, very caring, thoughtful, arrogant, short-tempered, always has to have the last word, entertaining – and with short, hairy legs.'

P.J.	♌	LEO

With many planets in water and fire, P.J. will always be pulled between the social and artistic limelight. At times he can be withdrawn and subdued, due to the duality of his personality and character; however, when Leo shines, he is a roaring flirt! He is very ambitious – *Big Brother* could well give him a kick-start. Lesson in *Big Brother*: to stay faithful to one woman.

He's proud of his academic achievements: he won a scholarship to uni, and was one of only five students in Europe to get it. He's an all-rounder: he's good at sport as well as being a high-achiever academically.

He admits he's not crazy by the standards of the other house-mates – the craziest thing he's ever done was to say 'I love you' to a girl. 'It was crazy because I'd never said it before, and I never thought I'd feel enough to reach the stage of saying it.'

His most embarrassing moment was when he was on a family camping holiday in Italy when he was 12. He went to use the toilet, which was a hole in the ground. As he walked away he saw a gaggle of girls looking at him. 'The old hormones were racing and I thought they were checking out my good looks. It wasn't until I got back that I realized I had missed the hole and it had gone down my leg.'

He jokes that he'll miss pornography while he's in the house. But he will feel bereft without satellite television, as his idea of a great night is good food, drink and something good on TV. 'That's sad, isn't it?' he says. He'll also miss pubs, clubs, shopping for clothes and his mates.

P.J. is generally laid back, but he does have a temper that can flare at times – although he reckons he's more likely to have a sulky mood than a fit of anger. 'A few weeks ago I went out with my mates for a curry but the place was shut, so I booted the guy's sign over. Really silly. But I don't usually lose my temper – I get in moods.'

One thing that is guaranteed to make him angry is a vegetarian who eats a Big Mac after having a few drinks.

He's really happy with his life. If he could be reincarnated, he would come back as himself 'because I've had a fab time. Or I'd come back as a Hollywood vibrator – for obvious reasons'.

The main thing that makes him happy is feeling wanted by his family and friends. But he also likes 'having sufficient funds for shopping and drinking. I've got lots of student loans and stuff'.

He says we won't see him cry in the *Big Brother* house, unless there was really bad news from outside. 'I'm an emotional chap when I'm on my own but I don't like to show my emotions to others. I don't think most men do, really. I'm definitely not going to cry in there.'

His way of hiding his emotions in the past has involved alcohol. 'I realized I really cared for a girl when it was too late. I messed her about, basically, and she pissed off to Australia. I was gutted and sank to the bottom of a bottle for weeks to get over it. I hid my emotions then with drink, and I never want to go through that again.'

The girl who went to Australia was P.J.'s most important love affair. 'I met her in my second year of university, so I was 18 or 19. I met her in a pub through a mate's girlfriend, and we hooked up for a few weeks after that. The first time I met her I knew we were going to see a lot of each other. It lasted eighteen months, which is the longest relationship I've ever had. I told her I loved her, I'm sure she loved me, but at the end of the day it got a bit stale and she wanted more commitment than I could give her. Our relationship turned into a Benny Hill show – me being chased with saucepans. Splitting up was shit, too horrible to talk about. I wasn't that nice and nor was she, so we spoiled what could have been a good friendship.'

He had his first girlfriend when he was 15. 'Before that, I was more interested in football. Girls came when my pubes did and my balls dropped.'

He values honesty in relationships, and say the most hurtful thing anyone could do would be to cheat on him. And it's not just in relationships with girls: 'I don't like people going behind my back and stuff.' But he admits he doesn't practise what he preaches; he's been unfaithful to lots of girls – he'd choose being unfaithful as his specialist subject on *Mastermind*. 'I have hurt a lot of women in the past, because I was just not ready for relationships.'

His ideal partner would be 'someone who makes me laugh, is intelligent and knows what she wants in life. A Natalie Imbruglia look-alike, please.' He says he hopes that on *Big Brother*, 'I'll meet the girl of my dreams.'

P.J. prefers being with people to being on his own, so he shouldn't find the house too hard to take. 'I sometimes enjoy my own company, but it can be very boring and depressing, and deep down I enjoy having others around.'

His heroes are George Best and Elvis Presley. 'I suppose they both wasted their talents, but what they gave us is amazing.' He'd love to be able to play football like George Best, and his favourite dream is of scoring the winning goal at Wembley. If he wasn't about to start a career as a lawyer, he'd like to be the England footie manager – or a top fashion model. 'Not much to ask, eh?'

He does play football as often as he can, and says he used to be good in the days 'when I was thin, fit and healthy'. He was selected for both Derby County and Port Vale youth teams, but broke a leg badly when he was 15, which ended his hopes of a professional football career. He also goes to the gym to keep in shape, but had to let that slip in his final few months of cramming for his degree.

He reckons his arrogance might annoy some of the other house-mates. 'Some people find it attractive, but a lot of people think I'm a twat. I'm vain too, and I don't know why because I'm an ugly bastard. My arrogance may wind people up. I can be arsey. And I snore!'

But he reckons the others will like him because 'I'm quite open, I can be a laugh, I understand when people have problems and I like to chat about anything. I'm sincere when I'm talking to people, and I'm sympathetic. I am good at offering satisfying compromises. I feel I can create and hopefully maintain a relaxed environment.'

He's a non-smoker, and his favourite drink is Foster's lager. He can drink more than ten pints on a good night out.

SANDY

Full name: Alexander Dall Cumming
Nicknames: Sandy, Sgt Bilko
Age: 43
Marital status: Married
Star Sign: Capricorn
Height: 5 feet 11 inches
Weight: 13 stone
Tattoos and piercings: Tattoo on right wrist.
Favourite food: It depends on the time of
day and day of the week.
Ambition: To never be alone.
What's in his suitcase? 1 card that says, 'Life is too important to
be taken seriously'; 1 pair goggles; 1 camouflage kilt; 2 bottles
of wine; 29 packets of chewing gum; 1 flag; 5 sets of ear plugs
(in case the others object to his snoring); 1 pair tartan trousers.

Sandy's a man of many contrasts. He was in the army for 14 years,
a sergeant in the Black Watch regiment. You don't get much more
macho than that. But now he's a personal shopper at Selfridges,
which means he dresses and styles women who shop at the store.
He meets clients, discusses the sort of look they want, then selects
the clothes, shoes, accessories and even lingerie for them. It's a job
normally done by women, and Sandy is one of very few men in the
country doing it. He loves it – and so do his clients. 'Together we
create stunning looks that make them feel confident, beautiful, and
vibrant. I can't imagine a better job,' he says.

He doesn't want the *Big Brother* experience to change his life. 'I
have a great job, a great relationship and great friends who will bring
me back down to terra firma.'

Of all the things he has done in his colourful life, he's most proud
of what he achieved as a sergeant in the army. 'You'd take a wee lad
from the backstreets of Glasgow or a little village, he'd have no
moral standards, no self respect and no prospects, and you'd turn
him into a proud, talented, respectable, trusted, honest and lively
person who would do anything for his mates – and all in 22 weeks,

by making him into a soldier. There are a lot of things I've done in my life but that's probably the one I look back on and think, that was a real achievement.'

He vividly remembers the sergeant who did the same thing for him when he was 16 years old. 'Sergeant Beveridge inspired me in my first career. He taught me always to go after my desires one at a time.'

The army also gave him one of the most difficult challenges of his life – leaving it, and going into civvy street. 'It was a bit like leaving prison – or the *Big Brother* house! I didn't allow myself to feel low, but I was starting from scratch with no money and no status. But I had the self-belief to keep me going, and my close friends all believed I would survive.'

He did a variety of jobs after leaving the army, including studying to be a landscape designer, and running a leisure club in a hotel in his native Scotland. He reckons his gardening training will help in the vegetable patch, his time at the fitness club will help him keep the others in shape, and his styling will mean that they all look their best when they leave the house. If only he'd stayed around long enough to put all these plans into action!

The craziest thing Sandy ever did was while serving as a soldier in Berlin – he stole the regimental colours of another regiment, the Gloucesters. 'If you understand the army, the colours are the most important thing for a regiment. I was dragged in front of the General in charge of the whole of Berlin and reprimanded, but I also got a pat on the back from our commander, so it was quite cool!'

The most embarrassing thing he can remember was dancing with the Queen Mother at a party for the Queen's staff at Balmoral – and he got the dance moves muddled up.

At the time, his regiment, the Black Watch, was providing the guard at Balmoral, and Sandy was the 'pony sergeant', in charge of riding out with picnics and wet weather equipment to the shoots on the estate. He taught himself and his men to ride in two weeks.

Traditionally, he and the other soldiers in the guard party were invited to the annual staff party, attended by the Queen, the Queen Mother and any of the other royals who are at Balmoral for the summer. Sandy was told by the Queen Mum's equerry that he had been selected to dance The Dashing White Sergeant, a Scottish country dance, with her. He and another sergeant who was also going to partner her were given a few lessons in the steps.

'There's a move called a paddy bar where the partners hold hands and go towards each other, first to one side and then to the other. I went the wrong way – I went left when I should have gone right. The Queen Mum told me I'd done it wrong. But she was very charming about it.'

The thing he'll most miss in the house is the freedom to jump on his bike and take off wherever he wants to go. And being able to pop out for a drink. But he reckoned, before he went in, that the only reason he'd leave is if there was a bomb threat or a fire – or if anyone snores louder than he does. He warned the others about his snoring in the first few hours in the house, and thoughtfully provided ear-plugs for any of his bedroom companions who struggle to sleep through his rumblings.

Sandy's an openly emotional man, and he's the only one of the housemates who thinks he's likely to blub a lot while he's in there. 'I cry very easily. Anything can make me cry, you wouldn't believe it. If we're having a conversation and I feel quite emotional about it, I'll cry. I've no fear of crying; I don't think anyone, whether you're a man or a woman, should try to suppress it. If you feel the emotion, you should use it. I cry at cartoons, at the news, at *Neighbours*, at things most people would think: Why's he crying at that? I cried at *About a Boy*, the Hugh Grant film.

'There's no special trigger that sets me off. I might go in there and not cry at all, and then again I might cry every day. Sometimes I find myself crying in the middle of the road, and then I have to pretend

SANDY	♑	CAPRICORN

An aspiring man who can come across as rather haughty, but one of his greatest strengths is to quietly bring order out of chaos. He is more introverted than the rest of the men in *Big Brother*. Sandy feels deeply about things, but full expression of his emotions will be difficult. Sandy is very self-contained; if he were placed on a desert island, he'd survive with no one else around for months! Lesson in *Big Brother*: to try and mix more, and not to be so self-contained.

it's just the wind in my eyes. The day I married Claire I cried a lot, it was very emotional, a big day for me. I had no qualms about crying.'

He's been with Claire for 13 years and married to her for eight, and says he will miss her most because, simply, 'I love her.' The only thing that would improve their relationship is 'more holidays'.

He has been married before, and he has had other significant relationships, but Claire is by far the most important. 'Quite a lot of people get married for the wrong reasons. We're pals, we can be together and we can also spend time on our own. We split up when I went to Australia, but we got back together. I was an arse to leave her. So when she said I had to woo her again, I did. E-mails, letters and phone-calls every day for months. Big bunches of flowers and poetry saying one simple truth: "I'm sorry and I love only you."'

He describes his ideal relationship as 'what I have now with Claire'.

'We met in a bar. Claire was in there having a coffee and reading the paper and I came in for an orange juice. I was carrying a great big poster, which was a wedding present for a friend. It was called The Kiss. I was dying for the loo so I said "Excuse me, will you look after this picture while I go for a piss?" After that we got chatting, mainly about my bike. We exchanged addresses. She lived about fifteen miles away but I cycled over there and said, "Hi, I was just passing..." She was having a dinner party at the time.'

Despite being very different to each other, they got together and it's been a stimulating and happy relationship since. They don't have any children: Sandy's explained to the housemates that he wouldn't like to be tied to bringing up a baby. He does have a daughter from his first marriage, but they have no close contact.

He was a late starter, romantically speaking. He didn't have his first proper girlfriend until he was in his early twenties.

The things that make him crotchety are almost all traffic-related. As a cyclist who goes to work by bike and does more than twelve miles a day, he hates bus drivers and taxi drivers, especially when they cut him up. If they do, they hear a few choice words that aren't in the dictionary, and he shows them the real meaning of hand signals. And as a driver he hates people who 'touch park', especially if the vehicle they are touching is his. He also gets exasperated by anyone with a negative attitude, who thinks the world owes them a living.

Things that make him happy are his wife Claire, his friends, his home, clothes, holidays, good food and drink, and his own company. He loves discovering London on his bike, especially if the sun is shining. 'I don't like it if I'm on my bike when it rains. I get wet and my clothes get ruined.'

Despite all the cycling, he still has to keep an eye on his weight – and if he could change anything in his life, he'd like the metabolism of a greyhound.

If he had to choose a specialist subject for *Mastermind*, he'd choose 'all the books I have ever read'. It would make a fascinating quiz, as Sandy has never read a book in his life. What he does enjoy doing in his free time is going to the cinema, listening to music and visiting art galleries.

He describes himself as 'passionate, observant, sensitive, funny, ironic, tough, vain, sometimes arrogant. 43 going on 16.'

He thinks he may find himself being nominated because some people think he is 'miserable', and he is open and honest about his strong opinions. He also thinks he appears 'chilled' when he's really quite excited, making him difficult to read. Oh, and that snoring thing again.

He also thinks he may find it difficult because he tends to make instant judgements about people which can prove to be wrong. 'I meet someone and I decide there and then what I think of them, and then sometimes – not invariably – I find I am wrong. But then if I am wrong, I will admit it and sort it out. I've got lots of friends who I get on with really well but I didn't like them at first meeting. So I'll probably walk into the *Big Brother* house and hate everyone, and then eventually get on with everyone. That's just the way I am.'

He reckons he will endear himself to the girls in the early days in the house, because he is used to working with women. 'I find myself attracted to women more than men in respect of conversation. Eventually I'll talk to the men. My whole life revolved around men for an extended period when I was in the army, and then I discovered talking to women.

'I am a good listener. I can listen to people for a long time without butting in, and eventually give my opinions on things.'

Among his assets as a housemate he lists 'broad shoulders,

quirky humour, a lifetime of wild and wonderful stories, all delivered in a unique style'.

'Some people think my age could be a negative thing in the house, but I actually think it could be positive. If people are having a hard time, it might be useful to have someone a bit more mature around. But I hope they don't look to me as a father figure just because I'm older; there are young people who can be as strong or stronger than me.

'It's important to remember that even though it is a competition at the end of the day, we do have to live together, and it's important that we make our time together positive. Although I expect we will have it in the back of our minds that it is being televised, I don't think we have to play up to the cameras. I think life for life's sake can be entertaining.'

He thinks the others may take against him because, although he's a sociable animal, he likes his own company. 'I might choose to sit by myself and not talk to anyone sometimes, though not for extended periods. That could quite annoy people if they want to talk and do things. I can see that could piss people off.'

Sandy enjoys a drink: his favourite tipple is 'fuck-off red wine'. He's a non-smoker.

SPENCER

Full name: Spencer Lee Smith
Nicknames: Spanky, Spen, Spence, Spennyboy
Age: 22
Marital status: Single
Star sign: Cancer
Height: 6 feet 1 inch
Weight: 13 stone
Tattoos and piercings: None.
Favourite food: Roast dinners, pasta.
Ambition: To marry a good woman and have
a nice family with no money problems.
What's in his suitcase? 200 cigarettes; 75 grams of hand rolling
tobacco and 4 packs cigarette papers; 1 lighter; 6 cans lager;
9 pairs of boxer shorts; 2 cans deodorant.

Spencer's one of the coolest, most laid-back guys you'll ever meet. He's so cool it's a wonder he stays vertical – and he doesn't if there's a bed or a sofa to lounge on. In the summer months he leads a dream life, punting tourists up and down the River Cam. 'It's great fun – beer, women, sun, cash. Unless it rains, of course. I meet new people and I always have a suntan. I meet women from all over the world.' He'd love to own a fleet of boats somewhere by the sea, to take tourists out fishing. And he'd also like to own a nightclub – even though he admits he doesn't like clubbing. 'I'm not a big fan of clubbing, but I'd love to own one. I'd run it well.'

When he's not on the river in the summer months, he works at a ski shop, selling everything to do with ski-ing and working as a technician on the equipment. There's a lot of downtime when nothing much is going on, and Spencer and his mates in the shop watch videos and play games.

He shares a house with a mate he has known since childhood, and four fish who are called Cool Modie, Eric, Vinny and Mike. His leisure time is spent at the pub, playing snooker or 'dossing about trying to write songs and learning the guitar'.

SPENCER   ♋   CANCER

The broody one. Even so, he will be popular with people. He thinks things through before taking action. He can be very laid-back, partly as a result of not being the most energetic of the group. There is a gentle strength that exudes from him, which other people will be drawn to. Lesson in *Big Brother*: to be a bit more energetic and do things.

The one thing he will most miss in the house is the pub. 'I like the pub and everything that goes with it.'

Like the other housemates, he keeps fit: he plays football once a week, does Thai boxing once a week and goes to the gym every now and then. But he doesn't need or want glamorous nightlife or expensive holidays: the best holiday he ever spent was in a cottage in Scotland in the middle of nowhere with his girlfriend of the time. 'We just chilled out, walking, fishing or getting beered up and stumbling home not knowing where we were. It was just a really relaxing fun time in a beautiful place.'

The person who has inspired him most is his grandad. 'He's great and I've known him all my life. We've always been very close. He's reliable, brave, full of good stories but never boring. He has indirectly taught me more than anyone.'

He's also close to his parents. 'They are loving and supportive people who have always been there to help even if they didn't agree with what I had decided to do. They are down to earth, and I can always have a laugh and a piss-up with them. I'm really close to my mum.'

He says he doesn't embarrass easily. He once took a girl round to meet a mate and the mate's parents, and 'she ended up getting pissed, threw up on herself and spent the rest of the evening asleep on the sofa. But that was her embarrassment, not mine.'

He did feel a bit sheepish when he went to the *Big Brother* audition and had to jump over the stick and introduce himself. His cynical slightly-distant approach didn't gel with all the wannabes. 'I didn't really know how to fit in to the whole thing. The guy before me said, "I'm not a geek, honest." So I said, "I don't like geeks like

SPENCER   PALM READING

Now here is a man with a plan. His heavy, square palm gives the impression of lack of interest and enthusiasm and his skin patterns show how he can be physically lazy. Don't be fooled as he waits for his time and will do some surprising things. Mentally, his longer, finer fingers show he is like a lay psychologist with a great sense of timing and this will be of interest, as he knows you're watching. He is a straightforward type when it comes to what motivates him most. Good food, good company and money.

Spencer likes to feel he has all bases covered. He knows that looking after others by offering no real resistance is disarming. His clear and straight lines show a need for a sense of order and possible routines and the non-threat good guy image he portrays in his everyday life. The short head lines (the lines in the middle of his hands) show that he can suddenly get bored with second guessing every situation. This will give rise to his erratic side. If he does give in to his feelings, he is liable to swing between being a hermit and liking his bed, to being an outrageous, subtle confrontationist.

His clear likes and dislikes may become extreme and he may not be able to remain Mr Cool. However, the real motivation here with Spencer is his desire to win the money. Spencer's hand has a sense of mystery about it. People with plain and simple hand lines are often not what they first seem.

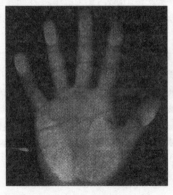 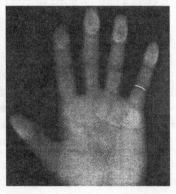

him." Nobody thought it was funny except me. They were all trying to show how sociable they were, how they get on with anybody, how funny they were.'

Things he can't stand include pompous customers who think his only role in life is to help them ski, arrogant people who have no right to have such a high opinion of themselves and 'Coke-heads who pin you in a corner and gibber on for hours because the sound of their own voice is like music to them.'

The things that make him happy include having peace of mind, spending time with beautiful women, playing on the river, having good health and having his friends and family around him.

He's a big Michael Jackson fan – one of the fish is named after the star – and he'd choose MJ's music as his specialist subject on *Mastermind*. His other hero is Eric Cantona, who also has an aquatic namesake: 'I respect his honesty and his skill, and I like the arrogance of the man. I don't generally like arrogance, but his is justified. I just generally like him. He is never afraid to be himself and say what he thinks needs to be said.'

He can't think of anything that he's especially proud of, but then casually adds that he 'saved a guy's life today. He was drowning and I pulled him out. When I filled in my *Big Brother* application form I put my running achievements down as the thing I'm most proud of, but that was a lie. I'm not particularly proud of it, but I couldn't think of anything else.'

He would be hurt if anyone did anything to upset his family, particularly his sister. The only thing that could make him cry in the house would be news of anything really bad about his family. 'I won't cry over being voted off or something like that. But the whole experience will be so mind-boggling that I just don't know. I'll probably cry if I stub my toe.'

He can keep his emotions under wraps if he has to. 'Everybody does it at some stage. I've had to be strong at funerals and stuff like that. Also, when I'm angry I tend to hide it.'

The biggest love affair of his life was with a Mexican girl he met three years ago. 'I had a girlfriend but I split up with her to be with the Mexican. She was only in England for a month. We got it on properly for about a week, we stayed in contact by e-mail, then she turned up at my house and we got back together. She was living in Paris and I went over to stay with her, at which point she changed her mind about me and now it's all over. I'm quite happy, though – I don't think about it that much.

'I was an interesting affair – it would make a great book, or a film. It would be really good. Your mother would love it, a real chick flick.'

He calls his ex 'the Spick'. 'I'm not being racist, that was her nickname and she didn't mind.' He says his feelings for her were the closest he's ever been to proper love, although he admits 'a few girls have done my head in for a while'.

Asked to describe his ideal partner he says, simply 'the Mexican'.

He first started having girlfriends when he was 15 or 16. He likes girls to be straight with him: the last time he can remember losing his temper was with a girl who tried to manipulate him. 'It all went Pete Tong and she made me dead angry.'

The most disgusting thing he can think of that he's done recently ('I do disgusting things all the time') was to wake up at his mate Charles's house, surrounded by lots of beer glasses, champagne glasses and beer bottles, all filled with a yellow liquid. 'I slowly realized I had slept surrounded by piss.'

He can't think of any flaws in his personality. 'I'm perfect, like Mary Poppins. Just joking. What some people like about me, others hate. Mates probably like me for being honest. I'm always there for them as well. I don't have lots of mates but the ones I do have are true friends. I've also got a sense of adventure that appeals to people.'

He reckons he'll bring organization, comedy and friendship to the house, and although he's up for a laugh, he can be serious when he needs to be. Unfortunately for him, he wasn't allowed to take his guitar in, and the housemates had better hope he doesn't practise another of his hobbies: knife throwing.

'On the downside, people can dislike me for all the same reasons that others like me. Honesty can be interpreted as arrogance, and all of a sudden you're a big-headed wanker. People do call me arrogant. I've got some surface bad habits: passing wind and snot rockets. But unless people are really looking and don't like me for some other reason, my habits are not a problem.'

TIM

Full name: Timothy Edward Culley
Nicknames: None
Age: 23
Marital status: Single
Star sign: Aries
Height: 6feet 2 inches
Weight: 13stone 8lbs
Tattoos and piercings: None
Favourite food: Steak, seafood
Ambition: To be rich and famous
What's in his suitcase? Two bottles of wine; 5 photos of
friends and family; box of Milk Tray; Oakley sunglasses;
Chanel sunglasses; 3 bracelets; 2 rings; 3 boxes of
contact lenses; lip salve; hair gel; wax.

Tim thinks that being in boarding school from the age of eight to 18 was the ideal preparation for life in the *Big Brother* house. He's the posh totty of the house: a good-looking university student with a wealthy background.

Although he was always at public school in England, Tim spent his holidays abroad with his family in Kuwait, Hong Kong or South Africa, where his father was working. It gave him a taste for life in a warmer climate, and he says that in ten years' time he wants to be living in South Africa, with a beautiful wife, a lovely house, a job running a multinational company and two children. He's even chosen the names for the children: Joshua and Jessica.

He loves travelling and enjoys joining in with local customs: he's eaten monkeys' brains and sheep's eyeballs.

He's an ambitious young man, determined to make a success of life.

'I set myself a lot of challenges, and to date I've achieved most of them. Probably the most major one was starting my own company last year. It didn't require much capital, but it was some-thing I knew nothing about, which is not what you do if you know anything about business. To follow through with that and do it all in one holiday from university, and be there at 9.00am on a Monday morning to start trading off my own bat, was a major step, a major achievement. And it ended up being good fun!'

The company, a promotions agency, was set up over a year ago, and Tim runs it in the afternoons and evenings, when he does not have lectures to attend at university – he finished his business finance degree a few weeks before going into the house. His dream is to one day have a successful agency for sports stars.

His role model is his dad, Neil, a retired pilot and now a hotelier and restaurant owner.

'He's the most successful person I know, and the most generous and the most supportive. He's made a lot of money by working very, very hard, and he's kept his family in a fantastic manner. He spends money like it's going out of fashion – but I'm like that, too. I respect his attitude to it: he doesn't hold back, he has a fantastic time and he gives me a fantastic life. He spends his money on those he loves, and that's a great quality to have.

'As far as money is concerned, I've done a few silly things and spent ridiculous amounts on things I don't necessarily need, like a sports car. I tend to live beyond my means: I live a champagne lifestyle on a house-wine budget.'

He says the one luxury he really could not live without is money: 'I'm quite materialistic.' In the house, what he will most miss are his friends, 'great sex', watching Arsenal play and playing sport – he's a keen rugby, soccer and tennis player, and also swims and regularly

TIM	♈	ARIES

Tim has a knowledgeable air about him, and is quieter than the others. With many planets in water, however, his intuitive and perceptive mind will be able to detect and observe the emotional state of others, and ascertain what makes them tick. Tim likes the nice things in life and will find it hard to rough it. Compassionate and sympathetic, he will want to get on with everyone. He is more of a blender than a leader. Lesson in Big Brother: don't try too hard to get on with everyone, otherwise you could become an emotional frazzle!

goes to the gym. What he won't miss is awful service in shops and 'the crap English weather spoiling plans'.

He says he's close to his mum Linda, who is a successful interior designer. 'She's very stylish and glamorous, and she loves me to bits and does lots for me.' He admits both his parents have spoilt him.

If he had to choose famous people to be his parents, he'd opt for Margaret Thatcher because 'she achieved amazing success' and Will Carling: 'a sporting legend and a legend with women'.

Although he says he's 'not a daredevilly sort of person', he admits he can act impetuously: 'I've flown off around the world at about two minutes notice more than once, just upped and gone really quickly. Once was to see a girl in Paris, once for a holiday, another time to play rugby'.

Sport takes up a lot of Tim's spare time and he says the only time he ever loses his temper is on the tennis court, when he gets angry with himself, and on the rugby pitch, where he joins in the usual pushing and shoving that goes on.

'If I don't perform well I get very angry inside and need to get back out there as soon as possible to do myself justice and put the poor performance behind me.'

His sporting hero is Andre Agassi and if he had to choose a specialist subject for *Mastermind* it would be Agassi's career.

He has a band of good, close friends and says he is at his happiest when he's with them. Other things that make him happy include children, animals and beautiful women.

If he could be reincarnated he'd like to come back as 'a beautiful lesbian – is there anything more fantastic?'

When it comes to his most embarrassing moment, there are two contenders: one was when he was given an intimate shave by a nurse before having a hernia operation, the other was when 'I tried to sing 'You've Lost that Loving Feeling' in front of about 400 girls at the sister school to my boys' college, when I was about 17. I wasn't as confident then as I am now, so it was quite a big thing, and seeing that I sing about as well as a strangled cat, I don't think anyone enjoyed it.'

Tim says that despite the impression he gives of being cool and ambitious 'I am quite a soft guy inside, I get attached to people very easily. I've got a lot of friends, boys and girls, and I'm very open with them. I've felt let down once or twice – luckily, not too often – when people have taken me for granted. It would be an advantage to be a hard, callous person, but I'm not like that. I leave myself open to get hurt.'

Despite this, he says viewers are unlikely to see him shedding tears in the house.

'I don't cry very often. I'd have to be very attached to someone to end up in tears. I don't think there's anything that could happen in the house that would reduce me to tears.'

He can, if he has to, conceal how he feels from the other house-mates. 'In different situations I've shown some of my qualities and played down others. I think it's important to be a chameleon, it helps you get where you want to be. For instance, at a job interview I'm going to show the confident side of me and try to hide the softer side, whereas in a relationship it would be less of the stern and strong side, more of the other side. It means I can relate to people right at the top down to people at the bottom, and just about every-where else.

'I like to think I'm a people person, I enjoy interacting with people and hopefully that will rub off on the other housemates, so they won't vote me off at an early stage. I'd like the public to have time to warm to me, to see the confident and ambitious side but also to see the inside of me, which is quite a nice bloke.'

He says his worst flaw is his vanity: 'I care about how I look, what I drive, my hair'. And as far as sharing a house goes, he rivals Alex in the Mr Clean stakes: 'I like people who take care of them-selves and are clean, and I like it if the house is tidy and nice'.

Tim said a sad goodbye to his Swedish girlfriend before he went into the house. Despite being very popular with girls, he was a late starter in the romance stakes. He had his first proper girlfriend at 18, which he blames on being at an all-boys' school.

'I'm not really into 'love affairs' – that sounds like something out of *Pretty Woman*. I'm not really a long-term person, most of my rela-tionships last a few weeks. I went out with my first love for six months, and because it's your first love and you're young you obvi-ously think everything's perfect and it will last forever, but after a few months I realised that the differences between us were huge, and that's why we split up.

'With my current girlfriend, it's fantastic. The only reason I can see that we would split up is because we come from different countries.'

Tim is looking to settle down soon: 'I really want to find the person who is that bit special. Otherwise, I just get bored and I finish the relationship because I don't want to waste time with someone who isn't really clicking with me'.

The perfect partner he is looking for will be 'stunning looking, well brought up, classy, independent, successful – but a little bit dependent on me'.

Tim thinks that the same qualities that will make some of the housemates really like him may annoy others:

'I'm ambitious and driven, and some people may not like that. But whenever I meet anyone like that, I respect them for being determined, so perhaps some of them will feel like that about me. I don't sit around doing nothing, I lead the way and try to get things done. I've always got an opinion and I'm pretty sharp witted, so that should keep the conversation going. I like to think I'm relatively charming, so that should do me OK, and as time goes on I think they'll see that I'm a nice guy and a caring person inside. I suppose different folks will appreciate different aspects of me, and I think there's something there for everybody. I believe there is always something in everybody to like.

'But I may come across as a bit full-on at first, because I'm outspoken and quite charismatic, and I prefer to be seen rather than not seen. If I end up being kicked out quickly I'll understand, because I may come across as a bit too ambitious and scare people off. Some people may see me as arrogant and right wing, or even a snob, which I'm not. But I don't take lightly to slackers or lazy people.'

He says he brings a 'rare combination of supreme confidence, intelligence and style to the house' and describes style and confidence as 'my trademark.' He says: 'I'm a leader who oozes charisma'.

He reckons he only goes out drinking once a week – but what a night he makes of it, knocking back twenty-five units of alcohol in Bacardi and Coke.

CHAPTER EIGHT

THE GIRLS

Now it's the turn of the *BB* babes, the super seven girls packed their suitcases for a stay *chez Big Brother*. Guess which one likes a saucy snog on a Friday? Which girl thinks the actress who could best portray her in a film is Kathy Burke? Who took in no makeup except mascara? Whose nickname is Pamela Anderson? Who worried about the camera showing her fat knees? And, unlike the boys, only one girl, Kate, thought she had a chance of going all the way and winning.

ADELE

Full name: Adele Claire Roberts
Nicknames: Della, Deli
Age: 23
Marital status: Single
Star sign: Pisces
Height: 5 feet 4 inches
Weight: 10 stone
Dress size: 10
Tattoos and piercings: Tattoos of Japanese symbol for mother on left foot; Japanese symbol for father on right foot; name Maxine, in remembrance of her auntie, on her left heel.
Favourite food: Chinese, chocolate, Sunday roast, watermelon, grapes and cereal.
Ambition: To make my own records and meet Michael Jackson.
What's in her suitcase? 1 lucky charm necklace; 2 bikini tops; 1 bikini thong; 11 pairs knickers; 4 bras; 1 photo of sister; 1 photo of girlfriend Vicky; no makeup except mascara; 28 hairbands and 4 hair bobbles; blue nail varnish.

Adele's such a great DJ she has appeared on the same bill as Judge Jules, Roger Sanchez and Scott Bond, spinning the vinyl in front of 5,000 people at a massive New Year's bash at Renaissance, a big club night in Stoke-on-Trent. Being a DJ is her main love, although she'd also like to get involved in music production. In the meantime, until her music career takes off big time, she needs a day job, and works in an office as a PA and admin manager. She says it bores her rigid, because it doesn't challenge her; but she gets a car and a good salary, and she likes all her workmates. But evenings and weekends are when she is 'really me – DJing, shopping and going to the gym'.

Ah yes, the gym. This is almost as important to Adele as her decks. She goes at least five times a week when she's in training – she takes part in bodybuilding competitions, and was in one just two weeks before going into the house. She had to lose 5 per cent of her body fat, and says she did it by having lots of sex – to take her mind off her empty stomach. There are a few fit housemates in *BB3*, and she's one of them. As well as weight training she does aerobics every day, and she loves playing footie.

She lives near the sea in Southport, but wants to move to London.

'All my life I've been near the beach and it's not something that means much to me because I'm used to it. Southport is a small town, and I want to be where the action is.' She was planning to move south in May – and she did, into the *Big Brother* house.

Adele is bisexual, and so far the two major loves in her life have been girls. 'I met my first girlfriend when I was 16. I used to work in a nightclub, and another girl introduced me to her. I thought she wasn't my type, but when I walked past her again ten minutes later I thought she was brilliant, unique looking, really striking. We were friends for a bit, then we hated each other for two years, and then when I was at college we met again when we both worked at the same fast food place. I was going to DJ at a club in Leeds so I asked her to come, because she's a really good dancer. Then she told me, after just being friends for absolutely ages, that she liked me in that way, and we got together.'

They broke up when Adele found out that her girlfriend had gone back to the hotel with a guy from a well-known band. They had a stand-up row – so loud that the hotel staff called the police. Her girlfriend insisted nothing had happened, but Adele couldn't take the lack of trust.

'I never thought I'd be strong enough to not want to go out with her, but now I am,' she says. Adele's in a new relationship, which she says is the best ever and which she hopes will still be going in

ADELE	♓	PISCES

Adele, with her quiet manner, will initially come across as compassionate, gentle, wise and mysterious. She will quietly seek the limelight with a strong mental determination and will reanalyse a situation until she is satisfied with the result. Adele has strong moral convictions and will have to fight off at least one suitor! Being a good listener and kind-hearted, some will seek solace with her. Lesson in *Big Brother*: to uphold her strong moral convictions.

ten years' time. They've been together five months, and her only wish is that they could live together.

'In an ideal set-up, in ten years' time I'll have an apartment in London, I'd be working in music, and with my girlfriend. I don't want any children, and it would be hard anyway. I really wouldn't want my life to be much different – I'm happy. I'd like to be going to the gym during the day and involved in music at night.'

She thinks her time in the *Big Brother* house will help her sort out what she wants from life.

'My big problem is that I never sit and think about the future. As long as I'm happy in the present, I trundle along. I think being in the house will teach me a lot about myself. I seem to be drifting through life, being content with what I've got, and maybe this is my chance to just go after something and put my all into it. I think it will teach me many important lessons in life – for instance, when I'm being selfish. It will highlight my strengths and weaknesses, and it will show me how I appear through other people's eyes. I think it will be the best experience of my life – and I wanna have a go because I'm hard enough.

'Being a Pisces I often have Walter Mitty syndrome and start daydreaming about being the greatest whatever! I usually daydream after reading a book or watching a film, like after seeing Ali I wanted to be a boxer, after *Moulin Rouge* I felt I was in love, if I watch the Olympics I want to be a runner, if I watch MTV Base I want to be a gangsta – well, maybe not…

'The biggest mystery to me is how I got into the house. I just feel so lucky. I'm hoping that being in the house will open up more avenues in music for me. I don't want to be famous particularly, but I do want to be known as a good DJ.'

Adele's proudest moment was the night she appeared at Renaissance. 'It was brilliant, all my friends were there, and they were all up for it.'

But she's got lots of other things to be proud of. She's got four A levels and 9 GCSEs, and she did the first two years of a degree in Pharmacology. She's very close to her family and says, 'I absolutely adore and love them. My sisters and brothers are bright, funny, beautiful and so individual.' As the oldest of six children, she's watched her mum bringing them up on her own and says, 'I really admire her.

She's a strong person and so generous and loving. Despite what life throws at her she always fights back, she's never bitter.'

She says both her mother and father are great role models. 'They don't drink or smoke or have extreme views, they let us make up our own minds about things.' They are the two people she loves most.

Adele describes her own personality as cheeky, funny, naughty, unique, brattish, considerate, thoughtful, spontaneous. Her family, she says, would see her as independent, generous, loving, confident and special – but they might also say she's scary when she's angry.

'When I'm in an argument I always think I am right, I never admit I'm wrong. I'm horrible to argue with. I'm bad, I never see other people's points of view. That's what pisses people off about me most. And I never apologize, on principle.'

She says the things she will most miss in the house are privacy, and music. 'Music changes my mood. I'll cope by doing press-ups to keep myself fit. I'll probably need to get away from the others at times – I'll go and see the chickens.' The people she will most miss are her mum, who she speaks to every day, and her girlfriend. What she will miss least is world news, because of all the unhappy things that happen.

Adele has experienced unhappiness, when her much-loved aunt Maxine died. It was after that that she had Maxine's name and symbols for mother and father tattooed on to her feet. 'I love and respect them all so much I will never regret having them done.'

She reckons the most hurtful thing that could happen to her in the house is people lying to her or deceiving her. 'That really annoys me more than anything.'

But she doesn't think she'll get close to any of the housemates. 'I don't think I'll have any proper feelings for them. I think I'll always be on my guard, knowing it's a game. I'll be thinking about winning, focussing on that. I won't let people get too close to me, no matter what it may look like.'

She doesn't think anything inside the *Big Brother* bubble will reduce her to tears. 'I hardly ever cry. The only people who can make me cry are my mum and dad. Even when I split from my first girlfriend, I was really upset but I never cried. It's not a conscious thing, like I make an effort not to. I'm just not a cryer.'

She thinks she will be able to hide her emotions. 'As I've got older I get really angry, I can feel myself shaking, and I try more and more to stop myself erupting. I get frustrated and angry at work, doing the same thing all day long. But you have to hide your feelings. I'm horrible when I'm angry, dead nasty, like a little thundercloud.'

Things that make her angry include 'men who think they can speak to you how they like and tell you what to do just because you're female. Also, when you are in a job serving people, customers who think they can act how they like because you're on the other side of the counter.'

She managed to control her anger and go away to calm down when one of her friends ran up a bill on one of her mobile phones; but on another occasion, when one of her friends was being bullied, she physically attacked the girl who was causing the grief – and had to be hauled off by bouncers.

She thinks she'll be an asset in the house because 'I can be quite caring when people are upset. I'll spend time trying to cheer them up. I don't like anyone being sad.'

The five things that most make her happy are, in order of importance, family and girlfriend; music; shopping, but mainly to buy things for family or girlfriend; good food (including chocolate); and sunny days.

Musically, she's into R'n'B, but although her favourite female artist is Missy Elliott – 'the most unique and talented female R'n'B rap artist in the world today' – Michael Jackson beats her into first place in Adele's all-time favourite top five, because 'his music is the soundtrack of my childhood'. Third on the list is Mary J Blige, followed by Alicia Keys and Whitney Houston.

She's lucky because she's already doing her ideal job, even if it's only part time: being a DJ. But if she could choose any other job, she'd like to be Missy Elliott's stylist 'because I could spend all day with her, get her to rap for me, and spend my days buying clothes'. She'd also choose Missy Elliott if she had to have a famous person as a parent, 'because she is the dog's bollocks'.

Adele's not a big drinker, but when she does indulge she likes grasshopper cocktails or Bailey's on ice. She went into the house a non-smoker.

ALISON

Full name: Alison Natasha Hammond
Nickname: 'Hammond eggs'
Age: 27
Marital status: Single
Star sign: Aquarius
Height: 5 feet 10 inches
Weight: 17 stone
Dress size: 24
Piercings and tattoos: None
Favourite food: Chinese food and Chocolate Oranges.
Ambition: To be happily married with four beautiful children.
What's in her suitcase? Gold shoes; Fiery Jack rubbing cream;
Toffee Crisp; Californian raisins; Galaxy; Terry's Chocolate
Orange; 26 pairs of knickers; 14 bras; 15 pairs of socks;
34 hair ties; Ribena.

Alison describes herself as 'big, black and beautiful.' The bouncing Brummie was once a successful holiday rep, and now works for a cinema complex. She's got huge amounts of energy, as the other housemates soon noticed.

Alison has packed a lot into her 27 years. She has seven GCSEs, two A levels, and she's worked in shops, bars, a computer company and has even appeared as a presenter on a schools' television programme. But it was her time as a holiday rep in Tunisia that furnished her with her wildest tales.

'I've done a lot of crazy things, but once in Tunisia I went on this boat with a rope on the back. The guys said 'strong swimmers only', but I had a go anyway. I was holding onto the rope behind the boat when my trousers started to fall down and everyone could see my bum. The worst thing was it was being filmed, but I held on anyway.'

Not that Alison has avoided her fair share of embarrassment in England. She doesn't worry about her weight: 'When I look in the mirror I think I'm quite slim.' But she has suffered because of it, and she hates racist and weight-related abuse.

'It's horrible bigotry. When I was on my way home from school once someone said, "How can elephants be brown?" I was with all my mates, and I was so hurt by it – it was racist and an attack on my weight. I didn't even have a comeback for it. I just carried on walking. But I've never forgotten it – all these years later I can still feel the hurt.'

But usually she laughs about her size. 'I once went into Topshop with my friend Emma. The thing is, I'm the sort of person who likes to fit into small clothes. I went into one of the cubicles to try on a tight little boob-tube, or so I thought, but when I came out to show Emma, one of my boobs was sticking out of the bottom. It was so embarrassing because there were blokes hanging around outside and they all saw my boob.'

Perhaps it was this incident that inspired one of Alison's ambitions.

'In ten years' time I want to be married with four children and running a clothes shop for big women. It would be really trendy, the kind of clothes you get in Topshop, but for big people, and I wouldn't charge the world for it.'

Realistically, she reckons she'll still be working at the cinema, although she'll have risen to the level of manager; and she'll still be looking for a boyfriend. The man she's looking for will be 'someone funny, who respects me and really does love me. Someone who likes talking.'

When it comes to romance, Alison has had her share. Her first serious relationship was at 20. 'But I had fancied him since I was 15. It only lasted six months in the end. That was it. But he's like my best friend now.'

It was Tunisia that brought long-lasting love into Alison's life. Although it's cooled off now, the last three years were one big holiday romance for Alison. She met the shy Mohammed when working as a rep and although he was a little stand-offish at first, she had soon got her man.

'He was really quiet at first so I just went up to him and said, "Hi, how are you?" but he just gave me dirty looks. I kept trying, and I made him laugh every so often, and I was thinking, "I'm getting through here." One day I went behind the bar counter and gave him a little peck on the cheek. After that we started to go out and everything was fantastic. His family were so good to me, they were absolutely lovely. We're not together now, but we've agreed to see each other when we see each other. It can't happen any more because I'm no longer working in Tunisia.'

However, it was not all love and happiness in Tunisia. After working hard to get her man she soon found that he was not as quiet and innocent as she once thought. 'He cheated on me, and the worst thing is I saw him do it. The girl was sixteen, but I didn't go mad, I just watched them and stayed dead calm.'

It was not long before he had come back, tail between his legs, asking for forgiveness. 'He was phoning me all the time, begging me to get back together with him, so I did. There was the trust thing at first, but he promised me I had nothing to worry about. I probably wouldn't have got back with him if his family weren't so great, so loving. They put me up, fed me, everything.'

Alison is a kind person, too. On Christmas day she cooked a meal for a homeless person and sat for an hour chatting with him – she says it is the nicest single thing she has done.

She reckons the only way anyone will see her cry inside the *Big Brother* house is if she is missing her mates and mother when she wants someone to chat to.

'I'm quite emotional, and I'll definitely miss my family. I cry if I'm angry, too.'

But she thinks she could conceal her feelings if she has to. 'I had to do it loads of times when I was repping. One woman made a couple of complaints about me, saying I'd been up all night playing music. The joke is I wasn't even in my room, I was at my boyfriend's. But I got into big trouble, and I really wanted to cry but I wouldn't let myself. I was so angry because I'd done nothing wrong, but I had to keep perky because I was working, and my job was to make people happy.'

Luckily for Alison, the one thing she couldn't live without is something she's allowed to take in to the house with her: her sports bra. 'It really does help me when I'm running or doing exercise. It helps my big baps retain themselves. If you told me I couldn't have it I wouldn't go in.'

| ALISON | ♒ | AQUARIUS |

People will be drawn to her magnetic personality, and her off-the-wall zany humour; though it can sometimes be too much for one person to handle. She loves the world and people. In between her zany moments, she likes to analyse humanity. Although big-hearted and optimistic, she can be a bit tactless, but nevertheless very entertaining. Lesson in *Big Brother*: that some quieter emotional souls would like the stage too!

She will miss special fried rice and spare ribs from the Chinese, Chocolate Oranges, her car, her mobile phone and, like everyone else in there, music. She won't miss television – she's not a big telly fan – and she won't miss her diet.

She's hoping that even though there's no music in the house, she'll be able to dance: she loves salsa dancing, and she can do the splits. She keeps fit at home by doing aerobics to a video for 30 minutes every day.

She enjoys her job because she gets to watch all the films at the cinema, where she usually works on the popcorn stall.

Her family is the most important thing to her and she says the most hurtful thing anyone could do to her would be to hurt one of them. She's the youngest and 'most spoiled' of three; she and her brother and sister were brought up in Birmingham by her single mum, someone of whom Alison is extremely proud.

'My mum is a big strong black mother with lots of confidence and love. She is my strength. She's also done things I would never dream of. For instance, she's now doing a degree. I admire that. And she's brought up three children alone and I don't think I could ever do that.'

'We are a very close family with a lot of love. We will always be there for one another.'

She's particularly close to her brother, and laughs at her memories of how the two of them behaved when they were children. 'When we were little, me and my brother were messing around. He picked his toenails and put them in a pan and fried them, then we tried toasting them. I don't know why we did it, but it was all instigated by my brother. That was the most disgusting thing I've ever done.'

She is very proud of her Jamaican roots and, along with the clothes shop, would like to open a Jamaican restaurant – if she can find a friendly bank manager!

She reckons the others in the house will like her because 'I'm quite charming and I do listen to people, so I would be there for anyone who had problems. I'm always game for a laugh. I'm the sort of person who has to be in on everything. If something fun is going on over there, I have to know about it. I'm always the last one to go to bed.'

But despite the relentless fun, fun, fun, Alison reckons she's tactful. And she says she'll also bring 'a different kind of sex appeal' to *Big Brother*.

The downside is that she thinks people will be put off by her bigness, and it might irritate the others that she's so irrepressibly happy all the time. 'There will always be someone who doesn't like you, and I think that if you can realize that, you stop yourself from getting hurt. They may not like my loudness. I do go over the top sometimes. Sometimes I don't know when to stop.'

She's a teetotal non-smoker.

JADE

Full name: Jade Cerisa Lorraine Goody
Nicknames: Pamela Anderson, Claudia Schiffer
Age: Twenty-first birthday in Week Two
Marital status: Single
Star sign: Gemini
Height: 5 feet 6 inches
Weight: 10 stone 3 pounds
Dress size: 12
Tattoos and piercings: Two tattoos on her back and
one on her right ankle. Belly button pierced.
Favourite food: Chicken, kebabs, everything. 'I love all food.'
Ambition: To do a duet with Rod Stewart.
What's in her suitcase? Photo badge of herself with her mum;
1 stuffed monkey; 3 rings; 2 pairs earrings; 4 bikinis; pink
satin diamante-encrusted dress with matching bag;
2 bottles white wine; reading glasses.

She's the youngest housemate, and she's the one with the high-decibel motor-mouth. Before the first night was over, almost every other contestant had asked her to turn down the volume. But Jade recognizes the problem: she reckons she'll get nominated 'because people will just want me to shut up. I go on too much, always chatting. I annoy people because I kind of bellow. I'm a lad, and that gets on people's nerves. And some people don't like me speaking my mind: if I think someone is taking the piss I tell them, not someone else. I guess I don't think before I speak.'

But there's a lot more to Jade than a big gob in a small space. She's full of energy. 'I'm always doing things for other people or for charity. You'll never find me sitting on my bum doing nothing.' She reckons she's a good team player, and she'll go out of her way to get things done. Once, when she saw a group of older boys beating up a younger lad, she stopped them and took the young boy home to his mum.

She says she's 'caring, funny, outgoing, happy, down-to-earth'. Things are certainly lively when she's around, which she reckons will keep the others on their toes. Her family, she says, would describe

JADE   PALM READING

Here is a case of a seriously wacky character, who has great ideas but seems unable to sustain them and ensure they happen the way she wants. She is without doubt a drama queen as her wide hand and breaks in her lines suggest. She is a sexy and bubbly personality and her very stiff thumbs show she cannot take no for an answer. No matter how many times Jade gets things wrong, she'll keep trying.

Her vivid imagination and periodic self belief and even disbelief are fed by a semi-simian line in her right hand. (We'll hear a lot of 'Did I say that?' and 'Did I do that?' later on interviews!) Despite a possible break, a line seems to traverse right across her hand from near her thumb to the side of her hand under the little finger. This means if Jade is in the right mood she could be up for almost anything. To laugh is this girl's tonic; laughter or tears and sometimes both at the same time, she'll get to others too. Like her or not, her audacity will shine through. Her rounded fingertips show she is a great idealist and at times everything can look black or rosy depending upon how much sleep she gets. Her emotions surge through her smooth fingers and have to be expressed. Her longer looking fingers show she is surprisingly good at working at details, but she can easily get bored and disheartened. Her family lines just inside her thumb line, and life line which runs around the thumb ball, show she will always have great support from her family.

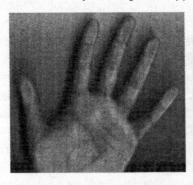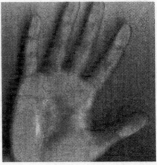

her as 'fun, loud, game for anything, do anything for anyone, and with a way with words'.

'There's never be a dull moment when I'm about, or so I'm told.'

She works as a dental nurse, which includes comforting nervous patients, mixing materials and being a chair-side assistant to the dentist. It's not her dream job; but she's happy.

She lives with her mum, but spends a lot of time with her boyfriend Danny. Before she went into the house she described it as a serious relationship: she said she'd like to be with him in ten years' time, living comfortably and being able to do what she likes. 'I'd like to have a nice house, a car, good health and enough money – and I definitely don't want to grow old on my own.'

She's very close to her mum, who she says has inspired her more than anyone. 'She has a lot to deal with and she still comes out on top. You can't hurt me because I've been through enough, but if anyone hurt my mum, it would kill me. We don't have much but she would give me her last 20p. She wants the best for me, and will always be there for me.'

She describes her mum, who lost the use of one of her arms in an accident when Jade was five, as 'one original lady. You will never meet another like her. She always points me in the right direction, she knows a lot about life and she is very strong. She brought me up and gave me all the love a person could give.'

If she had to choose celebrities for parents, she'd have Sophia Loren as her mum ('because then I'd know I'd grow old glamorously') and Sean Connery. 'Why not!'

Before she went in, Jade knew that her biggest problem was going to be missing people. Her twenty-first birthday came in Week Two, and that was always going to be a difficult time for her. 'When you get those quiet moments, I'll be missing everyone, and that may make me cry. If people inside make me cry it will be out of frustration. I won't be allowed to punch them, will I? I've never been able to hide my feelings. What's the point of putting a brave face on things if you're hurting inside? Just let it all out and you'll be alright again.'

True enough, homesickness did quickly get the better of her: Jade was the first of the housemates to have a good cry. She'd been in the house for 26 hours when she retired under her duvet for a

JADE   Ⅱ   **GEMINI**

A very bubbly, ultra-sociable chatty woman; friendly, wants to love and be loved by everyone. With so many planets in water, she is very sensitive, romantic and can fall in love easily. Jade will want to participate in everything this world has to offer. A highly-strung, childlike woman, who could grow on you if she hangs around for long enough... Lesson in *Big Brother*: to listen first, before all that chatter.

good sob, missing her mum and her boyfriend, and there were plenty more tears to come.

She admits she has a temper: she gets angry with people who tell lies, people who try to take control, and people who shout and point their fingers into her face.

Although she was very close to her boyfriend Danny, she could get mad at him – like the time he arranged to have a cheap night in at home with her but went drinking with his mates and turned up drunk. 'I hit him,' she admits. They were together for two and a half years before she went into the house.

'I met Danny through a friend. We had our ups and downs, but he was always a shoulder for me to cry on and I've been there for him. We support each other. It's been rocky at times, but we got through it mostly. The way I see it, you argue because you care, so all good couples will argue. He's really sensible, I'm not. I'm awful with money – I couldn't finance a bus journey.'

It's the best relationship she's ever had. 'We did our own thing, going out with our own mates, spending time together and he made me laugh all the time. He treated me like a girlfriend!'

Jade's first kiss was when she was 11, with a boy who had been her sweetheart at primary school. Her first serious relationship was when she was 15, with a boy who was living across the road. It lasted for three years.

She'll miss her mum more than anyone when she's in the house, 'because I worry about her and she gives me good advice. She's the best mum in the world'. She'll also miss her nan and grandad, 'because they're always there when I need a favour'.

Other things she'll miss are *EastEnders*, Graham Norton, and eating out in restaurants. And although she'll miss her dog, she won't miss her boyfriend's dog, 'because he's like a horse, barks a lot and always gets in the way of the TV'.

The achievement she's most proud of is getting into the *Big Brother* house. 'I'm proud to be me, because my family life has not been easy, and I've come through alright.'

The things that make Jade happy are her health, her family and friends, going out, having the money to go out, and gossip. Shopping is one of her great loves, and if she ever had to choose a specialist subject for *Mastermind* it would be shoes and bags, because she loves looking at them even when she can't afford to buy.

She's got a real phobia about tomato ketchup, and she hates flies and other flying insects. Eating ketchup is the only thing she would refuse to do in the house.

She's lucky because the luxuries she couldn't live without are all things she can have in the house: toothbrush and toothpaste, chocolate and moisturiser – as long as they pass the tasks and have money for shopping, that is. Otherwise, chocolate deprivation will set in.

The most daring thing Jade ever did was a 200-feet bungee jump to raise money for breast cancer charities. She closed her eyes and jumped – but she'd never do it again.

Under 'skills or hobbies' on her application form, Jade put: 'I can fit my body through an elastic band.' She even demonstrated the trick on her application video. But if that doesn't sound like a hobby that would while away many hours, she's also into *saroc* (French rock and roll dancing). She goes to the gym, but she's nowhere near as dedicated to physical fitness as most of the other housemates: she only goes about three times a month.

And she's a real party girl: she says she gets wasted when she goes out at the weekend. Her favourite tipple is Bacardi and Coke.

KATE

Full name: Kate Louise Lawler
Nicknames: Matey Katie, Pink
Age: 22
Marital status: Single
Star sign: Taurus
Height: 5 feet 7 inches
Weight: 8 stone 7 pounds
Dress size: 8/10
Tattoos and piercings: Belly and ears pierced.
Tattoo on tummy, below belly button.
Favourite food: Pizza, chicken, spaghetti bolognaise, crisps,
cookies, ice cream, pork pies, pineapple, strawberries, apples.
Ambition: To be successful in whatever I do. To be an actress
as good as Judi Dench, or run a hairdressers or a
bar abroad, probably in Tenerife.
What's in her suitcase? 17 thongs; 9 photos; 2 teddy bears;
2 bars milk chocolate and 6 bags sweets; 1 packet Blu-tac;
3 good luck cards; 5 bikinis; 3 sarongs; 5 bras; 1 face pack.

Kate's a fit girl, in both senses of the word. She's fit as in a stunning looker, a beautiful blonde with a great face and a fabulous body. And she's also fit in the athletic sense: she plays football, boxes and does weight training.

She's a city slicker, with a job working on an IT helpdesk in the City of London, but she finds the work 'tedious and boring'.

Her dream is that in ten years' time she'll be happily married, with four children and a husband who is absolutely devoted to her. She sees herself as a traditional mum, staying at home with the children. 'I want my husband to go out and earn all the money. I want to look after the children, and go to the gym every day so that I have a really fit body when I'm an old woman.'

Kate and her twin sister Karen have a very close relationship. 'She's always been a massive influence on me because we've always done things together and shared so much and we know everything about each other. She's always the one who pushes me

Spencer and Sandy share a companionable silence in the early days in the house.

Sandy's morning exercise routine.

Alison puts the housemates through their aqua aerobics.

'Three little maids from school are we.'

It's Davina!

LEE

The big adventure starts for Lee.

Lee growing up.

Sophie gives Lee the look of love.

Sophie and Lee holding hands in bed.

Lee bares his soul to Big Brother.

ALISON

'Wow, I'm really here!'

Alison in her early years.

Alison shows her strength.

Alison jumps off the kitchen work surface just before she leaves the house.

Snaps from Alison's family album.

Davina takes Alison down to
the crowds who love her.

Alison is reunited with her family.

JADE

Jade enters the house.

Age 2.

Jade, age 3½, and her dad.

Age 4½.

Jade modelling.

Age 8.

Jade at senior school.

Jade getting hammered.

Jade, age 12, at a karaoke night.

Jade's determined if she goes in the poor house, she won't be short of undies.

Funny head gear for Jade and Adele.

After the fight — Adele makes friends with Jade.

P.J.

P.J. goes in.

All dressed up.

What a cutie!

Modest as always!

P.J. as a baby.

Action hero P.J.

P.J., age 2, waiting to enter the house.

Proud parents.

P.J. and Tom in Ibiza.

Football mad.

P.J. proves to be the only housemate who can add up.

Jade wants affection but P.J.'s not giving in.

Did they or didn't they? P.J. and Jade in bed together.

SOPHIE

Sophie through the years.

A night out for the girls.

Sunning herself with Santa.

Lee turns his affections to Sophie.

Sophie lands a few punches.

Sophie demonstrates one of her great talents.

SPENCER

What a bundle of joy!

Spencer prepares to go in.

Age 2 weeks, with great grandad Cyril.

Age 5, with brother Tom and sister Emily.

Age 3, with brother Tom.

Spencer's mum, Maxine.

A Spencer sketch.

Spencer's grandparents.

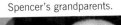

Spencer's mum and sister.

Age 17.

Punting on
the River Cam.

A tender
moment
with Kate.

Spencer
finally persuades
someone to wash
his clothes and
Sophie is the
lucky person.

Not kissing! Kate giving
Spencer a mouthful of
beer through the divide.

With the boys.

Tim's parents.

Shocks all round – a new housemate arrives.

TIM

Tim growing up.

Tim's nearest and dearest.

Kate, Spencer and Sophie get
down to the chores.

The boys get into the spirit of
things for Jade's birthday party.

The girls are determined to
keep their abs flat.

Fun and games at
Jade's birthday party.

Sandy dresses the part
for Lee's wrestling party.

Jade yawning, again.

when I'm down or whatever, and I do the same for her.'

She'll miss her twin more than anyone. 'We have a special bond, and I've never gone a day of my life without making contact with her in one way or another. We've shared our mum's tummy, and we've shared our lives since then. We've gone through ups and downs, goods and bads, and she knows all my secrets and I know all hers.' She'll also be missing the rest of her family, and all her girlfriends.

'My mum and dad are great, young at heart and very loving and supportive. They both encourage me whenever I choose to do mad things, like going to Japan. My mum will worry about me the whole time I'm in the house.'

She says her mum is caring and loving, and her dad is funny and strong. Her older sister is 'sexy, sensible, tall, gorgeous, loud', and her twin sister is 'sexy, hilarious, tall, big-busted and crazy'. Her younger brother is 'funny, nice sometimes, kind sometimes, moody and going through the teenage stage'.

If she could choose celebrity parents, she'd have Madonna as a mum: 'She's trendy, cool, young at heart, and I'd grow up strong-willed like her, and do everything and anything.'

There are lots of other things she'll miss, too: McDonalds, pizza, pick'n'mix sweets, television, boxing with her trainer Robbie, going to the gym, her favourite CDs, chocolate, bubblegum, alcohol and, extra specially, her West Highland terrier called Puppy Charles. But top of her list of misses is her mobile phone, which is normally 'glued to my hand', because she's always texting or talking to her friends. And she's not sure if the amount of makeup she's been allowed to take in will last: 'You have no idea how bad a girl can feel in the morning and how good she can make herself look with makeup.' She loves messing about with makeup, and enjoys paint-ing her mates' faces. She'd choose perfume as her specialist subject on *Mastermind*, because she has over 40 bottles and reckons she knows every perfume ever invented.

What she won't miss in there is her job. 'Staring at a PC all day waiting for the phone to ring, getting up at 6.15am to get there, checking my bank balance every day on the Internet.' But she'll miss meeting her friends at lunchtime to talk about men, and staring at her George Clooney screensaver. When she gets time to daydream, it's usually about travelling, George Clooney, Benicio del Toro, and food. She also fantasizes about becoming a DJ, and thinks there aren't enough women in the profession – she'll have plenty to talk to Adele and Sunita about.

She hopes that the *Big Brother* experience will make more friends for her, and that she'll learn something new.

'Perhaps I can change opinions – men's – about blondes, to show we're not all stereotypical girly type people.'

One person who has inspired her loads is her drama teacher from school. 'She knew so much about the world and was so intelligent. She made me do things I never thought I would be able to do. She taught me not to hold back.'

If Kate could have her life again, she'd concentrate on drama more – she was turned down for drama school; or she'd go to college to study fashion.

Kate doesn't claim to be one of the craziest of the housemates, although she admits to having a wild time with about ten mates in Ibiza two summers ago. They caused a sensation, a gang of stunning girls strolling around in thongs and chasing each other into the sea. 'We took over the beach. It was such a wicked day, because we all spent it messing around and trying to get each others' knickers off. I ripped off my twin sister's bikini in the sea, so she was stuck.'

The same holiday provided Kate with a horrible memory, as well as some fun ones. 'I got really drunk and fell over in a doorway with my skirt up and my thong on show. My mates took photos and were laughing themselves sick. I was so ill I slept on the floor next to the toilet all night.'

The most embarrassing thing that has ever happened to her was wetting the bed at a friend's house when she was 16. 'I hadn't wet the bed for years, but we watched a TV drama about a woman who abused her daughter and the girl used to wet herself. I always dream about what I'm thinking about before I go to bed. I woke up and I was weeing and I couldn't stop. I told my friend and she promised not to tell anyone, but she told her best mate and in the end lots of people knew. It was so embarrassing.'

She's really proud of running a mini-marathon through London

KATE	♉	TAURUS

A confident independent woman, with a sensitive vulnerable side if she feels left out. Kate is open, friendly and helpful. She is attracted to the limelight, but doesn't get too carried away with it. There is a competitive side to her; she loves danger and excitement, and wants to be treated as an equal to men. The desire to win will be strong, so the others will have to watch out! Lesson in *Big Brother*: to make sure she picks the right man, who can accept her competitive ways.

---

when she was only 15, competing against girls two years older. 'I was so skinny, I looked awful, but all my family were there to watch.'

She's also proud of her three A levels, because no one else in the family has done them, and her predicted grades were not high. She confounded everyone: 'I revised my bollocks off,' she says.

And she's proud of going to Japan on her own, to work for two months teaching English. 'It was a complete culture shock, and I coped on my own. I moved into an apartment and the washing machine instructions were in Japanese. I shrank half my wardrobe. But I overcame the shock by going out and buying new clothes!

'It was a weird experience, and they did laugh at me and call me a crazy English girl. It was very hard, and I used the strangest methods to try and get across what I was teaching the pupils.'

She came back without letting any of her friends and family know, and took them all by surprise.

More than anything else, she hates being betrayed, either by a bloke cheating on her, or by friends who break confidences. She also hates rain just after she's washed her hair, seeing her best friends stay with blokes who are no good for them, putting on weight and stroppy bosses. On the other hand, losing weight, eating good food, not being skint and looking good all make her feel happy.

She goes to the gym four or five times a week, where she does jogging, sit-ups and weights because she thinks her arms are too skinny. At weekends she loves shopping, going out with her girl-friends, listening to music and watching DVDs.

She's so concerned about her weight that one of the few things that might make her leave the house is putting on more than a stone in there. And about the only thing she'd refuse to do is eat a Brussels sprout.

If you see Kate crying in there, it could be because she's really upset – or it could be because she's hungry. 'I'm quite a fussy eater, so I don't always get the food I want. When I'm hungry I get funny, dizzy, and I do cry.' She says she may also be reduced to tears through missing people. 'If I do cry, I won't do it in front of everyone, I'll do it on my own. I'm quite emotional.'

She reckons she's had plenty of practice at hiding her emotions. 'I've done it loads of times, like when my ex-boyfriend dumped me. I was well gutted but had to put a brave face on it. It took me about a year to get over that.'

She doesn't always show her ice-cool side when she has boyfriend trouble. One ex who lied and cheated was always eating KFC, and Kate yelled at him, 'I hope you choke on a chicken bone, you w...er!'

She's only had three serious relationships. She split up with her last boyfriend four months ago. They met on holiday. She's finding the break hard: Kate still thinks things could work out between them.

She was a late developer in the romance stakes: she didn't have her first boyfriend until she was 17, and even then she only saw him once a week. Her sister was a dolly bird by the age of 15, but Kate was only interested in sport. 'I was a real geezer bird.'

Now she's on the lookout for her ideal man, who will have dark hair, brown eyes, Brad Pitt's smile, Mark Wahlberg's body and voice, big hands, a big manhood, sexy legs and the allure of Benicio del Toro, coupled with David Beckham's wages.

Before she went in, Kate expected to get on well with the others, 'because I seem to get on with anyone from any walk of life'. She thinks her positive attitude and optimistic outlook on life will help to make her popular.

'I look on the bright side and like to muck in. I like cooking and cleaning – I'm a big tidy freak. I'm the fastest bathroom cleaner in the world and I make a lovely spaghetti bolognaise. It will always be tidy when I'm there, unless the others are all really messy. I muck in with activities or chores.'

She describes herself as 'fun, out-going, feisty, flirty, girly, shy, sporty, active, friendly, confident, laidback, honest, genuine and experimental'. She believes she would bring warmth and energy to the house. 'I'm not boring, and I'm relaxed about being me. I'm not an extrovert, and I don't think getting my kit off on camera will win the game for me, but I think I'm entertaining.'

On the downside, she admits she can talk too much, and she'll happily sit up until 3.00am gabbing.

She's hoping her stay *chez Big Brother* will be the challenge she's been looking for. 'It's going to be the toughest thing I've ever done, but I feel deep down that my life would benefit.'

'Quieter people may dislike my personality, and although I think the tidying up is a good thing, others may think it's a tad obsessive. Some people may not like my character, or they may be jealous.'

Katie says she doesn't smoke – but admits to lighting up when she's really, really drunk. Her favourite tipples are passoa, vodka and cranberry juice, and wine.

LYNNE

Full name: Lynne Moncrieff
Nicknames: none
Age: 36
Marital status: Divorced/separated
Star sign: Aquarius
Height: 5 feet 7 inches
Weight: 9 stone
Dress size: 12
Tattoos and piercings: Tattoo on lower back.
Favourite food: Home-cooked Italian, Thai, Indian – best of all,
a bowl of cullen skink soup (a fish soup from the north-east).
Ambition: To make a living out of something I really enjoy.
What's in her suitcase? 15 pairs of knickers; 6 bras; 7 pairs
of socks; 3 pairs of earrings; 6 bracelets; 1 'feeling' blanket;
1 can Coke; biscuits; cheesecake; 2 bikinis; 2 boob tubes

While all the other contestants were holed up for security reasons in
London hotels, Lynne was sitting an exam in nineteenth-century French
Art at Aberdeen University, where she's a mature student doing a
History of Art degree. Let's all hope she passed – it must have been
terribly difficult to concentrate. No sooner had she put down her pen
than she had to dash to collect her suitcase and board the next flight
for London.

Lynne's not a material girl: she's used to living on student rations
and she thinks 'stuff is a disease of the twenty-first century'. She's
a free spirit who gets upset about global waste. She's travelled the
world, and she's still restless: she's hoping her time in *Big Brother*
will help her sort out what she wants to do with the rest of her life.
She has no clear idea of where she would like to be in ten years'
time, but she'd like to be 'quite successful in something I like doing,
and with someone I haven't yet met'.

While she is studying, Lynne works part time in a department
store and teaches Italian for a few hours a week. She learned the
language when living in Italy for a few years. She certainly won't
miss going to work: she's grateful to *Big Brother* for taking her away

from the prospect of temping all summer in her break from university. She's had a variety of jobs over the years, including being a kissogram girl and a picture restorer in Italy, but the worst was in a fish processing plant where she had to 'pick the little strand of shit out of prawns'.

She did well at school, but chose not to go on to university then – she was in her Gothic punk phase. 'I wish I had gone at 18, but I was rebellious, a punk, and I lived in London and then Italy for a few years. I wouldn't be the person I am today if I hadn't done those things.'

She's now making up for lost time, and spends her days after lectures reading, cycling, pottering around her flat, shopping, socializing, clubbing, going to the cinema and going out for dinner. And she admits that when she's supposed to be studying she spends far too much time e-mailing her friends.

She describes herself as 'game, honest, compassionate, real, vivacious, friendly, immature, sometimes selfish, forgetful, vain, creative, humorous, sincere, strange, self-conscious, effervescent, and with a bad temper'.

She lives on a tight budget, and buys her clothes in second-hand shops and 'semi-cool sales'. But she's not desperately materialistic and thinks she'd still shop at the same places if she was rich, although she might throw in the odd Fendi handbag. Even though money is something she can manage without, she does want to earn a reasonable amount one day, ''cos I dream of not having to put food back in the supermarket because I can't afford it'.

Her mum is the person who has influenced her most in life, simply because she's 'such a strong person'. Lynne's close to her,

LYNNE	♒	AQUARIUS

A woman with a strong character – she will be in competition with anyone who challenges her. This works in the outside world, but she will find it hard to adapt in the *Big Brother* house. She is attracted to the limelight but in a humanitarian way. Lynne is moved by the mind first; her emotions kick in later. Lesson in *Big Brother*: to try to be more flexible with views and opinions.

and will miss her more than anyone while she's locked away in *Big Brother* land. 'She's my best friend. She's strong willed and has taught me the basics of life: live, laugh and love. She really is an absolute diamond,' she says. She describes her parents, who celebrated their Golden Wedding anniversary earlier this year, as 'fabulous, spirited, honest, hard-working, funny, ahead of their time, long-suffering, law-abiding, intelligent'.

She has a married sister who she loves: she's auntie to her sister's two grown-up children.

Like Kate, Lynne went into the *Big Brother* house with a broken romance just behind her. She'd been with her boyfriend for four years, and knew him for eight years before that as a friend. They met at a party. They both agreed to the split earlier this year, because they were taking each other for granted.

Lynne's had half a dozen relationships, each lasting for at least a couple of years. She's had other boyfriends for much shorter times, too. The man she wants to share her life with will be 'fun, gregarious, compassionate, easy-going, intelligent, settled in a career and without any money problems'. But she knows he may be hard to find: 'I'm not asking for a lot, am I?'

She says that if she won the money, she'd buy her parents a new house and throw a weekend-long wild party for all her friends. Her heroine is Madonna, 'because of her single-minded determination, even though some people may think she's a bit of a bitch'.

Things that make her angry include snobbery, one-up-manship, stupid people, graffitti, being taken for granted and people with careless attitudes. Things that make her happy include dancing, singing, her family, giving presents, good service and food in restaurants, and good music. She also felt very happy after having a laser operation on her eyes for short-sightedness, when she found she could see clearly without glasses.

The craziest thing she ever did was a parachute jump, in Australia. She's got a video to prove it.

Like most of the other housemates, she's keen to keep fit and trim, and goes to the gym and goes for a long cycle ride at least three times a week. She's had a boob job – she says she was self-conscious about her breasts, 'so after ten years of deliberating I finally went ahead and got the op. It was the best thing I ever did.'

Lynne has had a couple of interesting trips in her life: once downstairs in a pub when she was wearing a Gothic punk outfit with a long veil, which caught in her heel. 'The second time was similar. I was working in a really awful bar in Australia where the waitresses were 'lingerie babes'. It was my first night, and all I was wearing was a thong and a bra and high heels. The heel of my shoe got caught in the rubber slip mat and I went arse over tit. I just picked myself up, dusted myself down and got on with the job in hand.'

She's really proud of her flat, which she did up on a shoestring – although she said in her application video that one reason she'd like to go into the *Big Brother* house was to have appliances that work; as, although her flat looks great, lots of things don't work. She also wanted to go in because 'I don't seem to be contented with my humdrum life, and it needs an injection of something quite bizarre – as Andy Warhol said, everybody should have their fifteen minutes of fame.'

She's also proud of having travelled around the world. She's been to south-east Asia and Australia, and carries with her some stunning memories: seeing thousands of fruit bats darken a pink and golden sky; visiting one of the oldest Buddhist temples; peering into a vast volcano and watching smoke billow from it.

One of her greatest achievements was getting down to the final ten in a nationwide singing contest in 1994. Unfortunately, she was so nervous that her performance at the final in a London nightclub was not one of her best. She says that if she'd had the confidence then that she has now, she'd have loved to make a career for herself singing.

Other careers she'd love to pursue include being a stylist or interior designer, but for people on a budget. Having done up her own flat so successfully without much money, she reckons she could do the same thing for other people.

The luxuries she really couldn't live without are, luckily for her, things she's allowed in the house: makeup and nice clothes. But she will desperately miss music.

She's allergic to animal hair, which is a sadness for her because she'd like to have a pet. If she was reincarnated she'd come back as a cat to be fed and stroked all the time. But looking after animals is the one thing she wouldn't be able to do in the *Big Brother* house.

She can get hurt, especially if people are nasty for no good reason. She reckons she may well cry while she's in the house, especially if she's been drinking. 'I have a tendency to cry when drunk.'

But she will be able to hide some of her feelings. 'I have done it when I've been very angry about something, and I just have to button it and not say anything, which is extremely difficult.'

She thinks her sense of humour and the fact that she can be very caring for others are the aspects of her personality that the other housemates will find endearing. 'I'm not a bad cook, I'm very tidy and clean, I'm a fun-loving people person, open-minded, and my philosophy is live and let live.'

And she reckons her quirky personality and her abilities as an entertainer will keep viewers hooked: 'I'm dynamic, dynamite, a free spirit of the times and I've got some wicked stories to tell.'

Unlike the rest of the housemates, who almost all say they enjoy listening to other people, Lynne admits she can be a poor listener – and she thinks it may exasperate the others. 'People can be talking to me and I'm nodding my head but not really listening. And I've got a bad memory, which can be annoying.

'Also, I might come across as loving myself too much. But hey, if you can't love yourself, who can you love? They may think I'm a bit insular, vain, loud and corny. Or loud-mouthed, opinionated and difficult.'

Her favourite drink is spiced rum and Coke. She doesn't smoke.

SOPHIE

Full name: Sophie Anna Bianca Pritchard
Nicknames: None
Age: 24 when she goes into the house, 25 when she comes out
Marital status: Single
Star sign: Gemini
Height: 5 feet 9 inches
Weight: 8 stone 11 pounds
Dress size: 10
Tattoos and piercings: Belly button pierced.
Favourite food: Mashed potato, cheese, chocolate,
baked beans, pasta.
Ambition: To qualify as a psychologist, to design my own clothes
range and to make a record (but I think I need a voice for that!).
What's in her suitcase? Teddy bear; 18 G-strings; 4 bikinis;
6 bras; 6 pairs of socks; spangly denim jeans and a spangly
denim skirt; 22 tops; 3 pairs of shorts; 2 bottles wine.

Sophie's world changed dramatically the day Sunita announced she
was leaving the *Big Brother* house. She was in the recruitment office
where she works, when her phone rang. It was Susy Price. 'Sophie,
we want you in the house. I'm parked outside in my car. Get your
things, and we're off to spend a couple of nights in a hotel,' Susy
said. Sophie, who was one of the stand-bys and knew a soon as she
heard Sunita was leaving that there was a chance she would be
going in, was staggered to find Susy waiting for her. She tried to stay
calm as she left work and was whisked away to a hotel for three
nights, and kept strictly away from television, newspapers and radio,
so that she had no idea how life was progressing in the house. The
production team chose her because they recognise that it is difficult
going in when the others have been there for a few days and already
know each other. They felt that Sophie was a strong enough character to handle it.

Then on Sunday, 2 June, just nine days after the other eleven, she
climbed the 23 metal stairs outside the house, walked past the big
orange eye logo and through the heavy door into the house. She

SOPHIE	♊	GEMINI

An introvert disguised as an extrovert, keen to interact and communicate with people. An attractive, sensuous woman, so watch out, *Big Brother* men! Sophie likes to chew things over so she will be slow to form an opinion, but that is not such a bad thing. A dependable person who can be possessive if the right man comes along. Lesson in *Big Brother*: to learn to make quicker decisions in some areas.

stood at the top of the steps for a few seconds, a bewildered look on her face, until Jonny ran up to take her suitcase and escort her down. With the exception of Kate, all the housemates stood up to greet her, and there was a round of kissing and introductions – noticeably much lower key than the excited scenes just over a week earlier.

Sophie describes herself as fun, caring, witty, with a good sense of humour, lovable, and nuts. As well as all that, she can wrap her legs around her head, lying down or standing up, which should come in useful for... errr, well, the housemates are bound to think of something...

Things that make Sophie happy include her family and friends, her music, chocolate, and anyone who can make her laugh. Music is so central to her life that she would choose it as her specialist subject on *Mastermind*.

She can get angry – she recently told a man who nearly reversed into her car exactly what she thought of him, in no uncertain terms. And she's got plenty of determination – after being told at school that she would never amount to anything, she set herself goals, and so far she has achieved some of them. She's most proud of landing a job travelling the world on a cruise ship for three years, for the first year as an entertainer and then for two years as a business manager. It was while she was with the cruise ship that she had one of the peak moments in her life so far, swimming with dolphins in the Bahamas. 'It was the most amazing thing ever.'

For the past six months, she's been working for a recruitment agency, helping to find the right people to fill jobs. She has her own list of clients, and builds a rapport with them – she helps them write their CVs and arranges interviews for them. She enjoys it because it's very varied, and she meets lots of people. But it's not her dream job. She would like to go to college to get a degree in psychology, and then work with disadvantaged or disabled children. She reckons the nicest thing she has ever done was to visit a boy with Down's Syndrome in hospital after he was hit by a car. The medical staff said there was not much chance of him making a full recovery, but Sophie spent hours talking to him. Six years on, he has recovered, and is talking again and enjoying life.

Not that she's always saintly – she told one ex-boyfriend that he was hopeless in bed because he had a small willy. She ranks that as the cruellest thing she's ever done.

Her most embarrassing moment was when she was dancing with a guy in a club, and one of her bra pads fell out onto the floor. 'I died. The poor guy didn't know where to look. So I picked it up and put it in my back pocket and carried on dancing.'

She was also pretty embarrassed when, aged 17, she had to persuade people to taste wine in a supermarket – dressed as a red wine bottle.

She works out at the gym three times a week, and like Kate and Spencer she's into kick boxing. She cares about the way she looks; if she could choose a celebrity parent, she'd go for Goldie Hawn as her mum, 'because daughters are meant to end up looking like their mothers, so I would have her figure and be laughing'.

But she's not exactly unhappy with her figure at the moment – when asked why people would want to watch her in the house for weeks, she says, 'Who wouldn't want to look at my body?!' She adds that it's her chameleon personality that will make compulsive viewing. 'Who knows which version of me they will get? That should keep people entertained and laughing.'

She's a romantic; in quiet moments she dreams of being on a beach with someone who truly loves her. She's single, and says she's met a variety of men in her life – 'some complete arseholes and some extremely lovely guys. I have just not met Mr Right yet – or if I have, the timing was wrong.'

The Mr Right she is looking for would be 'someone who is funny, who is my best friend and lover and not afraid to talk about his feelings. Someone who is proud to walk hand in hand with me. Someone who is as giving as I am.'

She's close to her family, especially her mum, who she describes as caring, loving, kind, supportive and wonderful. 'She has always been there for me, and she knows everything about me. I really look up to her, and if I'm half like my mum, that's an achievement.' Sophie's mum, Yvonne, is psychic and was always convinced that Sophie would make it into the house, even after she didn't go in on Day One.

She says her dad is strong, kind, forgiving, helpful and great, and she describes her brother as her best friend.

Sophie doesn't think the *Big Brother* experience will change her, except to make her a stronger person and open her eyes a bit more to other people. She'll miss her mum and her two best friends most: she talks to them on the phone all the time. On the subject of phones, her mobile is high on the list of things she will miss, together with her CD player, her car, going out, and sex. What she won't miss is work.

'Being out of the rat race for a while will be nice, and it will be great not having to get up early.'

She thinks the others may get upset by her bossiness, her dry humour and her tendency to speak her mind. On the other hand, she reckons she will contribute a great deal to the house because she's a good cook and likes listening to people and helping them sort out their problems. She's got a lot of team spirit and says, 'I'm always good for a laugh.'

She likes white wine, but she's not a big drinker – only about four glasses a week. And she also smokes, but again, it's in moderation – a pack of 20 cigarettes lasts a whole week.

SUNITA

Full name: Sunita Sharma
Nickname: none
Age: 25
Marital status: Single
Star sign: Virgo
Height: 5 feet 4 inches
Weight: 8 stone 4 pounds
Dress size: 10
Tattoos and piercings: None
Favourite food: Pizza, Mexican, Thai green curry and noodles.
Ambition: To bungee jump over the Grand Canyon from a helicopter. Also, to turn left when boarding a plane.
What's in her suitcase? 2 bottles white wine; 100 Marlborough lights plus 150gms hand rolling tobacco; 6 packets supernoodles; Spiderman vest; 10 pairs black knickers; 4 black bras; 9 pairs black socks; milk chocolate; 13 pairs of trousers.

Slinky Sunita isn't a girl to tangle words with: she's a qualified barrister, and she knows how to hold her own in any argument, as Jade found out before they'd all been in the house for 48 hours.

Although she doesn't work as a barrister, Sunita is very proud of her qualifications. 'I might not be practising but it's quite cool to be able to say it, people don't expect it. It's great to see the expression on their faces. Ridiculously, it seems to make them have more respect for me.'

She's obviously a bright lady, with loads of GCSEs and A levels, as well as a law degree. In her job as a legal clerk she represents solicitors in court, working closely with barristers to make sure they have all the information they need. She usually only works two or three days a week, and when she's not working she's jogging, exercising and learning to mix records – so she and Adele will have plenty to share, especially as Sunita's dream job is to be a 'superstar sexy female house or funky breakbeat DJ'. Despite all her academic achievements, the thing that she's most proud of is her flat stomach: 'Three years of sit-ups finally pays off!'

Although she's trained for the bar, Sunita's dreams include a different kind of bar: her idea of where she would like to be in ten years' time is running a bar on a beach, surrounded by all her friends, with alcohol flowing, music playing and having lots of fun.

The person who has influenced her most is her best friend from uni. 'I was a country girl and she was a city girl, really cool, and I learned a lot from her. She's very streetwise, really open-minded.' She was also very influenced by her primary school teacher, 'who taught me to have dreams and to turn them into reality'.

Sunita really values her friendships; she says her greatest fear is of being lonely and not having family and friends around. 'Everyone needs love and attention, and I'm so grateful that I have it.'

She is one of four children, and her parents split up when she was young. 'My mother is a saint. She's a traditional Indian woman who is deeply spiritual. She's a very mumsy mum, loved by every-one she meets. She is youthful, full of life, and she knows the impor-tance of love and laughter. She has been through a lot, yet she is one of the strongest women I know. She is completely unselfish and always does what she thinks is best for her children. There isn't a day goes by that I'm not thankful that she's my mum.'

She's very close to her family, and the most hurtful thing anyone could do would be to be spiteful to them, especially to her mum. She reckons they will all be proud and happy that she is in the house.

If she could choose celebrity parents, she'd have David Attenborough as her father because 'he seems so wise and passion-ate about life'.

The craziest thing Sunita has ever done was a parachute jump, but no ordinary one: she had to clamber out on to the wing and push herself off. It was for the Duke of Edinburgh's Award Scheme and at first Sunita agreed to do it 'because I thought it would be a bit of a laugh. I didn't know what it was going to be like, which enabled me to do it, but I would never do it a second time because I'd know what to expect. It was a bit frightening.'

Sunita admits that she can be a bit celebrity-struck – and can behave in a silly way around famous people. 'I embarrass myself. I once saw Mark Lamarr in a club in Leicester Square, and I ended up approaching him and saying something really lary. And I met Mel

SUNITA	♍	VIRGO

A very ambitious woman – whatever she puts her mind to, she does well. Sunita loves to analyse and observe situations before giving an opinion, but she can sometimes be indecisive. She needs to connect intellectually with people, or she loses interest in them. In order to thrive, she needs space, and freedom to recharge her batteries. If not, she will withdraw into herself, which is not necessarily a bad thing. Lesson in *Big Brother*: to learn to recharge with others around.

from *Big Brother One* and I kept telling her she looked just like Mel. She laughed about it, but it was about ten minutes before I realized it really was her. It was embarrassing. But I've chilled a lot now.'

Sunita's single: she's had a few short-term relationships, but nothing longer than seven months. She's looking for 'someone who is in touch with their soul and understands me. He would have to be loving, kind and generous. He would have a good sense of family and want to look after me.'

Inside the house, she's going to be missing her Playstation 2, especially Tekken and Metal Gear Solid, her television and, most of all, her music. 'I live my life to music, either in the background when I'm just pottering about or in the foreground, to satisfy my urge to dance.' Her hero is Kurt Cobain from Nirvana. 'They were the first and most influential band for me – before that I was into cheesy teeny bop music. Their music and lyrics were poetry to my ears. I was heartbroken when Kurt died.'

She's also going to miss her mobile phone. 'It's the bane of my life, but I get heart palpitations if I leave home without it.'

The other luxury item she wouldn't like to live without is, thankfully, not banned: it's Oil of Olay moisturising cream. 'My mum always uses it, and I love the smell. It is good for my skin and it will remind me of my mum.'

Sunita's worst fault, she reckons, is her indecisiveness. 'I'm not lazy, because I do get things done. But I go through massive phases of not being able to decide what to do and not doing anything. I can quite literally spend months not doing anything and not worrying about it, because if I can't make a decision about what to do I just put it off. I go through zombie phases. It's indecisiveness, not laziness. Funnily enough, I can always make decisions for other people.'

She reckons it will be homesickness, missing her family and friends, that could reduce her to tears in the house. She doesn't think it will be because of the behaviour of the others. 'If they were picking on me, I can give as good as I get. That wouldn't worry me.'

She'll be able to hide how she's feeling most of the time, she thinks. 'If you're upset you can't give the other person the satisfaction of letting them know. I am one of those people who holds things inside and deals with them in my own time, either on my own or when I'm talking to someone else about it. I don't hide my emotions all the time, but if the situation calls for it, then I can.'

She says she has been disappointed by friends who have not done for her the things she would willingly have done for them. 'But I don't say anything.'

Things that make her angry are racism, arrogance, and slow-moving tourists who clog up the centre of London. When she hears someone being racist or arrogant she's not afraid to stand up to them.

The things that make her happy include her family and friends, music, money, good sex and holidays. Like loads of other people, she dreams about winning the lottery and buying loads of presents for all her friends.

Her life, she says, is 'like one film scene after another. I'm always getting into the middle of hilarious or heated situations.' She says she lives it 'with the premise that you only have one life – so make the most of it. As I get older I realize how quickly time goes by – so I try to make the most of every opportunity, which usually involves having as much fun as possible. I used to be scared of change, but now I know it is a good thing, as it allows you to develop. I stay positive: if one door closes, another opens.'

She thinks she'll be up for anything she may be asked to do in the house. The only thing she'd draw the line at is country dancing: 'a bit too pansyish for my liking'.

She thinks the others might get exasperated by her loudness. 'For a little person, I'm loud. I can get over-enthusiastic and go over the top. I am a really full-on person, and I'm sure I can sometimes be a nightmare for other people. And I do say things that aren't politically correct, if they're funny. I don't mean them to be politically incorrect, but some people might not understand my humour. And if I revert to my zombie character, that might be irritating for them, too.'

She says she can also be sarcastic; her energy levels can sometimes be too much for others, and others may think she's argumentative. If they do all dislike her and she dislikes them, that would be enough to persuade her to leave. If she gets voted out, she won't feel rejected because she thinks you have to accept things that happen to you; it's fate, and life goes on.

'People can't remain indifferent to me; they either love me or hate me. I don't think anyone would call me boring.'

The plus points she brings to the house are, she reckons, her laughter, the mental support she can give to the others by listening, and her motivating skills: she loves getting everybody involved in group activities. She's good at sports, she's creative and artistic – she likes making sculptures.

'I give body massages to die for. I'm a clubber and dancing for me is more than just moving to music, it's an expression of the soul.

'I'm quite carefree, I love to laugh and I like to hear other people laughing. I like to be in situations where everyone is happy, and I go out of my way to make sure other people are not upset.'

What appeals to Sunita about being in the house is that it's different: she hates the idea of settling into a mundane routine. 'I like to live my life in different ways and do different things.'

For such a party girl she's not a big drinker – not because she doesn't like the stuff, but because she says she has a low tolerance of alcohol. But she does enjoy a few glasses of wine during the week, and she's got a weakness for vodka. She also smokes – which came as a surprise to her mother when she went into the house. She's a vegetarian.

CHAPTER NINE

THE HOUSEMATES' REAL MATES

You love them, you hate them. They irritate you, you can't get enough of them. Everyone reacts differently to the housemates, choosing their own favourites and wondering why others survive the nominations, because they're just dying for the chance to vote them out.

But however passionately you feel about them all, there's a gang of people who are even more fervently involved in the goings-on in the house – watching the television with their hearts in their mouths, just hoping that their own personal housemate doesn't say or do anything that will upset the voting public. They're the housemates' real mates, their family and friends, the people they hugged and kissed just minutes before they entered the strange world of *Big Brother*. How do they find it, watching their loved ones every day but not being able to talk to them? We asked some of them whether the contestants we see on our screens are the people they recognize from real life.

LEE

Lee's dad Peter is amused to see his son helping out with the chores in the *Big Brother* house – he's not keen on cleaning and washing up at home.

'Perhaps I'll be able to get him to do a bit more about the place after this – the only thing he does at home is keep his bedroom tidy.'

Lee lives with his dad and younger brother Pete, and they are both missing him like mad while he's in the house.

'He's so close to Pete. They spend a lot of time messing around together and playing practical jokes – usually on me!' says his dad.

'It's really quiet without him around. The house was always full of the sound of him and Pete laughing.'

Lee's big smile has been with him all his life; his auntie Diane says it's the thing she most remembers about him as a baby.

'He always had a big grin for everyone, and that's never changed. The whole family are very fun-loving; they don't take life very seriously. Lee feels life is to be lived and enjoyed.

'But he's a gentle giant. Despite looking so big and strong, there's a really sensitive side to him. He's a good listener and he's good at spotting people's problems, and helping them sort them out.'

His dad Peter says that as a baby it was a constant struggle to stop Lee eating the wrong things – he was once discovered having a feast of snails in the garden.

'Everything went straight into his mouth. And he's loved his food ever since – not that he ever does any cooking.'

The family had a shock when they saw Lee strip off for his audition tape. His day says:

'He didn't tell me he'd sent in a tape – I didn't know until he got chosen for the audition. I asked him what was on his tape and he said he just talked about himself. I said that was probably why he got selected, because so many people make fools of themselves by taking their clothes off. He said nothing, and the first time I saw it was the day he went into the house. I was watching with my mum, Lee's gran, and she said, "The last time I saw that bottom I was putting a nappy on it."

'He's going to get some teasing about it.'

ALISON

Alison's mum Maria says her daughter loves parties, 'and she treats the *Big Brother* house like the best party she could be at'.

Alison has always been a bubbly, outgoing person. 'Nobody ever forgets Alison once they meet her,' says Maria. 'She is just like you see her in the house – always on the go, very energetic, never down.'

It was Alison's older sister Saundra who suggested she apply for *Big Brother*.

'Me and my son Matthew were really big fans, but Alison didn't know much about it because she'd been working abroad. We kept saying to her that she should be in the house – it really is the right place for her. She's so relaxed, so laid-back – she went in to have a good time, and she will.'

Saundra is nine years older than Alison, and remembers her arrival in the world.

'She hasn't changed – she was a noisy baby, and she's still noisy. She was always dancing, entertaining us all. She's very much a family person, very generous and warm-hearted.'

Alison lives at home with her mum 'and the house is very empty without her'.

SANDY

Sandy must be the only person in the house who never watched any of the two previous series. He applied because so many people kept telling him it was a hard thing to do – and Sandy loves a challenge.

'He's always set himself challenges,' says his wife Claire. 'It's probably his army background.'

He raised thousands of pounds for children's charities by climbing the height of Everest on a stair climber, and by working out nonstop for 12 hours.

'He was working in a gym when he decided to do the workout challenge. His friend Gavin Hastings from the Scottish rugby team came and started with him, and called back at the end to finish with him.

'Two years later he did the Everest climb, and then did it again as a ringer for the Scottish rugby team when they were challenged by Everest double glazing to do it. The third time he did it, Paul Gascoigne was staying in a lodge at the country club where Sandy was working, and he was so impressed by Sandy's efforts that he handed over £800 for the charity appeal.'

Claire says Sandy is a complex person.

'He's very forthright and honest, both in what he says and what his body language shows. He's also very content with himself, which may be misinterpreted as him being a bit stand-offish. He loves company, but he's also very happy on his own. He's not afraid to say, "Right, guys, I'm going to bed now," when he wants to.

'The rituals he has developed in the house, when he gets up and sings a bit and does his resistance training in the pool, that's very like Sandy at home – he has his own morning rituals when he doesn't talk a lot. That's because when he gets to work he has to do a lot of talking – persuading people, coaching them, and he likes some moments of peace and silence.'

Three years ago Sandy suffered a major accident which, Claire says, has helped make him very philosophical about life.

'He was cycling to work when someone opened a car door just in front of him. He was impaled on the door: it went right through his chest to his heart. Luckily, he fell off his bike into the arms of an off-duty fire officer who knew about first aid, and astonishingly there was a German thoracic surgeon and two Canadian A & E nurses nearby – they were in the queue to buy tickets for the show *Chicago*. Between them they saved his life, but he was physically debilitated for about two years, and he still has problems lifting things.'

Claire reckons Sandy's calmness and maturity may go against him in the house.

'He may seem a bit on the sidelines, not part of all the hyperactivity. But he's much more interesting and complicated than he appears initially. He's also great fun. When he was in the army there was a huge formal photograph taken of the entire Black Watch regiment, and the photographer only took two frames of it. On the first one, he's perfectly well behaved. But on the second he has slipped on a red nose, and there's a ring of soldiers around him who are creased up laughing.'

Claire is convinced that Sandy's time in the house will not change him. 'He's done so many interesting things – he'll just regard this as another one.'

KATE

Kate's twin sister Karen switches the television on every day to get a fix of her sister – because the two of them have never gone for more than a day without being in touch with each other.

Karen and Kelly, who is their older sister, both knew as soon as Kate applied for *Big Brother* that she would get in.

'She's great fun,' says Karen. 'She can do impressions, accents, you name it.

'She's also really hard-working. She stayed on at school and did very well in her A levels. She's an all-rounder.'

Kelly says that even before the final shortlist for the contestants was drawn up, she knew her sister would make it. 'I kept dreaming of seeing her in the diary room, in the bedroom. Deep in our hearts the whole family knew she would get in.'

Kelly has a toddler son, Alfie, and on the day Kate was whisked off into *Big Brother* world, she insisted on waiting until she saw Alfie to kiss him goodbye.

'She's frightened of commitment, which is why she never settles down with a boyfriend,' says Karen. 'But she loves her little nephew to bits. And she's very close to all our family.

'The personality you see in the house is her. There's no side to her at all.'

ADELE

Adele's cousin Diane is younger than Adele – and remembers how, all through their childhood, Adele would always stand up for her and look after her. Even now that they're grown up, it's Adele that Diane always turns to when she wants advice.

'For the first few days after she went I kept going to the phone to ring her, and then remembering that I couldn't. Because she was there on the television screen it felt like she was close. She's always been very caring and a bit motherly, worrying about how other people feel, and always wanting to do things for you. If you told Adele you wanted something, even though she didn't have the money, she'd somehow find it to give it to you.'

Diane knew as soon as Adele went in that she would get on with the others in the house.

'She meets lots of new people through her job as a DJ, so she's used to it. I think she's enjoying it – you'd be able to tell if she wasn't. She's basically a very happy person, a very family person.'

Adele's girlfriend Vicky says she went into the house to win the money, 'so she can give it away, buying presents for everyone. She's very generous, always thinking of others. She's caring and strong and lots of fun, and I don't have any worries about her being in there, because she can cope with anything.'

Adele's sister Lesley says it's really weird seeing her sister on television every day. 'I don't miss her as much as I would if I couldn't see her and know that she's alright – although I often want to talk to her and find myself nearly speaking to the television screen.'

Lesley and Adele were very close as children – and still are. 'She was the good one who worked hard. I was always the wild one. She teases me terribly because I didn't work hard at school. We were talking recently about how we had a Speak and Spell toy when we were little, and she said I couldn't even spell cat! She has always been very kind – even when we were little she shared her toys with me, and now she's forever buying presents for everyone.'

ALEX

Alex's mum and dad Hannelore and Richard reckon that moving into a house with a bunch of strangers wasn't very difficult for their son.

'He's been travelling the world as a model for five years now,' says Richard. 'He's used to finding himself in strange places with people he's never met before.'

Alex's stunning good looks have been with him all his life – he was a lovely-looking little boy.

'As his mum, I didn't see it,' says Hannelore. 'But whenever I took him to see my family in Germany they always said how good-looking he was. We just took it for granted; we are more proud of the fact that he has a great personality.'

'Thank God he took after his mother's side of the family for his looks and sporting skills,' says Richard, 'Hannelore's family are all tall, athletic and good-looking.'

'But he gets his heart from his daddy, ' says Hannelore.

They don't think he will hook up with any of the girls in the house.

'He always has beautiful girlfriends, but he doesn't just go for looks – they have to be decent, good girls as well. He's looking for a girl with the right heart, and I don't think she's there in the house for him.'

As a boy Alex was always entertaining people, always full of energy. The headmaster at his junior school commented that he spent five or six years trying to get him to sit still – and now he's on television jumping around.

'Whenever we had babysitters for him, we'd get home and they'd say they didn't babysit him – he entertained them,' says Hannelore.

The couple don't care how long Alex stays in the house. 'If he's unhappy I hope he will have the strength to walk out and come home. The bed is changed and made up for him, he can come home whenever he wants.'

JONNY

There are two Joannes in Jonny's life – his fiancée and his sister. And they both think he's fantastic.

'It's surreal watching him on television. Our mam can't watch – she's missing him so much she says it would make it worse,' says his sister Joanne. 'I was having my breakfast the other day at the same time he was having his in the house, so I rang mam to say I was having breakfast with Jonny.'

Jonny applied last year, so when he decided to have another go, Joanne his fiancée says, 'We all said "Yeah, yeah, have another go." But we didn't get excited until we knew he was in the final few.

'It's surreal being able to watch him and not being able to talk to him.'

As a fireman, Jonny has had to cope with some harrowing situations.

'I think that's why he has developed a black humour – it helps him cope,' says Joanne. 'The lads at the fire service are 100 per cent behind him. They love him, even though they think he's mad. He doesn't talk about things he's seen much, although he saved a woman's life not long ago by giving her the kiss of life. When the paramedics arrived they said that if he hadn't done that, she would have died.

'All the lads in the fire brigade do a lot for charity. They think up some mad things to do – and Jonny is always madder than anyone else.'

His fiancée Joanne says that although Jonny loves clowning around, there's a quiet side to him.

'He's quite chilled down when he's just with me or with his family. He's also very sensible. He sometimes likes a bit of space – he'll need to get away from the others in the house now and again. But he wants everybody around him to be happy; he doesn't like seeing anyone down in the dumps.'

WHICH PART OF YOUR BODY WILL YOU MOST WORRY ABOUT PEOPLE SEEING ON TV?

ADELE: My chest.

ALEX: My toes. I don't like my toes, they're hairy.

ALISON: I'm not really worried about anything being seen. I suppose my love handles don't make me too appealing. I've got really saggy tits but I just don't care about it. It's just my rude bits, really. I'm like anyone, shy to strangers but show everything to someone I'm going out with.

JADE: My lulu.

JONNY: My torso because I'm skinny. I'm thin, no matter what I eat. I've got no problem with being nude, I'd just like to be more in shape, but there's nothing to be ashamed of.

LEE: None. But if I have to choose one, my stomach.

LYNNE: My legs. They're not good. I've got fat knees.

P.J.: My arse. I hate it. The lower half of my body is quite short and stubby.

SANDY: I'm carrying a bit of weight so at first I thought my tummy. But it's only a part of me. I suppose like most guys I don't really want people to see my willy. It's not the prettiest sight in the world, unless it's in a state of readiness. But again, it's part of me, and there's nothing I can do about it.

SPENCER: The soles of my feet are hideous. They look like I've been in the bath for ages. When you work on the river your feet get wet and you forget to wash them and stuff. If I wash them every day they look alright.

SUNITA: My bum.

TIM: 'I like my body. I suppose my hair first thing in the morning. Or my feet – I'm not a big feet person.'

His sister Joanne describes him as 'the most fab brother you could ever have. He's always doing things for people – the day before he went into the house, even though he had lots to organize, he drove 20 miles out of his way to pick something up for my husband.

'And on the Saturday night before he came in, he wanted to go out for a last drink with all his mates. But he couldn't tell anyone where he was going, or even that it was a special occasion. So when he rang around, some of them said they were staying in, because they didn't have any money. So Jonny persuaded them to go out, and he paid for everybody.'

LYNNE

Lynne's close friend Kizer reckons her early dismissal was a major mistake by the other housemates.

'She needs time for her personality to come across. She's intelligent, sensible, a really good friend and she's got a great sense of humour, but she didn't have a chance to really get into her stride.

'She's been holding herself back a bit in the house, because of course she never knew there'd be a vote to get someone out in the first week. If she had stayed in, everyone would have seen the true Lynne, and I think she would then have been able to stay in right to the end, at least down to the last five.

'She's not really a girlie girl; she's more of a boys' girl. But she gets on with everyone, she loves to laugh.'

Her ex-boyfriend Paul says, 'She's kind, generous and funny. She was my best friend for years, and then we went out together for four years. I think I was worried about going out with her because I really didn't want to lose her as my friend – she's such a great lady. Thankfully, we have managed to stay friends.

'She's a very loyal friend, and she loves her family. She's a people person, but at the same time she will always be very forthright and direct, very strong in arguments. But I think those are plus points.'

SPENCER

When Spencer was a little boy, his mum Maxine felt as if she had a season ticket to the local hospital casualty department.

'If there was a scrape to get into, Spencer got into it. If someone was going to end up being driven down to the hospital, it would be him,' she says. 'He always had to learn things the hard way. He was very strong-willed, a typical boy. He never had any serious accidents, but that was more luck than anything else.'

But despite getting into trouble with his mum and dad and his teachers on a fairly regular basis, Spencer was a happy child.

'He never lets things get to him. He's quite calm for someone of his age,' says Maxine. 'Also, he takes a while to get to know people. He's not one of the ones who makes instant friends – he takes his time assessing people. But he has got lots of friends, really good friends.

'I don't think of him as a ladies' man, although obviously he's had girlfriends. But then, I'm his mum so I don't expect to know everything about his life!'

P.J.

P.J.'s dad Pete says his son might as well have been christened P.J. rather than Peter James, because ever since he was a baby that's what the family and all his friends have called him.

'He's a great son, we couldn't ask for better. He was a very demanding little boy. From about five years old he was always organizing everybody, and everything had to be done the way he liked it, because he's a perfectionist.

'He adores his little sister and he's very sensitive to women, which I don't think has really come across in the house. He talks to girls and understands them; he likes discussing fashion with them. He always seems to attract girls, but he's not the womaniser he seems to be in the house. He says he's had 65 sexual encounters with girls – well, that's only ten a year from the age of 16, and although that may sound a lot to an older generation, it's a couple of weeks in Ibiza for a lot of young lads today.

'And there's been a lot made about him going in not wearing underpants. He never wears underpants; he hasn't since he was a child. He's taken a couple of pairs in to sleep in, but that's all he owns.'

P.J. is a talented footballer, and his dad still reckons he's good enough to play professionally.

'Unfortunately his career ended when he broke his leg badly, but he's still amazingly good. But he also worked very hard academically. He's a bright boy, but he didn't get where he is without hard work.

'He was nicknamed "The Boff" at school, but he's friends with a whole cross-section of people from all walks of life, and some of the tougher ones described him as "a safe boff" – in other words, they liked him even though he did work hard in class. I always stressed to him that he should study in the classroom and play in the playground.'

Peter says he and his wife Marian have not been shocked by any of P.J.'s anecdotes and stories. 'We're a very close family and we don't have secrets from each other. If I haven't heard some of the actual stories, I've heard plenty like them.'

He says that P.J. won't flaunt his intellectual ability.

'He'll downplay it. It's a defence mechanism – he wants to fit in and make others feel they fit in. He's basically warm and generous, and hates to see anyone being exploited. When the boys squeezed toothpaste onto Spencer when he was asleep, P.J. appeared to enjoy it at first, but within seconds he said, "That was dreadful" – and he apologized when Spencer woke up.

'He's got a sarcastic sense of humour, and that takes a bit of warming up – he has to know how far he can go when he's teasing someone before he will say anything sarcastic to them.'

SOPHIE

Sophie's mum, Yvonne Gordon, has always encouraged her daughter to have a go at anything she wanted to do.

'I told her that you only regret the things you don't do in life, not the things you do do. I don't think there's any point in parents trying to harness their children: you bring them up and then let them get on with what they want to do. And Sophie really wanted to go into the house, so we're all thrilled that she made it.

'She was a very easy child. She always woke up happy and singing. She was a real girlie girl, not a tomboy: she loved playing with dolls. She's a Gemini, and she definitely has two personalities – one minute she's this sexy, vivacious girl; the next time you see her she's like a small girl, really vulnerable. I just hope the livelier side of her comes through in the house.

'She's a smashing daughter. She's only got one fault – she won't ever share her Maltesers with me!'

JADE

Jade's mum, Jaqueline Budden, is really proud of her daughter for getting into the *Big Brother* house – and surviving so well in there.

'When I'm watching her I just want to jump into the telly and bring her home, I'm missing her so much. But I'm really excited that she's there, although it's nerve-racking, too. I was a bundle of nerves when she got nominated in the first week, and so relieved when she didn't go out. I knew that if people had time to get to know her, they'd love her.

'The thing about Jade is that she's totally honest. What you see in the house is her – she hasn't changed at all, she doesn't try to play up to the fact she's on TV. She's always been the way she is: a bit noisy, full of fun, loves everyone. It's so quiet at home without her. I don't think winning is the most important thing in *Big Brother*: it's such an amazing achievement just to get there.'

TIM

Tim's mum Linda was surprised when her son told her, just a couple of days before he went in, that he was going into the *Big Brother* house as Sandy's replacement.

'It's not out of character for him to want to take part in something like *Big Brother* because he has a lot of confidence and he likes mixing with people. But I was totally unprepared for him going into something as successful and as much in the public eye as *Big Brother*. The media interest has come as a complete shock, and I'm sure Tim will be just as shocked when he comes out.

'It was surreal watching him go in. I could tell from his body language that he was really terrified. It must be much easier being there from the start.

'He's not a big drinker, and he hates people who get stupid on drink, particularly girls. He's very clean and tidy, although probably not as obsessed about it as Alex. Even as a small boy he always kept his room tidy, and he always helps clearing up after a meal. He loves his food.'

Linda, who works in a pharmacy, was touched to hear Tim telling the other housemates what a great interior designer she is. 'I think he exaggerates. I used to do it, now I only do it for friends.'

She says her son is 'kind, generous, never malicious. He can hold his own in an argument and will speak up if he doesn't agree with something. But he is not at all devious or unkind.'

Tim is missing his graduation ceremony from Durham University by being in the house.

'I hope he doesn't regret that – it's something that only happens once in your life.' He's due to start work with a headhunting company, and his mum is hoping that will still go ahead when he comes out of the house.

DOODLE ANALYSIS

Is the Big Brother house your idea of a dream home? If you could come up with a blueprint for the house you'd love to live in, would it be a castle or a cottage? Cosy or imposing? Modern or medieval?

Before they went into the *Big Brother* house, the contestants were all asked to doodle their own ideal home. Ronnie Buckingham, a psychic and doodle analyst, has been looking closely at their sketches, to find out what they say about the characters in the *Big Brother* house.

ADELE   DOODLE ANALYSIS

She's written on her sketch that she hasn't got the colours she would most like to use: pink and purple. The fact that she wants purple shows that she's a very spiritual person, and pink shows that she's soft and feminine. She's coloured the roof of the house red, which shows she is a very guarded person, someone who protects herself from being hurt. The flowers leading up to the very smart front door show that you are welcome up to her door, but not beyond it – the flowers are red, which says keep away; but they are edged with green, which compensates and means you are welcome so far, but no further. The black picket fence also shows that she's very protective of her own domain.

KATE — DOODLE ANALYSIS

Her house is so bare. She's not a home-lover. She's drawn a large post box, which shows she wants other people to give her things – approval, love, admiration. The red front door suggests she has a temper. The flowers have no colour in them, which says she has a lot of maturing and growing up to do. The blue curtains are very sketchy; she doesn't want to stay around at home, she wants to be out all the time. The lack of detail in her house suggests she's not making the most of her full potential at present: there's a great deal more to her. She isn't the most passionate of women; if she never finds a lifelong partner, she'll be fine on her own.

ALEX — DOODLE ANALYSIS

This is the smallest house of the lot, and it is very red with a brown roof and black bits. The colours show he is a dark person, with a lot of anger and a lot of sadness and hurt. The windows are interesting; one of them has a blind pulled down, which says that he has a lot to hide, a lot that he doesn't want to expose. One of them has nothing – no curtains or anything – which is an attempt by him to open up; but he's not really comfortable with it. The massive garage shows that he wants to go up in the world, materially speaking, and he loves cars. The smallness of the house shows he lacks confidence, isn't sure of himself, but wants everything in his life to get bigger and better.

SPENCER — DOODLE ANALYSIS

He's drawn the most beautiful house of the lot. It's very welcoming, and shows he puts his home above everything else. When he settles down in his own house, it will be very important to him. But he won't keep it to himself – the steps he has drawn leading up to the front door show that everyone is welcome. There's lots of smoke coming from the chimney which shows two things – warmth towards others, and sexual passion. Although he's drawn a bungalow it has a dormer window, which suggests there is just one huge bedroom upstairs: the bedroom, and what goes on there, is very important to him. The bright sun in the sky shows that he has a bright, lively personality.

SANDY — DOODLE ANALYSIS

The smoke coming out of the chimney is a mixture of colours – red, blue, yellow, green. This shows he is a dreamer, and his dreams are generally very positive. He sees the best in life, and gets on with it. All the windows are different shapes, which represent several very distinct and different phases in his life: he has moved from one environment to another. The doorframe is bowed in shape, which suggests that there is a lot of pressure on him: he has had hurt in his life, and he has had plenty of worries. He sees himself as a loner, but when the chips are down he's a very reliable person to have around.

P.J.   DOODLE ANALYSIS

The chimney is yellow, which is the colour of love, and there's smoke coming out of it, which shows he is passionate. The downstairs windows are very plain and the upstairs are elaborate: he's a ladies' man. The green grass has been drawn like little kisses, which shows he is a dreamer, and perhaps more of a  romantic than he likes others to realize. He's very vulnerable to criticism. He has drawn a red roof, which shows he is angry and is suppressing things. He has a brain for detail.

SOPHIE   DOODLE ANALYSIS

There's a lot about this drawing that tells me Sophie has been let down or disappointed in some way in her life. The winding path to the door suggests life has not been easy, and the very dark door means that she feels there is a darkness inside her, a sadness. Why did she choose number 13 for the number? It's bad  luck, and she feels she has had her share of that. She's a pessimist, inclined not to see the best in things or people. She's drawn in some brickwork, which suggests she pays attention to details. She's very particular about how she looks, and may be particularly careful about small things like having a perfect manicure. The bedroom windows are small and the ones on the ground floor are larger, which suggests she's had an unhappy romantic life. She's a very loyal friend, a kind person, and she needs a lot of reassurance because of her insecurity.

SUNITA   DOODLE ANALYSIS

She's drawn a sun with a smiley face, which shows there is a lot of brightness and warmth to her personality. But the house is so bland – there's no colour to it except black. It's not a house that you would want to stay in for long: she's not ready to be tied down. The picture is actually quite boring, which emphasizes that she's honest and straightforward; she doesn't have secrets. The black suggests she may have worries about her health, whether real or imaginary – she could be a bit of a hypochondriac.

TIM   DOODLE ANALYSIS

He's drawn a big house, with nine windows, a swimming pool and tennis court. But he's drawn it in the corner of the paper, which suggests that although he wants a large, expensive house, it's more because he wants it for prestige and show than because he is deeply interested in his home environment. Home is important, but not central to his life, which fits in with the fact that he has been away from home, in boarding school, a great deal. The fact that there are no curtains confirms that he's not a home body. He's also rather detached from his own life: he views it like he would if it belonged to someone else. There are no flowers, which suggests he likes material possessions rather than natural ones. He's drawn the house from an angle, with two sides showing, which says there is a lot more depth to him than you see at first acquaintance. The porch is like a sentry box: he's guarding himself, he doesn't easily admit people into his life at anything other than a superficial level.

ALISON — DOODLE ANALYSIS

Lots of red in this drawing, which shows she's a larger-than-life lady. The red also shows there's some anger and hurt inside her. But the bright yellow door is very welcoming: she loves people and she has a very good soul; she's kind and generous. But the red door handle, knocker and letter-box say that she doesn't want people to dig too deep – she wants to keep her secrets. Three windows upstairs and two downstairs means that she's keen to have a deep sexual relationship. The flat roof is interesting – it means she's not very ambitious; she's content with life the way it is. The tiebacks and butterflies on the curtains show that she's got a very sensitive, feminine side.

JADE — DOODLE ANALYSIS

She's drawn a very basic house, which suggests she's not really a homebuilding cosy person. The twin chimneys show that she needs a partner: she's someone who wants to be loved. And the fact that the smoke from the two chimneys intertwines shows that she is deeply sexual. She's even numbered the door 69. And she's got more elaborate curtains upstairs in the bedroom area, showing this is where she intends to spend a lot of time. The fruit trees with bright red apples suggest that she's a girl who wants to have children, be fruitful. She needs to be protected, and she'd thrive with an older man who can look after her.

JONNY — DOODLE ANALYSIS

This is more like an architect's drawing than a doodle. Everything is symmetrical, which shows he likes to have things his own way. There's a nice yellow path, which welcomes people, but the roof is red, which shows there's a lot of suppressed anger – something he's keeping the lid on. There's plenty of glass and no curtains, and even a naked lady at one of the windows: he's an exhibitionist – doesn't mind taking his clothes off, doesn't mind other people seeing into his life. The black shading that he's put around the drawing shows he likes to keep control; his own home will be neat and orderly. But the long grass outside shows that when he's away from home, order goes out of the window; he can be a slob. He's a chauvinist – he doesn't see women as equal partners.

LYNNE — DOODLE ANALYSIS

There are no sides to the house and the path is very twisty and windy; she hasn't followed a straightforward path through life, and she's not yet sure of her own boundaries. She doesn't know what she wants or where she wants to go. She's an idealist; the seagulls show she loves nature, peace, idyllic surroundings. She appreciates beauty. The red butterfly shows she is feminine, but it is very plain, which suggests she lacks confidence. She's a possessive lady – when she's in a relationship she likes to own someone. The flowers in the long grass suggest she's been cut down to size at some point, suffered a real knock-back.

LEE DOODLE ANALYSIS

This is the weirdest drawing of them all. He's tried to draw in the individual bricks, which shows he's a stickler for details and likes every little thing to be right. The two enormous windows upstairs show that he likes a lot of bedroom activity. It's quite a grand house: he's hoping to move up in the world. The little animal, a dog or a cat, shows he feels protective towards  others – he'd like to protect the woman in his life. He's sure of himself: the lack of curtains and the bright light bulbs show that he wants people to look at him. He's not self-conscious; he's proud of how he looks. The two garages suggest he is into flashy cars, or would be if he could afford them. The bright red door with the tiny window, like a spyhole, shows that he is quite private, deep inside; there are complex parts to his character, and you would have to know him very well to understand them. The half-sun in the corner shows he has moods: he can be bright and cheerful, but he can also be down.

CHAPTER TEN

UPPING THE ANTE

Well, it certainly came as a bombshell to the housemates. How was it for you? In one amazing swoop, millions of people watched the big divide separate the haves from the have-nots in the *Big Brother* house. For the contestants it was unexpected, unforeseen – and unforgettable. For the viewers it was an astonishing, gob-stopping, overwhelming television moment. As the glass bars went up, the reality sank in: the group who thought they were sharing a house together were suddenly leading separate lives.

The contestants knew something was afoot when they were asked to pack their suitcases and strip their beds a couple of hours before the task on Saturday 8 June, Day 16 in the *Big Brother* house. Were the task losers going to be evicted? Kate wondered. Spencer thought they were all going on holiday; Sandy speculated that they were being moved to a different house.

It was their second task, and they were expecting it to be like the one the week before: all in it together with a pot of £400 shopping money to be won. But when 10.00pm came, and they were live on Channel 4, Adele read out the announcement that the task would split them into groups of five – one group with luxuries and loads of money; the other with nothing but basic supplies and no access to their clothes or belongings.

Every one of them had to pack a small canvas bag containing the essentials they would need for a week. There was hardly room to pack anything more than underwear, socks and a few toiletries. Then came the actual task: the first five to put a basketball through a hoop would be in the rich side of the house, the rest in the poor side. It was a starkly arbitrary way of splitting them: Spencer and P.J. didn't even get a shot at the hoop, because five other housemates had already scored goals. Sandy, Jonny, Kate, Lee and Sophie were the lucky ones, and amid recriminations that Sandy had jumped his place in the order and that Jonny had been standing too close, the two groups were ordered by *Big Brother* to go to their separate bedrooms.

For nearly two hours, they were holed up while a team of black-clad *Big Brother* staff moved into the house and erected the division – 91 glass bars which hived off two-thirds of the house and garden for the lucky winners. In the rich bedroom, Kate felt bad about it all; Lee was worried that without P.J. they wouldn't be able to add up the shopping list; Sophie didn't want to celebrate her birthday the next day without her friends. Sandy was enjoying it, planning to change his clothes about four times a day to irritate them, and debating what food to cook that would send the most delicious smells wafting across the divide.

In the poor bedroom, everyone was still smarting about the way the split had been made, but they were being very positive about it. When the doors were unlocked, with cries of 'Oh my God,' and 'That's mad,' they ran to the divide, Kate hugging first Jade and then Adele, before each side set off to explore their new territory.

In the run-up to the launch of the show, the division of the house was a colossally difficult secret to keep – and it nearly worked. Despite some very early press speculation that there might be a rich house and a poor house, it wasn't until the unsuspecting contestants were in the house that rumours began to fly round.

For Markus the designer, it was a huge constraint: he had to design a house that could, after the first two weeks, be divided into two – and yet would fool both the contestants and the viewers until the moment of the big split.

'It was essential that the place didn't look schizophrenic for the first two weeks, so I had to work out how to unite the two worlds into one whole, yet still have a marked difference between them when we separated them,' he says.

The decision to split the house was taken by Phil, Helen and Gigi after many head-banging sessions: they knew they wanted to raise the *Big Brother* ante, but they weren't sure how to do it.

'We didn't want to compromise the essence of *Big Brother*,

which is a group of strangers creating a life for themselves in isolation from the rest of the world,' says Phil. 'But we knew there were a couple of things that drag the house down. In the first two series the task didn't seem to matter much, to the viewers or to the contestants. They could wager their spending money, but they realized that by only wagering small amounts, it didn't make much difference whether they passed or failed; they'd always have enough money to manage on, and nobody had to bust a gut getting through the task – or even feel guilty if they were the one who let the side down. They put bonding with their housemates as a higher priority than getting a bit of extra money for cider, or better food.

'And the other problem, we felt, was that contestants could hide in the house – not literally, but they could hide their true motives and feelings. They could play a waiting game, being non-confrontational, getting on with everyone, biding their time. Therefore nobody felt strongly enough about them to nominate them, which was very frustrating for the viewers who were itching to evict them. We wanted to find a way of forcing them to show their hand. That's why we've toughened up on the nominations procedure, not allowing them to give excuses instead of reasons for nominating. But we wanted to expose them even more, to their own housemates.

'That's why we wanted the tasks to be more illuminating about them and their attitudes to one another. Most of all, we wanted to ensure there was something big riding on the results of the tasks.'

The feelings of the top team were confirmed by a Channel 4 focus group of viewers which showed that, although they all loved the show, they really didn't engage with the tasks; they even thought that they sometimes got in the way of relationships that were developing in the house.

Phil and co agonized over how to change the tasks. It was clear they were too long – when they lasted over three or four days both viewers and contestants lost interest, and every day the task had to be re-explained in the voice-over, which was repetitive and often complicated.

'And there were whole days when they were supposed to be practising the task but did nothing, which confirmed that we were dragging it out,' says Helen. 'At first we thought we would make them simply one day long. Then we thought it would be great to film the tasks live, happening in real time, completed within half an hour during the show on Saturday evening. Saturdays are always down days in the house, following the evictions. Viewers learn about the task at the same time as the contestants, then watch them either pass or fail within the running time of the programme. And by putting the task show out live, the viewers get much more of a feeling of being involved in it. We deliberately have no presenter – we want it to feel slightly raw and real.'

So that's how you make the tasks more entertaining. But there was still the question of how to increase the jeopardy.

'One of the things we are always doing is looking around the world at other shows. The French had pitted the boys against the girls and had two winners; the Dutch and the Germans had divided contestants into 'rich' and 'poor', according to how well they did in the tasks. In the Dutch version they had a 'battlefield' in which the contestants fought guard dogs for shopping money,' says Helen.

'We knew that things like the battlefield wouldn't work here: we believe it is one of the sacred rules of *Big Brother* that there is no contact with the outside world, and they had camera crews running around filming the action. In America, as a treat, two contestants were whisked away by helicopter to the Emmy awards ceremony. That's just not our idea of *Big Brother*: it has to be a complete cut-off from the world. But we did wonder about the 'rich and poor' idea.'

Phil, Helen, Gigi, Petrina, Markus and Ruth Wrigley, Head of Entertainment at Endemol UK, went over to Amsterdam to see how the division was made in the Dutch series. The programme was still running, and they were able to watch the Dutch housemates living it, as well as talk to the Dutch production staff.

'It took us about six hours to work out what they were doing,' says Gigi. 'We couldn't get the hang of it at all. They had one house that was all deep-pile carpets and gold lamps and statues – it looked like something designed by a footballer's wife. Then the poor side was like a Hansel and Gretel cottage, there were rustic tools hanging from the walls and fake cobwebs festooned about the place, and the housemates slept on straw.

'We were thinking, what on earth are they doing? This isn't going to solve our problems. But just as we were leaving to drown our sorrows the Dutch executive producer said, "It is still *Big Brother*. It is about how a group of people interact with each other, and because success or failure in the task is so important, you get a clearer view of how they see each other."

'And when we looked at it like that, we could see it: all they had done was increase the jeopardy, making the results of the task mean something big. We'd been distracted by the rusty tools and the ornate lamps. But they didn't have to come with the idea, which, like all the best *Big Brother* ideas, is basically simple.

'We've always done the show our own way. British viewers have different expectations. They're a more sophisticated viewing public than in most countries. And there were other aspects of the Dutch version we didn't like: they put tasks into the house at random, whenever the production team fancied it. We felt that wasn't fair, and Big Brother may be firm but he is also always fair. They also divided the housemates into two teams for the tasks, and pitched them against each other, which we found confusing. It didn't feel like one set of housemates, with one house and one winner.

'We were determined that, even though we divided them into rich and poor and they had different experiences of the house, it would still feel like one environment and they would still be able to interact with each other.'

Phil, Helen and Gigi made two lists – one of the fundamental elements about *Big Brother* that they would never change or compromise, and the second of elements they wanted to change or were willing to change to improve the format. One of the other things they had learned from the focus group was that viewers loved surprises (like the arrival of Josh and the eviction of Elizabeth on a Thursday in *BB2*), even if the housemates weren't always keen on them.

'We obviously couldn't do the same things again,' says Helen. 'But we definitely wanted something fresh and exciting. Each year, the contestants are more savvy, more knowing, and we have to come up with things they are not expecting. We don't just want the decor to be different – we want them to feel a bit wrong-footed, a bit unsure of what is going to happen next. Most of all, we wanted to make it impossible for them to come in with a game plan of how they are going to survive for nine weeks.'

So the decision was made that the tasks would be all or nothing, win or lose, no in-betweens. And the 'all' would be a great deal: a sum of £400 to spend on shopping (a huge increase on last year's money, which was £1.50 per day per person. Even if they wagered the maximum 90 per cent on it and won, the total would never come to more than £200), a luxury all-mod-cons home, and the chance to buy extra treats like videos, or buy an exercise bike. What's more, the sum of £400 would not diminish as the number of housemates dwindled, nor when half of them were living in the poor side of the house.

'When you have nothing else to do to break up the week, food and shopping become incredibly important,' says Helen. 'From the outside, viewers may think they would cope quite well with this limited vegetarian diet. But in the house, with nothing else to fixate on other than negative thoughts like, "Does everyone like me? Am I going to get nominated? Will I be evicted?", food takes on a huge significance. It is a source of comfort, entertainment, a subject for endless conversation – it's one of the few things they have to look forward to. This doesn't just apply in the *Big Brother* house: for the people who took part in the American Biosphere experiment, things like having a pizza or even a cup of coffee became disproportionately important.'

But it was important not to be cruel to the poor side of the house.

'They have enough food not to be hungry, and in a funny sort of way they may enjoy it more than the other side. We see it as a choice between hedonistic and monastic, rather than rich and poor. The vegetarian no-alcohol diet will actually make them feel healthy after a few days, and they will have plenty to do – and we all know that boredom is one of the biggest enemies in the house. Roughing it can be a lot of fun.'

The designer Markus agrees. 'The divide between rich and poor is about more than just material possessions: it's a whole lifestyle. While the rich can go to the tap, fill the kettle, plug it in and make themselves a cup of tea, the poor have to light the fire and boil the water on it.

'It makes them aware of things we take for granted,' he says. 'To some degree I believe they will have a better lifestyle than those on the rich side. It is simple, basic, but involves doing more. If boredom

FENG SHUI

The *feng shui* doctor and Chinese astrologer Paul Darby has been looking at the design of the house – and he thinks that stagnant *chi* energy is the cause of problems in the first few weeks for the housemates.

'There are missing areas of *chi* energy in the west, the *feng shui* location of creativity, pleasure and new beginnings. This undermines the yang energy, which means there will be difficult times in the first few weeks, as relationships develop and grow.

'There is some west energy in the garden, so if the housemates find the right spot out there, between the living room and the big bedroom, they could find their creativity and pleasure blossoming, and it is a great space to sit chatting with new friends.

'The north-east sector is almost completely missing, except for a small area near the diary room. The north-east is a very strong, lively sector associated with inner growth, deep wisdom and thought, as well as knowledge. The lack of this energy is the root of the slow start, with the housemates tending to shy away from each other and not always being understanding of other people's needs.

'The south-west sector is also not strongly represented. There is a part of the garden that is in this sector: quite a lot of the lawn is in it, a couple of the sun loungers and some of the other garden seats. This is the area that would bond the housemates together into a strong relationship, and would also help small alliances and romantic liaisons to develop. As dusk falls, this is the area that couples who are interested in each other will be attracted to.

'The south sector is small, and has the swimming pool in it. This is really bad, as the south is a fire element area, and fire and water don't go together. This is the area for passion, fame, energy, enthusiasm and public reputation, but the water douses these forces. I think some of the housemates will be reluctant to use the pool. The area around it is where arguments may develop. Watch for trouble between housemates sitting on the decking near the pool.

'There are some good basic earthy and fiery colours used in the living areas of the house, and the circular rugs do help to circulate and move the *chi* energies around. But the steps that lead down into this area from the door are a really bad idea. Stepping down into a living space tends to take away the vital yang (lively energy) and encourages stagnant puddles of yin energy – not good for lively interesting conversations.

'In the kitchen the cooker is extremely well placed in the fire element sector of the south, bringing good energy to whoever is working there. But there is a lot of metal in the kitchen that will be draining, and will generate feelings of 'can't be bothered'.

'The seating area, near the main entrance and steps, is an interesting area with some good and some bad seating positions. But it has lots of straight edges pointing towards it – these are poison arrows that put people on edge, making them argumentative and prickly. The orange colours are lovely, but they do not suit the north area – the housemates with their backs to the steps will feel very insecure. The sofa opposite is in the north-west, a much better position, and housemates sitting here will control the conversations and situations. The north-west is the sector of influential people, important meetings, protectors: it is called 'the boss's position'.

'The girls' bedroom, the comfortable one, is also in the north-west, and is therefore a good place for meetings and sorting things out. This is the best area of the house; it will fill the housemates with energy and make them strong, so that they develop friendships and alliances. The colours in this bedroom suit the sector it is in, much more than the colours in the other bedroom, which is in the east. The wood in the boys' bedroom is really good, because the east is the wood sector – the area of ambition, growth, health and family. But the metallic colours that dominate the room are in conflict with the good energy. This is a room where confusion, niggling and getting the wrong end of the stick will all happen.

FENG SHUI continued

'The area around the chickens and the vegetable patch is very good, strong and well planned. People who use this area alot will become richer – not necessarily in money terms, but in terms of the enrichment of their lives. It should be a very good plot for vegetables, and the housemates should eat as many of these as possible to supplement their sagging *chi* energy levels.

'The area inside the house nearest the entrance to the garden is a good place to sit, with very strong energy – good for recharging batteries. The dining table is also a good place to be, except for those whose backs are towards the stairs.

'The bathroom is a good chill-out area, a place to recharge batteries and restore peace and calm.'

is one of the problems of the house, having to tend the garden, the chickens, and cook everything over an open fire will give its own essential rhythm to life in there.

'I think some of them will prefer life on the poor side, especially if they are resourceful and enjoy the chance to reflect on themselves and their lives.'

It was decided not to introduce the divide for two weeks to give the group time to bond. For the first week, when they were all brand new to the house, they had no task and lots of spending money, and they then played all-or-nothing as a group at the beginning of Week Two.

The generous amount of shopping money caused a minor headache for the production team. In previous years, housemates asked for items that weren't on the short shopping list that *Big Brother* provided for them – which meant someone had to cost the extra items and let them know whether or not they could afford them. That worked fine when the budget was tiny. This year, the team knew that they could spend hours costing a long list of extras, and discussing it with the housemates; the shopping would be severely delayed. So instead of the short list, the housemates have been given a massive 12-page detailed list of things they can buy. It has made planning the shopping a bigger diversion than ever inside the house.

Supplementary rules also had to be drawn up: the secret rules of the House Divided. The most fundamental of these is that nothing can cross the divide – it's a very serious breach if anyone tries to pass anything through. But housemates can still touch each other, even kiss if they want to, and they can spend as many hours as they like chatting through the glass bars.

One aspect of it all that fascinates the production team is assessing its effect on nominations and viewers' voting. Will viewers feel sorry for the ones in the poor side? Will being ruthlessly self-interested in order to win a place in the rich side actually be a bad move, in that the housemate may scoop up a few luxuries at the cost of being voted out? Will housemates deliberately lose in the tasks in order to win sympathy?

'It changes the whole dynamics of the task, the nominations and the voting,' says Helen. 'And that's exactly what we wanted. People who play a waiting game, trying to be nice to everyone, will find it much, much harder. This *Big Brother* house gives them nowhere to hide.'

The change in the evictions procedure in Week One – getting the public to make nominations and giving the vote to the housemates – was also introduced to shake up both the contestants and the viewers.

'The housemates just weren't expecting it, because they didn't have to nominate anyone. The viewers had to vote for people they hadn't had much chance to get to know – maybe they voted just because they didn't like the colour of a shirt or a hairstyle. It just added to the tension and the excitement,' says Gigi. 'All the contestants have been through a great many hoops to get on to *Big Brother* – yet it could be all over after just seven days.'

THE HOUSE DIVIDED

The decision made, it was down to Markus to put it into effect – to somehow create an environment that would fool the housemates and the viewers (and even the press who were shown around three weeks before the show started).

'To engineer the divide I devised a system of concrete panels to clad the walls. Individual panels can be taken out and softer panels put in, but it still seems like an integrated whole.'

Markus was determined that the two-way mirrors, essential for the cameras to peer unobserved into the lives of the housemates, should seem unobtrusive, part of the whole design, fitting in to the modular panel system. It was the dimensions of the mirrors that determined the size of the panels. Sample panels were then made in plaster and resin, and in the end Markus chose pre-cast resin with a veneer of concrete, all manufactured specifically for the house.

'The panel system means that when the house is divided, one side can be very plain, monastic, simple, with the only relief being the variations in the grey colour and texture of the concrete. On the rich side we have softer panels covered with carpet, walnut, cherrywood, white suede and bright plastic to put an injection of colour into the environment. But the feel of simplicity runs through both environments.'

The tag that summarizes the feel of the third *Big Brother* house is 'urban Zen'. (The first house was 'penal chic', the second was 'cabin fever'.)

'Being in the *Big Brother* house is like being in transit – like being on a ship that's between one land and another, and not part of either. They leave their old lives behind and they don't know what their new lives will be like, but in the meantime they have to get on with the day-to-day existence of the house, living with people they have never met before. And they're stuck there, just like being on a vessel. The whole show is a vessel.

'So I wanted to design an environment that almost has a transitory feel to it, not something cosy and homely.'

It was the division of the house into poor and rich that gave Markus the idea of the staircase, with a stainless steel handrail, leading to the doorway.

'In a sense, one element of the house was going to hover metaphorically above the other – rich above poor – so it seemed to make sense to enter the house by descending into the space. The idea works: it also means that when contestants come out of the house they are raised above the audience, which allows the crowds to be closer than in previous years.'

The staircase also makes a natural shelter for the diary room, the heart of the house, which is underneath it. In keeping with the rest of the house, it is a muted grey colour, with the *Big Brother* eye made in ripple glass on the wall, and sensual-looking blocks of tiles that are functional (they absorb sound) as well as decorative.

The diary room chair, the most vital piece of furniture in the house, is a big red armchair that looks like a squat Buddha figure. It was only put into the house an hour before the contestants arrived.

'We commissioned a chair specially. It had a white fibre shell with mulberry coloured padding,' says Phil. 'We designed it so that people could use it in different ways: they could drape themselves across it like a chaise longue, or sit upright as if they were in a bucket chair.

'But when it went in, it didn't look right. Three hours before we launched the show and brought the contestants in, all I could think was that it looked as though someone had thrown a huge lump of chewing gum into the middle of the Diary Room. I said it looked awful and that I wanted to change it, however late it was. Julian Bellamy, the commissioning editor from Channel 4, agreed with me. So Helen and Gigi spent a frantic two hours finding another chair. Markus had already seen the one we finally settled on, and had liked it, but he had sent it back to the shop because we had our own. Luckily, they were able to whizz it round to us again, and we all liked it. It was taken in covered in blankets – the audience were already assembled outside to watch the housemates go in.

'The next problem was getting the other one out. God knows how they got it in, but in our last-minute panic we had to take a chainsaw to it and cut it in half. That's why Jade got locked in the diary room on the first night: we broke the lock getting the chair out.'

With the advantage of knowing the limitations of the last house, this year the camera run, the passageway that surrounds the whole building and allows the manned cameras to move between mirrors to follow the activities of the housemates, is more spacious, and covers the whole circumference of the building.

As well as designing the physical layout of the house, Markus also had to organize all the furniture, fittings and furnishings. The company that has supplied most of the distinctive *Big Brother* furniture and accessories is a shop called Aero, in the Kings Road, London, which specializes in designer classics, contemporary furniture and homeware.

'I told them very precisely what I wanted. I had a very clear and

RICH AND POOR: WHAT THEY GET

THE GARDEN

The rich have sun loungers, a red cube-shaped table and red and grey stools and chairs made of glass-reinforced plastic.They have a heated swimming pool, hexagonal in shape and measuring five by five metres. It is 1.5 metres deep, and surrounded by wooden decking. One of the few chores they have to do is to clean and maintain it.

The poor have concrete seats. Their part of the garden includes the vegetable patch, where potatoes, carrots, turnips, swedes, radishes, cabbages, lettuces, broad beans, spinach, rocket, tomatoes, and basil are growing alongside strawberries, rhubarb and gooseberries. They have to tend and water the vegetables.

The chicken coop, designed by Markus to look like a chicken, also belongs in the poor part of the garden, where it houses six rare breed chickens who supply the housemates with eggs.

'It looks more like a chicken than I hoped it would,' says Markus. 'It's a complicated structure, and I hoped it would end up looking like a piece of origami, almost as is if it were about to take off in flight. Instead, it looks like a chicken!'

FOOD

The rich have as much as they can buy with £400.

The poor have an organic vegetarian diet, with enough calories and vitamins to keep everyone healthy; but it's boring – vegetables from the garden and eggs from the chickens, supplemented by supplies of brown rice, lentils, porridge and flour. No alcohol, cigarettes, chocolate, meat or fish – until Big Brother took pity on nicotine addict Spencer, and let him have tobacco.

HOT WATER

The rich have hot water for two hours in the morning and two hours in the evening.

The poor have warm water at the kitchen sink for the same hours each day.

BATHROOMS AND LOOS

The rich bathroom includes a whirlpool bath, a shower in the middle of the room with a large head, and two washbasins. There is another washbasin in the rich loo. The bathroom is predominantly white with blue glass tiles, and panels of ripple-effect glass supplied by a company called Ozone, who special-ize in architectural glass and have their own unique method of melting and moulding it. Behind the glass panels, which give an appropriately watery effect, there are lights. There are bundles of soft white towels and supplies of bath salts.

The poor have a shower and loo, reminiscent of the days when lavatories were at the bottom of the garden. The shower is outside in the garden, with cold water only. The towels provided for the poor are rough linen.

BEDROOMS

The rich bedroom contains two double beds and four single; its carpet is grey with subtle flecked stripes of brown. On the walls are panels of fabric, specially made by a company called Bute, which uses old dyes and materials. It is a gentle, subdued lichen colour.

'I wanted a sophisticated feel, whether the housemates are aware of it or not,' says Markus.

Each bed has a cupboard next to it, and on the cupboards are Japanese paper lights that look like over-sized shells, or square blocks containing a round circle of light, designed by a potter. Against the walls are stainless steel panels with coat pegs.

The poor bedroom consists of a series of futons set into walnut benches, each bedspace with a drawer beneath it. The six beds are close to each other. 'So close that they can smell each other's breath,' says Markus. Next to each bed, a hole has been drilled in the wood to hold a water glass. The only colour in the room is the rich brown of the wood and the varied shades of grey in the concrete cladding. The bedding, all of which in both bedrooms has been supplied by House of Fraser, is neutral in colour.

RICH AND POOR: WHAT THEY GET *continued*

'It's a very prescribed environment. I wanted to create the sort of room you wouldn't normally see. There's a Zen simplicity to it: it's the kind of room you might see in Japan, but it's totally alien to people brought up in Britain. It challenges the accepted ideas of the rituals of bedtime that we all take for granted.'

BED LINEN
The rich have a constant supply of freshly laundered bed linen.
    The poor have to wash their own.

THE KITCHEN
The rich kitchen has a vivid, vibrant feel, with red and orange panels mixed with the stainless steel appliances. Behind the panels are more lights. They have a fridge, freezer, and cooker.
    The poor have only one cooking pot, an open fire to cook on, and brushes for cleaning their area.

THE LIVING AREA
The rich living area has grey carpet with an irregular decoration of different sized circles in vibrant colours, and there are thick rugs.
    The poor living area has a wood laminate floor and a plain bench with beech block stools and hard chairs. Orange panels which decorated the wall before the great divide were removed, leaving the unrelieved concrete panels.

THE DINING TABLE
The dining room table is a large wooden walnut refectory table, which both rich and poor share – but the rich get more of it than the poor.
    The rich dine off white china dishes with two kidney-shaped sections, one for the main course and one for a side salad or vegetables. They were designed by new young designer Caterina Fada and supplied by Aero.
    The poor have simple wooden bowls specially made for Big Brother by a carpenter.

exact idea, and they were able to more or less find everything that I wanted, with very few compromises.'

Many items and features in the house are unique, and were commissioned specially. The carpet, made by Miliken, was ink-jet sprayed to Markus's specification. The kitchen was made by Messon in Venice and shipped over. There are interesting radiators, made by Bisque, which look like stainless steel sheaves of corn, and another one in the bathroom that looks like a child's building set. There are what Markus calls 'interactive' pieces of furniture, like a stainless steel bench that rocks when you sit on it, and seven round stools dotted about the house, all in primary colours, which light up when someone sits on them.

'The aim is to have beautiful, poetic elements around the house. I think that it will affect the housemates and they will grow to appreciate it, if only at a subliminal level. My idea is to demonstrate that things don't have to be mass produced. There are creative individuals working today, and I think it is important that someone has loved this environment into existence rather than nipped down the shop and bought the same as everyone else.'

He says he doesn't mind that the contestants will probably hang their socks to dry on his poetic radiators.

'It's always the same in architecture. At the time it's painful; you create a beautiful environment and then people move in and stick their Kylie Minogue posters over some detail you are really proud of. But it's natural. We're all human beings and we like to put our own stamp on our environment, to build our own nests, to let our own personality rub off on the space we live in.'

One of his aims with the design was to give the housemates plenty to discover, so that they won't know all there is to know about the house after a couple of hours.

'Designing it and building it and then watching complete strangers move into it is weird. It's like giving birth, but then the baby is whisked away to be brought up by someone else.'

Markus designed the 180-square-metre garden, and contractors came in to install it. From January, the vegetables and ornamental plants were being nursed, ready to be transplanted on to the site.

Even in the garden, Markus stuck to his design themes, going for a simple layout with unusual features, like wooden slatted deckchairs that are back-lit and seem to grow out of the wall, and grass that sweeps up the wall, forming a wide frame for a central light.

'The chairs could be anything: it's a bit like sitting on the branch of a tree. And the grass growing up the wall – they can use that for games or anything they like. I wanted elements in the garden, and in the house, that will enable them to decide themselves what they want to do with them; and I like transposing objects, putting them in unusual situations.'

There are more lights behind the wooden louvres that break up the flat planes of the walls in the poor side of the garden. 'I like the louvres because they have a kinetic feel to them; they're like the bristles on the back of your neck.' The rich part of the garden has a backdrop of white and orange walls.

Light is a constant requirement in the *Big Brother* environment, which has to be bright enough for the cameras to be able to film everything, and Markus has found loads of ingenious ways to inject it. A large stainless steel frame in the garden, about the size of a billboard, contains a whole series of different shaped lights.

'I wanted the light in the garden to have an ethereal effect; I wanted to diffuse the harshness of spotlights and security lights with different qualities and sources of light. It's the same inside the house; there are soft panels of light. People gravitate towards dark corners, and we want to encourage that by giving them corners to go to.'

'The garden is another room; it simply doesn't have a roof,' he says. 'I've kept the solid contemporary feel, with the emphasis on natural – I love the juxtaposition of the natural and the manmade.'

Markus couldn't get everything he wanted: there were always financial constraints. True to his belief that design should be carried through to the smallest details, he drew up plans for his own door handles, but there simply wasn't money in the kitty to have them made.

'I wanted to put one small window in the house, with a floor that sloped up to it, with only one thing that the housemates could see through it: a weathercock on a spire. The weathercock would move, showing them that the outside world was moving on without them. But things like that dissolved away: it is impossible to do everything.'

CHAPTER ELEVEN

BIG BROTHER BODY TALK

Want to know who fancies who in the *Big Brother* house? Who is trying to hide their dislike of who? Who has found a really good friendship that may well go on after the lights go out and everyone goes home?

Susan Quilliam, body language expert on *Big Brother*'s *Little Brother*, has drawn up some guidelines to help us all read and understand the silent signals that the housemates send out all the time – the secret clues to how they really think and feel, whatever they may say.

Body language does not lie, and it often reveals far more about a person than a torrent of words. Susan, a relationship psychologist, is a professional people-watcher, able to interpret all the non-verbal messages that the housemates are sending to each other without even being aware of it themselves.

'The important thing is not to judge too quickly, not to put a major interpretation on one single gesture,' says Susan. 'For instance, most people know that folding your arms across your chest is a defensive gesture, closing you off from contact with one or several other people.

'But it's never that simple; you always need to look at the broader picture – all the signals, over time. One gesture can be made for lots of reasons, and may only last a few seconds. So we need to check and see if it is part of a whole pattern.'

When Susan studies the housemates, these are the signs she is looking for.

ATTRACTION

People who are attracted to each other naturally pay each other a lot of attention, listening closely and laughing at each other's jokes. They turn their bodies towards one another when they are talking, and they use their hands to make pointing signals – actually gesturing towards the other person, or opening their arms in an inclusive way. Their legs will be slightly apart; they won't have their arms across their body.

They also make a lot more eye contact that we would in normal situations. Conversationally, we only glance at each other for a fraction of a second; but when people are interested in each other they hold the gaze for two seconds or more.

Once contact has been established, and both partners have been giving off these early signals, the classic flirting behaviour is to withdraw slightly – to look deeply into someone's eyes and then glance away or down, to see if the other person is interested enough to follow. It's a teasing look, as if to say, 'I'm here, but now I'm not here. Are you interested?'

Another easily recognizable sign of attraction is blocking behaviour – when one of the two subconsciously tries to stop anyone else muscling in on the act, perhaps by standing between the one they fancy and the rest of the group; leaning an arm across and resting it on a counter; or putting legs up on to a coffee table to make a barrier that prevents others joining in. Voices also go lower and softer, more indistinct, so that the two have to put their heads closer together to hear each other; this also creates a bubble around them that excludes others. And they mirror each other's poses: if one puts a hand to the back of their head, the other may well do the same; if one stretches their legs out, the other will follow suit.

By this stage the couple want to be together, and follow each other about; they might go out into the garden together. They begin to stand closer than usual. In normal British society we stand three to four feet away from each other – that's the distance we feel comfortable with. (The Spanish, Italians and Latin Americans naturally stand closer to each other; the Scandinavians maintain the same distance as us, but keep it for longer before moving closer to someone they fancy.) When people are attracted, the distance

> ### WHO WOULD YOU CHOOSE TO PLAY YOU IN A FILM ABOUT YOUR LIFE?
>
> ADELE: Jada Pinkett Smith, because she's a really good actress, quite small, brilliant. And she's dead pretty. I wouldn't like someone ugly to play me, not because I think I'm pretty but if I've got the chance to choose, I'd go for someone who looks good.
>
> ALEX: Ewan McGregor.
>
> ALISON: Whoopi Goldberg.
>
> JADE: Patsy Palmer.
>
> JONNY: Paul Whitehouse.
>
> KATE: Courtney Cox, I think she's a bit like me.
>
> LEE: Will Smith.
>
> LYNNE: Kathy Burke.
>
> P.J.: Dustin Hoffman – you've seen my nose!
>
> SANDY: Robbie Coltrane.
>
> SOPHIE: Julia Roberts
>
> SPENCER: Brad Pitt.
>
> SUNITA: Ally McBeal – the character, not the actress.
>
> TIM: A cross between Tom Cruise and Hugh Grant, or, better, I'd play myself.

goes down to two feet or less, and touching begins. They reach out and touch the other person's arm, they brush past them, they find excuses for horseplay.

The *Big Brother* house has slightly different body language rules to the rest of society, at least at first. In the early days the housemates are so desperate to bond and get on well with everyone that they may give off some of these signals, even to people they are not particularly attracted to. But after a week or so, all pretence has gone and their body language is telling the truth. In fact, in the pressure cooker environment of the house, the signals become stronger and clearer.

ANTAGONISM

Real open aggression involves a lot of the same body language as passion, but there are plenty of clues to show it has a different root. Again, it can involve closeness and eye contact, but in a threatening way. The voice can get lower, too, but it becomes very distinct and menacing. Often, though, the voice gets louder.

But in the *Big Brother* house we are less likely to see overt aggression; people will use body language to show that they dislike each other, without anything being said.

One of the first signs is turning the back and excluding someone. Another is a series of nervous gestures: tapping feet or fingers, fiddling with small objects. These gestures show tension and stress, not necessarily dislike. But someone who is struggling to conceal their dislike will exhibit these stress signs, and they are the first body language clues. Look at the hands – clenched fists are another secret signal of serious dislike.

Sometimes the person who is trying to suppress their feelings will actually put a hand across their own mouth, as if trying to stop themselves saying something aggressive. Or they may put their hand to their throat, as if subconsciously stifling the breath, let alone the words. They may lean backwards when talking to someone they don't like, and even give little shakes of the head.

EMPATHY AND SUPPORT

People who are getting on well, but are not sexually attracted to each other, mirror each other's postures while sitting next to each other. This sends out the signal that they like the other person, like the way they are behaving, and are happy to be similar to them. It's a very overt sign, and usually comes at the beginning of a friendship. They may even start dressing alike, and women especially may start grooming each other – helping with hair and makeup. Usually, as time goes on, those who are genuinely close will drop this behaviour. There will still be physical signs of their friendship, but they will be hard to spot on the screen: their heartbeats and their breathing will sync with each other's.

Although the cause is psychological, this kind of physical manifestation is quite possible. The best example is of girls menstruating: when they live together, their cycles quickly become synchronized. It only takes four to five weeks for this to happen.

UNHAPPINESS

Unhappy people cut themselves off from others – although not all people who are cut off are definitely unhappy. An unhappy person lacks confidence, and it shows in their body: they don't have a straight spine, their shoulders are tense, their body looks somehow off balance. Their head droops and their gestures may become slow and weary-looking. They instinctively comfort themselves, which means touching themselves, because it was with touches and cuddles that we were reassured when we were little. The most usual places to touch themselves are the head and the hands: they lean their cheeks on their palms, they stroke one hand with the other, they pinch the fleshy part of their thumbs. They may even rock their bodies rhythmically, or drum their fingers in time with their heart-beat. Men may put their hands down their trousers.

Unhappy people may actually begin to look unwell, although there is nothing physically wrong with them; their faces may become tired and pinched, or puffy and swollen – childhood signs that tell parents that their children need sleep and looking after. Unhappiness makes people feel cold; they'll seek comfort in hot drinks, wrapping themselves in blankets, and eat carbohydrates or childish foods.

GIVING COMFORT

We all use body language to help others feel better. And the language of comfort is touch. The people in the *Big Brother* house tend to be tactile – they give each other hugs and kisses. When someone is low it is natural to stroke them, groom them, nurture them.

LEADERSHIP

Leaders have strong and effective body language. They seem confident, their heads are up, their movements are sure, they make strong gestures to show others what to do. They look directly at people. They don't have to shout to make people listen to them; they speak clearly and commandingly. Their gestures are open and include people; they are quick to spot the defensive signals of others who don't want to be part of the group, and they pay special attention to them.

HOW PEOPLE SHOW THEY ARE
UNCOMFORTABLE WITH A LEADER

Folded arms, an irritated expression, a loud, sharp tone of voice – these all show direct opposition to a leader. Looking down or away, fidgeting, turning their bodies slightly away, all show lack of support for a leader.

JADE   **HANDWRITING ANALYSIS**

it's amazing what you can tell about a person by their handwriting

Jade, although obviously young, is likely to remain childlike for quite some time. Uncomplicated and immature, she will tell it how it really is, calling a spade a spade no matter what. By no means a loner, she in fact needs the company of others, if not their approval and affection. Her sense of humour is very much to the fore and will stand her in good stead. Tending not to overthink matters, she lives each day at a time and will form closest relationships with those she feels least threatened by.

LEE   **HANDWRITING ANALYSIS**

IT'S AMAZING WHAT YOU CAN TELL ABOUT A PERSON BY THEIR HANDWRITING.

Lee is impatient to get on in life and appears to have little regard for the subtle nuances of other people's emotions. He is a go-getter and in many respects an idealist. Living as an optimist but also a perfectionist, he can be exhausting to live with. Lee may leave the more sensitive individual reeling in his seemingly cavalier attitude to feelings. He is practical and has a no-nonsense attitude to life. What you see is what you get – love him or hate him!

SPENCER   HANDWRITING ANALYSIS

Its amazing what you can tell about a person by their handwriting.

Spencer is able to transmit an easy-going and relaxed impression to the house when, in fact, he is deeply sensitive and cautious with his emotional displays. He is a hard worker and keen to help others in order to gain brownie points. Spencer hides an irritability which will come out into the open if he feels threatened. Basically, he is someone who needs to feel part of a team and will behave accordingly.

PJ   HANDWRITING ANALYSIS

It's amazing what you can tell about a person by their handwriting.

PJ seeks communication with others on all levels and is socially versatile. His strong creative side ensures exciting, if not dynamic, interaction with others. However, he is easily bored and the constant thrill-seeking on all fronts, coupled with a strong sensuality, can make him unpredictable. There is a tendency to resort to sarcasm to get the upper hand in a social situation and if this doesn't get results he is not above a good sulk! Although secretive about his own emotions, he can be indiscreet and outspoken when his guard is down.

ALISON — HANDWRITING ANALYSIS

It's amazing what you can tell about a person by their handwriting.

Naturally extrovert, Alison will exude a confident and infectious enthusiasm wherever she goes. Not everybody will be bowled over by her manner, however, as she can be demanding and selfish in a social setting. Deep down she is conservatively minded and would rather shock others before they can shock her! Given half a chance, Alison would make a great nurturer of others and in fact this is one of her great strengths. Honest and open, she can sometimes act as an unwelcome reminder of others' more devious motives.

ADELE — HANDWRITING ANALYSIS

It's amazing what you can tell about a person by their handwriting

Adele is no-risk taker and thinks extremely carefully before saying or doing anything. Some may say she is a schemer, others that she is merely guarded and cautious. Either way she is an excellent planner and negotiater, as well as a logical thinker. She is likely to be the member of the house who others call upon for advice, certainly, her powers of mediation and negotiation are second to none. However, it would be a mistake to think that she is unambitious for herself because, at the end of the day, Adele wants to win in all that she undertakes...

SOPHIE   **HANDWRITING ANALYSIS**

It's amazing what you can tell about a person by their handwriting

With a pronounced intuition, Sophie is well versed in the emotional nuances of others and has a generally open and receptive generosity. People will feel relatively easy in her company and will trust her almost as a replacement mother. However, Sophie finds it almost impossible to ask others for the attention that she, in fact, craves from them.

JONNY   **HANDWRITING ANALYSIS**

IT'S AMAZING WHAT YOU CAN TELL ABOUT A PERSON BY THEIR HANDWRITING.

OR IF I'M WRITING A LETTER
↓

It's amazing what you can tell about a person by their handwriting.

Jonny is rather a difficult character to get to know as he very much wants to be in control. He is an emotionally cautious individual under a facade that is anything but! It would be too easy for others to see him as a young man who can appear cocky and certainly brimming with self-confidence. The fact is that he wants to be liked and, coupled with his need to have the last word, he often has a precarious tightrope to walk in life. He can be stubborn and prickly when under pressure to reveal his feelings.

KATE	HANDWRITING ANALYSIS

It's amazing what you can tell ▬ about a person by their handwriting !

Kate chooses to print her letters, thereby creating a barrier to her own personality. She, in fact, wants others to see her as straightforward and down-to-earth when, in reality, she is constantly analysing and assimilating others' behaviour and reaction to her. There is a deep insecurity at play and it is most important to her that she is liked. Those in her vicinity will need to work hard at winning her trust before she opens up her heart to them.

ALEX	HANDWRITING ANALYSIS

Its amazing what you can tell about a person by their handwriting

Alex keeps his emotions very much in check and his feelings to himself. This trait alone will make him one of the more difficult members of the house to get to know. He finds it hard to fully relax in front of others and is therefore quite hard on himself and certainly self-critical. However, he is well balanced and mature and will cope well under pressure. His self-discipline will help carry himself and others through a crisis.

CHAPTER THIRTEEN

AN EVICTION
DAY IN THE LIFE OF PHIL,
BIG BROTHER BOSS MAN

7.45am. It's Day 15 in the *Big Brother* house, and the housemates are all asleep.

Phil Edgar Jones is driving to Elstree when his mobile phone rings. It's one of the producers, to tell him that Lee's girlfriend has phoned in to *Ri:se*, the Channel 4 breakfast programme, slagging her boyfriend off for his flirtatious behaviour, and announcing to the world that she is pregnant. Phil is worried: he understands how hard it is for friends and family of the housemates to watch them and not be able to talk to them.

8.00am. The security barrier rises and he drives into the film studio complex, and along the narrow road to the *Big Brother* studio and offices. Ahead of him sits the strange white shape of the house. There are a couple of uniformed security men with walkie-talkies on the metal staircase: it looks quiet and deserted from the outside.

First stop for Phil is the gallery, to talk to the producer who has been there overnight. The bank of camera screens shows scenes from the house: they're all still asleep. Phil wants to know what happened before they went to bed. Has anyone said anything interesting? How are Alex, Alison and Sandy reacting, with an eviction pending? Fridays are always strange days in *Big Brother* land. 'It's as if they are waiting for a public hanging, and a weird mood descends on the place,' he says.

There's good gossip for him: Lee has been telling Sophie he fancies her, and she's admitted that in the real world she would find him attractive and go out with him. So where was Adele when all this was going on in the early hours? The producer fills him in on all the details.

Then it's off to look at the house. He walks around the camera run, the moat-like passageway that surrounds the place, from which the cameras film through two-way mirrors.

'I'm like the captain of a ship – I have to make sure everything is polished and ship-shape. I check that the drapes are properly closed behind the mirrors, so that the housemates can't see anything beyond their own reflections. There's rarely anything wrong, although once I had to remind one of the runners not to bellow into his walkie-talkie, because the housemates can hear loud noises. Usually I just twitch the odd curtain, like a fussy housewife. Everyone who works on *Big Brother* takes the programme so seriously, but I like to check everything anyway.'

9.00am. He goes up to the second floor of the George Lucas studio building, past the plaque saying it was opened by Prince Charles in 1999. Instead of going straight to his own office, he goes along the corridor to find Matilda Zoltowski. Matilda's in charge of all contact with the friends and family of the contestants: she looks after them when they come to the studios, and she liaises with them all the time about their worries and problems. Phil tells her about the phone call to *Ri:se*, and she immediately rings Carmen, Lee's girlfriend.

In his own office, which he shares with five other people, Phil clicks on to the fans' websites. 'I always like to know what people are talking about, what they want to know, which bits of the show they love and which bits they are criticizing. It's all good this morning: they seem to be as fascinated as we are by what's happening between Adele and Lee and Sophie, P.J. and Jade, and Kate and Spencer.'

9.10am. An e-mail from the company that supervises the eviction vote tells Phil that Alex is most likely to go – he is 8 per cent ahead of Alison. Sandy isn't in contention – only about 20 per cent of the voters want him out. Interestingly, Alison is getting more phone votes than Alex, but more people are voting for him interactively and by text messaging.

9.15am. Matilda comes in to give Phil some good news: the call to *Ri:se* was a hoax. Carmen is not pregnant, and she's not even upset with the way Lee is flirting with the girls in the house – she thinks he's got a game plan, and as far as she's concerned she's standing by her man. 'I feel relieved. None of us likes the idea that someone is getting hurt.'

9.30am. Down to the portable cabins in the studio to view the half-hour programme that has been made overnight about what happened in the house on Day 14. It will be shown as part of the 8.30pm programme. Phil is joined by Helen Hawken, the series editor, Katie Brosnan, the Channel 4 commissioning editor, and the producers

'The programme was great. I asked for one or two little tweaks, but we have such a fine team of producers there's never any need for major work. I watch it to make sure we're covering all the angles the viewers want to know about: who does Lee fancy today, is Kate still throwing herself at Spencer? Most of all, I want to make sure that the three who are up for eviction are featured prominently, because everyone wants to see how they are coping.'

10.45am. The viewing is over, and Phil and Marion Farrelly, the live series producer, go through the questions Davina will ask whoever's evicted. With three up for the chop, they have to prepare three sets of questions. They also have to make sure three sets of clips of the best moments of the nominees are ready.

News comes in from the voting: the gap between Alex and Alison is narrowing, it's down to 4 per cent, but it still looks as though it will be Alex who has to pack his suitcase tonight. Sandy is still a rank outsider, but the team can't ignore him: you can never take anything for granted in *Big Brother* land – especially when the Friday voting frenzy begins.

12 noon. Davina arrives, casually dressed in jeans and T-shirt, carrying a bag decorated with an England flag. Today is not just the day of a *Big Brother* eviction: it's also the day that England's World Cup team face their arch rivals Argentina, and it's all set to kick off in half an hour. Phil's Scottish, but even he can't remain impervious to the excitement pervading the production offices. In the house, Spencer, Lee and P.J. are feeling the strain, and are desperate to hear news of the match.

For the first half hour after she arrives, Davina, Phil, Marion, Katie, Helen and other members of the team gossip about the goings-on in the house while they eat lunch in the meeting room on the second floor. Davina eats a plate of meat, cheeses and vegetables. Phil tucks in to chicken, followed by a cherry pudding with custard – it's 'Fat Friday' for the production team, a day when they all eat puds, ice-creams and sweets, because they work such long hours under high pressure.

Gossip over, they get to work on the three different scripts that Davina will have to be comfortable with before the evening. She adds some questions of her own, and puts her individual gloss on the ones the team have come up with.

'She's very good at questions, and she's so knowledgeable about every aspect of the show that she knows just what the viewers are going to be keen to hear.'

Every so often, someone pops out to get an update on the match. It's still 0-0.

1.14pm. A huge cheer goes up, and everyone in the meeting room leaps to their feet and scrambles to the room next door, where the match is being shown. Michael Owen has been fouled; David Beckham is taking the penalty. Breath held, work forgotten until the ball is safely in the back of the net and the crowd are going wild, then it's back to business. Phil is convinced that Spencer, sitting out in the garden, will have heard the cheers.

2.30pm. Davina goes to her dressing room for half an hour, to chill out and get herself ready. Phil gets an update on the voting. It's even closer, but Alex is still ahead.

3.00pm. Down to the studio for rehearsals for the 8.30pm show. This year the format is slightly different. 'I wanted to show more of the story from the house, and also I wanted to make sure the viewers can see what happens in the house immediately after the eviction announcement,' says Phil.

CHICK, CHICK, CHICK, CHICK, CHICKEN, LAY A LITTLE EGG FOR ME

The other inmates of the *Big Brother* world who have to get on together are the hens. There are seven hens and one cock, all rare breeds and rather beautiful. But the contestants are more concerned about how many eggs their feathered friends lay than how lovely they are to look at – especially as eggs are a vital part of the diet for those living in the poor side of the house.

The hens are:
- One Speckled Sussex, a dark brownish black hen splashed with white.
- One Dark Brahma and one Gold Brahma, which are large hens from Asia with placid temperaments and soft feathers. They are easy to handle, so shouldn't cause the housemates any problems.
- One Black Araucana, who lays a pretty blue egg.
- One Barnevelder, a heavy, soft-feathered brown hen originally from Holland.
- One Black Orpington, a traditionally British breed, huge and gorgeous. The Queen Mum loved them.
- One Silver Spangled Hamburg, a big softie with a pink comb.
- The cock is a Gold Brahma, a big fellow who weighs around 12lbs.

After this rehearsal, they rehearse the interview with the evicted housemate. Matilda stands in for the evictee: she knows as much as anybody on the team about the contestants, so she has a go at answering Davina's questions in the way she thinks they may respond. But everyone knows that the essence of *Big Brother* is its unpredictability, and there's no way of forecasting how any individual will react to being booted out of the house.

'Davina is amazing,' says Phil. 'She reads the interview questions off cards twice, and then she can remember it all, in exactly the right sequence. It's very impressive.'

They also go outside to rehearse the walkout, the moment when the evictee comes through the double doors at the top of the 23 metal steps. One of the production runners plays the part, but it's not a bit like a real eviction because everything has to be kept very quiet and subdued, in case the housemates hear anything.

'We rehearse it every week, to check camera angles and other technical bits and pieces – but we can't begin to recreate the atmosphere of the real thing.'

In the yard outside the house, metal crash barriers are going up to pen in the crowd who will turn up for the eviction. Again, the men work quietly. Security is on full alert: four or five attempts are made to get the football score in to the housemates. In the end, Phil gets fed up and tells a *Daily Star* journalist with a megaphone to go away. As the reporter is standing outside the film studio grounds, he takes no notice and continues to bellow the 1-0 score-line through the megaphone. The housemates spend the afternoon cooped up in the house.

In the studio adjacent to the one where Davina is rehearsing, *Big Brother*'s *Little Brother*, which goes out live on Channel 4 on Friday evening, is also rehearsing. Excitement is building up: there's an air about an eviction night that is quite unique, which infects everyone on the team.

6.00pm. It's dinnertime – more pudding and custard for Phil.

6.30pm. Davina is in her dressing room, having her makeup done and getting changed. She always wears something slinky and black for *Big Brother*.

'It's part of the tradition of *Big Brother*, and it's one that works so well we want to carry it on. She always looks great, and it's a look that's identified with *Big Brother*,' says Phil.

He watches the *Little Brother* programme from 6.30pm to 7pm. 'It's a great show tonight – they talked to the neighbours who live in the houses nearby, and they all identify with the show and feel it belongs to the town.'

7.00pm. The dress rehearsal starts. 'It's a highly complicated show, technically speaking. The director has five cameras in the studio, and another 35 in the house that are being directed by others; he has to take what they are directing and feed it into the gallery. And every eviction show is a bit different.

'We also rehearse all the graphics, and check the amount of time the phone numbers of the evictees appear on screen. We use a stopwatch, so that we are scrupulously fair. We also triple- and quadruple-check that the numbers on the screen are the right ones – it would be the worst possible nightmare for them to get muddled up. You can never assume it's OK, you have to make sure.'

Another voting check shows that the gap is still closing, and it's getting very tight between Alex and Alison, although Alex is still slightly in the lead.

A representative from the electoral register arrives to monitor the voting, and make sure that it has all been carried out fairly. Checks are made with British Telecom that the voting has not all been coming from one or two telephone numbers.

8.30pm. It's live on air. The tension inside the house is matched by the tension in the studio. There are three minutes left for voters to make their choice, and it still looks like it will be Alex: he's just under 2 per cent ahead of Alison. There has never been a *Big Brother* vote like this one. The production team are thinking it will be the Alex eviction show that will go ahead at 10pm. Surely things can't change in three minutes? Davina tells the viewers the figures: Alex has 39 per cent, Alison 37 per cent and Sandy 24 per cent. Then it's into the clips of what happened yesterday in the house.

8.43pm. The advertising break. The woman from Audiocall, the voting company, literally runs from the cabin at the far side of her studio over to Phil, who is in the gallery. She's red-faced and very excited: there's never been such a close result in the history of *Big Brother*. Even more exciting, in the last three minutes the voting has turned against Alison – enough to tip the balance. She's going to be the one evicted, by the narrowest of margins. Out of 1,405,191 votes, Alex got 38.44 per cent, Alison got 38.52 per cent, and Sandy got 23.04 per cent. Alison has topped the poll by a meagre 1,027 votes (she received 541,214, and Alex received 540,187).

DAVINA AND DERMOT

'Hello *Big Brother* house. This is Davina. You are live on Channel 4 television. Please do not swear.'

The familiar voice rings around the sitting room and the contestants suddenly become serious – and scared. One of them is about to hear that they have been voted out of the house. It's a sombre moment: even those who have not been nominated feel strained and anxious on behalf of their friends, and worried about the dynamics of the group after another one goes.

But there's also excitement and anticipation in the air: the compensation for being voted out is the chance to meet Davina, to run the gauntlet of the crowd with her arm around your shoulder, to give up the sofas in the house for the sofa in the studio, sitting next to the presenter who has become as much a part of the *Big Brother* experience as the diary room chair and the chickens.

The Davina moment is a high for every contestant, whether they leave in week one or week nine. It's part of the thrill of the whole game – Davina's name crops up on a great many application forms; she's part of the reason so many people want to get into that house.

'Davina is totally and utterly the public voice and face of *Big Brother*,' says Phil Edgar Jones, 'She's the biggest *BB* fan there is. She never misses watching it, she phones me every day for updates about what's going on, and if there's something exciting happening on the E4 live streaming she calls me to make sure I'm watching. She's very perceptive about the people in there, and she's fascinated by what they're doing. She gets the show, she totally understands it, it's in her DNA. She told me she couldn't bear it if anyone else was presenting it. She feels it's hers, and it is. She's also a hugely nice person, very easy to work with. The crew all lover her.'

She feels motherly towards the contestants who are evicted. 'I always feel very protective of the housemates when they come out, as they're very vulnerable then,' she says.

Davina isn't the only presenter who is now closely identified with *Big Brother*. Dermot O'Leary, who fronts the live *Big Brother*'s *Little Brother* programmes, is fast becoming as much a part of the *Big Brother* mythology as Davina. When Sunita decided to walk out, it was Dermot, not Davina, who greeted her and questioned her in the studio about her decision to go home. When the family and friends of the housemates want to have their say about the way their loved ones are appearing on screen, it's Dermot who takes the flak. It's the *Little Brother* programme that brings a lot of the fun, frivolity and irreverence to *Big Brother*, and Dermot's up for all of it. Like Davina, he's a huge *Big Brother* fan, totally hooked on the goings-on of the contestants' lives.

'Dermot's perfect for *Little Brother*,' says Phil, 'It needs a cheekier tone of voice, and he's got it. He's got the wit to handle the live parts of the show, he's a good interviewer and quick with a funny reply. I think he's one of the most underestimated presenters on television at the moment, and we were really pleased to get him for *Little Brother* for this year and last. He's got star quality. And like Davina he's another huge *Big Brother* fan.'

Now it is Phil's turn to run. He dashes to Davina, who is as shocked and excited as everybody else. The news ripples through the studio, and there is a tremendous buzz in the place: eviction nights are always tense, but this is something else.

8.46pm. Back on air. Kate and Alison have been doing impressions of Davina's voice: within a couple of minutes they hear the real thing, as she speaks live to the house and tells them, 'The third person to leave the *Big Brother* house will be... Alison.' For a few seconds, the housemates sitting on the orange sofas seem frozen. Nobody moves. The only one who speaks is Alison, who says one word.

'Gutted.'

Then her face breaks into a wide smile, and the others start to crowd round to hug and comfort her. Alex looks more worried than relieved, but a small smile plays around Sandy's usually impassive lips. He pours Alex a glass of the 1994 claret that he has saved ever since coming into the house, and says, 'Here's to us.' What he says next, amid all the hubbub of hugging, kissing and tears, upsets all the girls. 'Somebody out there knows the truth,' he says, enigmatically.

Davina tells Alison she has one hour to pack and say her good-byes: for much of that hour the debate will be about what Sandy meant. Eventually he tells the boys, 'I don't suffer fools, and the public don't either.'

9.00pm. Off air, and time for another rehearsal. This time, finally, the team know which show will be going out at 10.00pm. The links are practised, and Davina, Marion and Matilda have a last minute run through of the questions, just in case there's anything vital that's been forgotten.

9.30pm. The crowds are coming in, chattering excitedly and carry-ing their banners. Phil goes outside to see them.

'It's always a great feeling, when they are beginning to pour in. It feels good that they participate so much. The banners are brilliant, and they're now a real feature of *Big Brother*.'

They're up to scratch tonight, and the audience seem to share the feeling that it is Alex's night, as there are at least three banners about him to every one about Alison or Sandy: 'Alexander the Great,' 'I piss in the shower too,' 'Alex is Competitive, Likeable, Educated, Attractive, Normal,' with the adjectives on top of each other so that their initial letters spell CLEAN, '3-2-1, will Alex please leave the *Big Brother* house,' 'God Save the Queen,' with a picture of Alex, 'We Wee,' 'Alex Clean, others Mean,' 'Cleanliness is next to Godliness,' 'Anal Alex,' 'Golden Jubi-wee.'

The Alison banners are kinder: ' You can break my bed any day,' 'We love all of you.' There's the usual collection of Spencer banners – he's building up a committed fan club, although one or two have a go about his smelly feet. And, in the week of the Queen's Jubilee and the day of the famous football victory, there are loads and loads of white banners with the red cross of England on them. There are some bizarre ones: 'When Red Light Shows Wait Here,' and the totally surreal 'Golf Sale.'

Inside the house, tears are being shed and promises made. Jade and Kate are both upset, but Alison puts a brave face on it for them. It is only in a touching moment with her mate Jonny, when he gives her a chain to wear round her neck, that she breaks down and sobs. 'Come on, you daftie. It's only a crappy metal chain, but it's all I've got. Trust me to make you cry,' he says, hugging her.

10.00pm. Back on air. Davina, followed by a security man, dashes past the crowd to where Alison's mum Maria and sister Saundra are standing. During a ten-minute reprise of what's been happening in the house for the past hour, Davina reassures Maria that everything will be alright when Alison comes out. Everyone is a little bit worried: Lynne, who left a week ago, was booed when she emerged. From the mood of the crowd, it seems unlikely that this will happen to Alison, but there are a lot of crossed fingers.

10.10pm. '*Big Brother* house, this is Davina.' When the call comes, Alison is in the loo. When she appears she's wearing a black T-shirt with the spangly message 'Big and Beautiful'. The housemates do the hokey-cokey round the room, and the 10-9-8 countdown begins. When Alison is asked to leave the house she is still dancing, jumping on top of the kitchen units and fooling around. The production team realize that the sound link with the house is down: she hasn't heard the countdown or the instruction to leave. The producer in the gallery is hurriedly told to go into the sound booth and ask her, as the voice of *Big Brother*, to leave. She passes under the now-traditional archway of arms and runs up the white steps. At the top she seems to fall over: it's a joke routine the housemates have been doing all week, and she gives them one last pratfall to remember her by. But even then, she can't leave the house: the electronic door lock is jammed. After a brief heart-stopping moment it is released and she emerges, carrying her case, to run down the first ten steps to Davina, who hugs her and says, 'It's OK girl, they love you.' And they do: the crowd cheer wildly.

'It's a relief,' says Phil. 'This is the biggest moment of our week, and we want it to be a happy moment for everyone. The sound breaking down and the door refusing to open caused me a few seconds of anxiety, but everyone knows what to do and in the end the tension just made for great telly. We may have rehearsed it, but we actually never know what's going to happen at an eviction, and we watch it like viewers at home. There's only a limited amount of control you can have: you can control what you film, but not what happens.

'Davina is brilliant with the evicted housemates. In the first few seconds she tells them we love them, they're great, they should enjoy the crowd and the cheers. She's also really good at getting the crowd involved.'

10.15pm. It's the ad break, and Phil goes up to Alison to say hello, and congratulate her on how well she's doing. He gives her a big hug. 'I'm sad when anyone leaves. I wanted them in there in the first place. We all love Alison – and we love her even more when she does a really good interview with Davina. She answers well, she's funny, she's confident.'

10.35pm. The show is over, and after a brief chance to speak to her mum, Alison is whisked upstairs to the meeting room. On the way along the corridor she spots an ice-cream machine, and can't walk past it without getting a Cornetto. Then she chats with Helen, Phil and Susy Price, who will be her chaperone for the weekend.

'She's going through a real mixture of emotions. She is upset that people wanted her out, and she's gutted that she isn't with her mates Kate and Jonny. People form very intense bonds in that strange environment, and friendships mean a great deal. We reassured her that she'd only been voted out by the narrowest of margins.'

Susy gives her back her mobile phone, her first real evidence that she's outside the *Big Brother* house. It beeps the moment it is switched on: there are loads of text messages waiting, mainly from friends saying, 'What the hell are you doing on telly, Alison?'

'She was a bit teary, it's such a huge emotional occasion,' says Phil.

She has a chance to sort out her feelings more when the

HOW LONG DO YOU THINK YOU WILL LAST IN *BIG BROTHER*?

ADELE: I hope to get to the last three, but I won't win.

ALEX: To the end.

ALISON: Two to four weeks.

JADE: About Week 3.

JONNY: The last few weeks. I'd like to win it.

KATE: I could go all the way – I've got to win something some day.

LEE: All the way, there's no reason why I can't do it.

LYNNE: I think I'll be voted out quite soon, after two or three weeks. I don't want to disappoint myself by thinking about winning.

P.J.: I either go in the first couple of weeks or I win it.

SANDY: I have no preconceived ideas. I don't think I'll be last out, and I won't mind being first out. It's not important when you go, it's what you get out of the experience.

SPENCER: I think I'll win.

SUNITA: Midway – if I don't go mad in the first week.

TIM: To the end. I think I could win it. My attitude to life, my will to win and my determination will mean I do well.

---

production team leave her alone with Brett. She spends half an hour with him.

'It's totally confidential and Brett never tells me anything, other than to say that she's alright,' says Phil.

Davina has left to go home. 'But before she goes, she makes sure she has a chat with Alison's family and friends – she always does it, at every eviction. It's a very bewildering and emotional experience for them, especially as they can't be with Alison for a couple of hours, and Davina's brilliant at making them feel happy. She kinda feels it's part of her role there: not just to front the programmes, but to make sure things go smoothly for everyone else.'

11.30pm. It's time for Alison to meet the press. Fifteen journalists from national daily and Sunday newspapers, magazines and radio stations are waiting in a viewing theatre in the next studio block.

They've been at Elstree all evening, watching the programmes in the press room, and phoning in to their newsdesks with voting figures and the reactions in the house to the eviction. Now it's their chance to meet her in person. Like the crowd, they love her, and while they wait to be ushered to the viewing theatre there's a great deal of discussion about how they should greet her. They want to order her a Chinese – she's already told Davina that the thing she missed most in the house was Chinese food. But none of the local takeaways can deliver in time. *BB* Aled, the reporter from the Chris Moyles Radio One show who is a veteran of three series of *Big Brother* (and is now so well known as *BB* Aled that it's how he introduces himself) literally runs from the press room to the giant 24-hour Tesco supermarket next door, and returns with a selection of Chinese dishes to put in the microwave. The staff in the press room obligingly heat up the food, put it on a plate and cover it with foil, and he presents it to a delighted Alison at the press conference. The rest of the journalists put chocolate bars on the table in front of her when they place their tape recorders. Small things, but a big gesture from the cynical journalists, who have taken her to their hearts. She's the only *Big Brother* evictee to ever be given presents by the hacks.

Phil, Helen, Brett and other members of the team pile into the back of the room to give Alison support during her press grilling. Not that she needs it: she answers with great aplomb, giving her opinions on the house and the other housemates in a witty but not too bitchy way. She describes living with Alex as 'like having your dad in there', and says that although she thinks she's generally pretty picky about hygiene, he's 10 per cent worse ('No, make that 20 per cent – no, 50 per cent').

There's a running gag on the Chris Moyles show: whenever an interviewer runs out of questions to ask a celeb, they throw in, 'What's the capital of Australia?' It's amazing how many people say Sydney, but when *BB* Aled tried it on Lynne last week, she got it right: Canberra. So this week Phil and the others have primed Alison – she knows the capital of Australia. Unfortunately, Aled doesn't ask for the capital of Australia – he asks for the capital of Norway. At the back of the press room the production team are all mouthing 'Oslo' to Alison, and she either knows the answer anyway or she can lip read, because it comes out pat.

The press conference over, Alison is whisked away to rejoin her family and friends, and to spend the next few nights in a London hotel, looked after by Susy and by Julian Stockton's Outside Organization, who will be arranging her schedule of interviews and television appearances.

Phil hugs her goodbye as she leaves the press conference, then chats for a few minutes to the *Daily Star*'s *Big Brother* correspondent, Peter Dyke.

12 midnight. Phil goes to the bar, where members of the live show production team have now gathered. He's too late to join them for a drink: the bar has just closed. Besides, he's driving, so it would only be a soft drink. But he's got time to speak to Marion, Helen and any of the off-duty producers who are there. Everyone is agreed that this was one of the best eviction nights ever, partly because of Alison's winning personality and partly because of the terrific tension caused by the close vote.

12.15am. The day ends the way it started: with a trip to the gallery to ask the producer on duty what's been happening in the house. He hears Kate has been in the diary room, in tears and wanting to leave because of the loss of her friend Alison. The producer who talked to her thinks she will be all right. The housemates have been drinking solidly for over two hours, and the usual post-eviction depression is setting in.

12.25pm. Phil drives out of the Elstree gates and heads home for bed.

CHAPTER FOURTEEN

WHY DO WE WATCH *BB*?

It's the most fascinating, compulsive, addictive TV show ever invented. But why? What is it about watching a dozen complete strangers doing nothing very much for nine weeks that makes us all put our own lives on hold to live it with them?

Phil Edgar Jones says, 'It gives us permission to gossip without being caught. You can't beat nosing into every detail of what people are thinking and doing. We're fascinated by other people, and *Big Brother* shows us more about other people than we are ever going to see in the world around us. Even the boring bits are compulsive viewing, because it's when the smile slips and the mask drops that the real person emerges; and we're all waiting for that.'

Peter Grimsdale – who is in charge of developing programmes that go out over more than just the television screen – believes we all watch it compulsively because we know that the television production team have no control over it. The only people who dictate what happens in *Big Brother* are the contestants, and that makes all of us feel more powerful.

'We like the idea that there is nothing between us and the *Big Brother* house, other than the technology that beams it into our homes. It's a very interesting development in the history of broadcasting. In the 1930s, when radio reporters went out to interview fishermen, they didn't broadcast the fishermen's own voices; they got actors to say what the men said. The feeling was that ordinary people shouldn't be able to contribute to this wonderful medium of radio. In the early days of television, if an ordinary person ever got the chance to talk, they only gave two-word answers: this wasn't their world.

'But since the 1960s, when portable cameras came in and people could be filmed more easily, we've had a shift towards putting ordinary people right into the centre of the picture. Fly-on-the-wall documentaries started showing us how people really live – but even then, if we thought about it, we knew there were camera crews and producers influencing everything.

'Gradually, we've all become more and more telly literate; we understand how television programmes are made a lot more than we did, and we aren't deceived any more. When we see a nature programme with somebody pretending to be battling against the elements, we ask ourselves, "But why, when the camera crew is there?"

'So with *Big Brother* we've moved to the stage where we know there are people making the programmes – but we know that those people are not the ones dictating the content. There is no script, and if you watch it live there is no editing. It is, at last, the real thing, without interference. So that means we watch the contestants with total fascination, knowing that the behaviour and attitudes we see on the screen are genuine, and it's the best chance we ever have to observe it.'

CHINESE ASTROLOGY   **GOAT**

Spencer, Adele, Alex, Tim and P.J. are all goats. Goats do not like rules or authority. They are creative, inventive and often eccentric. When goats get together, there may be long silences and deep thoughts. But when they do speak, they may put their foot in it by not thinking through what they say, and then having to apologize afterwards. They tend to ramble, and they are daydreamers. They are sensitive, seductive and sensual, with strong creative talents, often to do with music.
They get on with: Alison, Sunita, Lynne, Lee, Kate
Friction with: Jade, Jonny and Sandy
Famous goats: Laurence Olivier, Mick Jagger, George Harrison, Joni Mitchell, Sophie Ellis Bextor

Every week the *Big Brother* team helps us to understand what we see in the house by getting experts – psychologists and psychiatrists – to interpret the behaviour of the contestants in ways we may not have thought about. Paul Coueslant, the series producer of the Sunday psychology show, reckons the appeal of *Big Brother* is largely based on the fact that we all think we are amateur psychologists.

'The Sunday programme offers expert views that may challenge the way we've been looking at what's going on in the house, or help us see things that we haven't noticed. There are undercurrents, tensions, ways of detecting people's real thoughts and feelings that the experts can point out and interpret for us.

'The change in the format of the show, with the division of the house, gives us a much richer seam to mine than in the first two

---

CHINESE ASTROLOGY   SNAKE

Sophie is a snake, a lucky lady with guaranteed beauty and wisdom. A snake lady is always well dressed and lovely to look at. She adores style, class, luxury, has a seductive charm and smile, and socializes well. She does need her private moments. She is intuitive with people and knows when to advance and when to back off. When young, she tends to dabble in relationships rather than get deeply involved and committed. She can be very jealous, and has a vindictive, deceptive streak. She will never give up on what she wants: just when you think she is down she will bounce back up again as strong as ever. She is the master of the double cross, and her smile can hide ulterior motives. With her quick brain she is good at manipulating people to get her own way. She likes to win and hates to be put down. She is very sexy, great in bed – and she knows it!

She gets on with: Jonny, Jade, Sandy
Friction with: Alison
Famous snakes: Tony Blair, Peter Mandelson, Julie Christie, Andre Previn, Mao Tse Tung, Grace Kelly.

series. But essentially the strength of the show is that we are all fascinated by watching other people.'

He says it is important for the experts not to judge the behaviour in the house according to preconceived ideas.

'The starting point of our show is what happens in the house. We don't make programmes to illustrate particular theories the experts may have: we ask them to explain things that have happened. However thoughtful you are in advance, there is a huge element of unpredictability. We want to reflect the lives of the contestants, and understand them more, but not manipulate them to fit anyone's ideas of how they should behave.

'That's why, although viewers are probably not aware of it, the commentary that goes out with the programmes during the week is totally impartial and factual: no interpretation or angle is given at all.'

Three of the shrinks who work on *Big Brother* – two on the Sunday psychology show and one behind the scenes – have given us their ideas on what makes *Big Brother* the best game in town.

Peter Collett, a social psychologist who helps us interpret and understand the behaviour we see in the house on the Sunday programmes, believes the deep appeal of *Big Brother* lies in the fact that watching it forces us to think about people and the way they interact.

'It is essentially a psychological programme, which caters to the very deep fascination we have with other people. Soaps partly satisfy this fascination, but the characters are two-dimensional; they act according to a formula, and we are aware that they are scripted and contrived. *Big Brother* is the diametric opposite. We find it very difficult to second-guess the housemates. We form opinions of what we think they are like and how we think they will behave, but time and time again our preconceptions are mistaken. People are much more complex and complicated and mercurial in real life than they are in a soap. *Big Brother* gives us a multi-dimensional view of people that we don't get elsewhere.

'One of its appeals is that we see the world differently from the

CHINESE ASTROLOGY — COCKEREL

Jade is a cockerel, very over-the-top in dress, in manner and in speech. A cockerel fusses over small things and this can irritate other people. Her moods are very high or very low, with nothing in between; she needs to recharge her batteries very regularly, or she becomes very cranky. She's flamboyant, feisty, colourful, theatrical, a downright show-off. She is honest and plain speaking – perhaps too much so! She can be very entertaining, as long as she does not overdo it. She has dramatic mood swings, and can be insensitive to others' feelings.

She gets on with: Sophie, Alison, Lynne, Sandy

Friction with: Jonny, Lee, Kate

Famous cockerels: Joan Collins, Dolly Parton, Eric Clapton, Nick Faldo.

housemates: they have a worm's eye view and we have a bird's eye view. We can see A currying favour with B then going to C to slag off B. We have the illusion that we are seeing everything, which gives us a Godlike sense. I believe it empowers us as viewers more than any interactive technology. It gives us a sense of superiority, which comforts us and enhances our self-esteem.

'But it also poses questions to us about our own network of friendships. We assume our friends are consistently our friends, but when we see the double-dealing that goes on in *Big Brother* we become doubtful about the certainties of our own relationships.

'Also, because we see people in all their complexity, we have to deal with whatever stereotypes we may have attributed to them. We have to change our opinions as we watch them interact. We can't be lazy about our perceptions. It places a psychological demand on us; we have cognitive work to do as an audience. You can't watch *Big Brother* in a mentally passive state. You have to be engaged, working out what the hell is going on. It's a piece of detective work, trying to work out who you like and who you don't – and why. It's hard work, mentally, to understand them properly, which is why this is so much more engaging and addictive than other programmes.

'The contestants become part of our lives; we assimilate them, and we react to them and about them in the same way that people living in small communities react to each other. We recognize ourselves and our lives in what happens in the house, even though it's a very concentrated version. We call it reality TV, but it isn't entirely real. If you put a bunch of people in a house with cameras trained on them, but allowed them to carry on with their normal lives – going out whenever they wanted to and mixing with other people – it would be nowhere near as interesting as *Big Brother*, for two reasons.

'The first is that by isolating them psychologically, they turn inwards towards each other, not outwards, and become obsessed and preoccupied with each other.

'Second, the format is constructed in such a way that it brings co-operation and competition into conflict. In our normal lives, we manage to keep these two things apart, although we do sometimes compete with those we love, adore and get on with. In *Big Brother*, though, there is a stark conflict: the housemates have to compete with

---

CHINESE ASTROLOGY	TIGER

Alison is a tiger. Tigers are winners. They have beauty, intelligence, shrewdness, cunning and charm, and a gorgeous smile. But they have claws, and they will use them if necessary. Tigers have torrid affairs: they are usually very attractive and have a string of lovers. They can be beguiling, with a great capacity for achievement and getting what they want. Generally they are lucky, but can be foolhardy and even self-destructive. Tigers sum people up, watching them and learning all about them before becoming friendly. They can play mind games and be ruthless underneath a front of calm authority.

She gets on with: Spencer, Jonny, Sunita, Lynne, Sandy, Adele, Tim, P.J. and Alex

Friction with: Sophie, Lee, Kate

Famous tigers: The Queen, Princess Anne, Demi Moore, Groucho Marx, Germaine Greer.

the others, in terms of nominations and evictions, while at the same time getting on well with them and genuinely liking them.

'The juxtaposition creates a kind of pressure cooker; it turns the screw several times psychologically. It doesn't necessarily make people uncomfortable, but it accelerates the process of relationships. In our normal life, relationships move at a manageable pace, but in *Big Brother* everything is shorter; things happen with much more rapidity, which makes for more interesting relationships because of the internal conflicts – and also much more interesting viewing.

'There is also no escape. It's an enclosed, hermetically sealed world; there is no connection with the outside world, and they forget about it. At the beginning of each series they look around and check the positions of the cameras and feel very self-conscious. This rapidly declines until they only occasionally remember the presence of the cameras; they never completely forget – there is a little filter in their heads that stops them doing certain things. But 95 per cent of their behaviour is perfectly natural.

'Some are more conscious of the cameras than others, and some occasionally play to the cameras. Essentially, there is nowhere to

---

CHINESE ASTROLOGY — MONKEY

Lee and Kate are both monkeys. Monkeys are bright, quick-witted, sociable, youthful-looking and can be manipulative, making good friends with people who they think could be useful to them. Their real motives are often deceptive. They thrive on fantasy and hidden agendas. Monkeys are very sexual: they are often preoccupied by thoughts of the opposite sex. They have a childlike enthusiasm for everything and a quirky, fun sense of humour that can sometimes annoy others. Under pressure they may crack.

They get on with: Jonny, Sunita, Sandy, Jade, Spencer, Tim, P.J., Alex and Adele

Friction with: Alison, Lynne

Famous monkeys: Elizabeth Taylor, Bob Marley, Omar Sharif, James Stewart.

hide in the house. Even though they can dive under the duvet or try to find blind spots where the camera can't see them, almost everything they do is recorded. A major part of the success of the programme is that we know they are trapped.'

Peter believes that the new format, with the house divided into rich and poor, makes *Big Brother* even more psychologically fascinating than ever.

'It's potentially very divisive, but also has the interesting potential to bring people together. It allows people in the rich house to gloat and laud it over the others, and be ostentatious about their privileges; but they may choose to conceal their privileges and enjoy them out of sight of those in the poor half.

'The people in the poor house also have two completely different ways to behave – they can make the best of a bad job, be upbeat, and look on the bright side. Or they can become morose and withdrawn.

'It is how each individual reacts to this division which makes *BB3* much more interesting than *BB1* or *BB2*. But it is also fascinating to see how the division of the house affects the voting by the public. We don't like gloating, and being British we also expect the losers in the poor side to make the best of things. We may have some saintly people who will volunteer to go into the poor side even though they could be in the rich side, which would endear them to the audience – but even that could rebound on them.

As an experimental social psychologist, Peter knows that the consequences of success or failure can be profound.

'Winners become elevated; their moods are positive, their self-esteem is high. The consequences of losing may also be dramatic, but they need not be. Again, the house provides us with a microcosm of life, in that we can see before our eyes what happens to people who become disadvantaged for the flimsiest of reasons, just because they didn't do well at a particular task. It doesn't seem a fair way to apportion privileges – it's a bit arbitrary. But privileges are apportioned just as arbitrarily in real life; people end up at the bottom of the heap for random reasons. We can see in *BB3* a reflection of the way society is structured.'

He believes *Big Brother* has also 'blasted a lot of myths about viewing audiences out of the water. We've always assumed that young people are only interested in things that move fast. But what characterizes *Big Brother* is that is it very slow-moving; there are lots of longueurs. Nothing much happens a lot of the time. Yet young people have resonated with the programme and what it has to offer. They've shown that they can take the long view, and they are interested in an intimate close-up view of people, even though it is certainly not fast-moving.'

Brett Kahr, the psychotherapist who provides a lifeline for all the contestants, has his own ideas about why we can't get enough of *BB*.

'We live in a world of text messaging, faxes, e-mails, answering machines, mobile phones – we are probably at a point in history when we have more contact with more people than ever before, and yet it's very rapid, not particularly deep, it's not face to face and it has very little profound emotional content. We have the illusion of being connected to lots of people, but it's very superficial.

'In a typical day I make about forty phone calls, and perhaps only one or two of them have substantial emotional content. The others are quick and businesslike. That's sad, but this is a true reflections of our surrent world.

'We need emotional continuity in our lives, and there is something about the return of regular characters that satisfies our need for richness and continuity. What *Big Brother* has tapped into, perhaps quite unwittingly, is the fact that we get to know a group of characters with whom we have regular contact – perhaps even more contact than with anyone else, except our partners or our children or our parents. We spend more time with the *Big Brother* contestants for nine weeks of the year than we do with our best friends. It's a one-way relationship, but it is satisfying, because we feel we really know these people and are part of their lives; at the same time, we are not overwhelmed by all the intimacy of having to meet them and have relationships with them. *Big Brother* gives us the illusion of intimacy without the associated problems.

'The continuity, reliability and dependability of the characters helps us to triumph over our internal feelings of loss and deprivation. We could get a lot of this satisfaction from soap operas, and people

---

CHINESE ASTROLOGY   **DRAGON**

Sunita is a dragon. She's charming and crafty, used to using her feminine wiles to get her own way. She loves to be in charge and give orders. A dragon does not like weaklings. She loves compliments, may be susceptible to flattery. She can be selfish, strong-willed, straight-thinking and silver-tongued. She can also be sad and sentimental. She may make enemies quickly and can be resentful and vindictive. She can have a 'take it or leave it' attitude to other people. She likes glitter, wearing flashy clothes; she loves to stand out from the crowd and be the centre of attention. She is suspicious about people, but often has a good instinct about them. She makes partnerships and alliances to protect herself.

She gets on with: Jonny, Alison, Jade, Lee, Kate, P.J., Alex, Adele, Spencer, Tim

Friction with: Lynne, Sandy

Famous dragons: John Lennon, Al Pacino, Che Guevara, Paul Getty, Pele.

---

do. But there are important differences, the most obvious being that the *Big Brother* characters are real.

'Another big difference is the eviction procedure, which serves two very important psychological functions. The first is a result of being asked to choose who goes – there is an aggressive element to voting. It helps us to discharge angry feelings about people, and it helps us deal with our own feelings of failure by projecting them on to the person being booted out.

'The second function is that of helping us deal with our anxieties about death. If you think of the eviction process as someone being "killed off", it's quite a reflection of our life cycle. We're plonked on earth and every year someone else we know dies off, often unexpectedly, without a good reason. We're all preoccupied by death, even if we are not conscious of it. Yet it's not something society lets us talk about. We receive virtually no help with our fears of death.

'The eviction gives us the experience of seeing people get killed off, and this helps us deal with death. It's brutal, beyond our control, just like death. But it's safe, because in the final episode all the contestants are magically restored "to life".

'So the eviction procedure helps us deal with powerful emotions like aggression and death. But more than anything else, I think *Big Brother* vindicates the ordinariness of our own lives. It shows us just how interesting the minutiae of human life are. It shows us that a group of people who sit around doing not very much are endlessly fascinating; this reassures us that we don't have to be doing exciting things in our own lives to make us interesting and worthwhile people. We don't need to feel failures because we are not spending our lives jetting about the world, clubbing every night, rubbing shoulders with celebrities. Ordinary life can be just as rich. And by becoming engrossed in the tiny details of the housemates' lives, we can accept the minutiae of our own lives, which may, at times, be fulfilling and at other times more humdrum.'

Sandra Scott, a psychiatrist on the Sunday psychology show, says:

'Watching *Big Brother* is like peeking through the curtains into other people's lives. We've never before been allowed to watch our neighbours' lives so closely. You really feel you are seeing their lives – their whole, normal lives. We realise that there is a TV effect, but in time they cannot keep up a facade, and we can tell when they are playing to the cameras. At the same time, it is important to realise that we are no seeing the whole of them: we are seeing their personality under pressure, which can bring out extremes and this may not reflect totally the person their friends and family know.

'Other reality television formats don't work so well because they put people into extreme circumstances, and the viewers know it is not natural. It becomes more like drama, and second-rate drama at that.

'But *Big Brother* is what it says it is, and that's why it is so much more interesting, and done so much better than other shows.'

Sandra is fascinated by the motives that entice people to apply for the house.

'Financial gain is not the only aim. It is much more about making a mark, becoming "someone", having their fifteen minutes of fame.'

CHINESE ASTROLOGY   **HORSE**

Lynne is very special – a 1966 fire horse. A horse always signifies fire, but 66 was also a fire year, so this is an animal that only occurs once every 60 years. The double dose of fire means she is very powerful, extremely argumentative, very sure, strong, domineering, ruthless, curious, questioning. She is not patient with others and will ask personal and difficult questions. She can upset people very quickly. She can be charming, as long as things are going her way. She loves style, class, image; she likes everything to look right. She can be bitter and vengeful, and she is also wilful and stubborn. She does not enjoy asking for help and cannot see why she has to – she considers herself better than most other people.

She gets on with: Alison, Sandy

Friction with: Jonny

Famous horses: Mike Tyson, Paul McCartney, Janis Joplin, both Helen and Brian from *BB2*, and Lisa Stansfield (who is also a fire horse).

The contestants get invited to celebrity parties, they write columns, one or two of them may launch television careers.

'Even though they may not make the top rank of celebrities, they are invariably higher up than they were before they went in, and they are higher up than what they consider the average person to be.

'They now go in with a very good idea of what reception they will get when they leave, and what sort of rewards it may bring. They are going in with their eyes open wider, which is no bad thing.'

She says that as an expert, she is always trying to comment on things that will make *Big Brother* more interesting to the viewers, things that they may not have noticed or realised are important, and to add a psychological perspective to what they have seen.

'There are many things to look for, but essentially the housemates dictate the pace and it's important to look at them with an open mind. There is a certain amount of well-established research about group behaviour, and we can look at that if certain things are developing – for example, the selection of a scapegoat or the election of one person to a leadership role. But rather than just looking for things like that specifically, I also see my role as trying to bring a great depth of understanding to what is actually going on, and getting viewers to look at things again, and maybe understand more about them.

'I strive to make people notice things they haven't picked up on. Some things are blindingly obvious – everyone can see when a romance is developing – but it may not be obvious to see the impact this may have on the group.

'I never found their behaviour completely inexplicable, although perhaps I am surprised that there isn't more romance. A major factor in romance is proximity: if you spend time with someone enough, a relationship has the chance to develop, whereas if you can't see someone it withers much more easily. And they certainly are pushed together within the small confines of the house which, with the divide this year, is even more reduced. With so little to do (no music, television, books) you would imagine romance would provide a welcome distraction. However, exposing such intimacy on television

---

CHINESE ASTROLOGY   **DOG**

Sandy is a dog – a good organizer, planner, list maker. He is caring and unselfish, making time for others and listening to their problems. He rarely reveals his own problems, and can be moody and pessimistic, often affected by miserable weather or the moods of people around him. He loves to socialize and works well with people. He can feel nervous and insecure, and tries to cover this up by trying too hard to make friends. He will take on responsibilities, help others, sort things out, show genuine friendship and concern.

He gets on with: Sophie, Jonny, Alison, Lynne, Kate, Lee
Friction with: Sunita, Spencer, Adele, P.J., Alex, Tim
Famous dogs: Liza Minnelli, Elvis Presley, Sylvester Stallone, Brigitte Bardot.

CHINESE ASTROLOGY	RAT

Jonny is a rat. A rat works off nervous energy and needs to be liked – he can try too hard at this. When cornered, a rat can become verbally aggressive. He worries about his image, falling for anyone who flatters him; monkeys often do this for rats. He's honest and very shrewd, a good communicator, but sometimes speaks too hastily and regrets his words later. He likes to impress and can be very persuasive and sensual. A rat always considers himself to be right. He will complain about others and never accept any blame himself.

He gets on with: Sophie, Lee, Kate, Alison, Sunita, Sandy

Friction with: Alex, Lynne, Jade, Spencer, Tim, Adele, P.J.

Famous rats: Diego Maradona, Marlon Brando, Hugh Grant, James Taylor, Yves Saint Laurent.

seems to have been an inhibiting factor in *BB1* and *BB2* – an interesting point, given that most people think of the housemates at natural extroverts.

'Another factor is having something substantial in common with the person you form a relationship with, and all the contestants have one very big common experience: being in the house.'

She says that although the housemates quickly forget that they are on camera, the periodic reminders of the outside world – trips to the diary room, the voice of Big Brother – remind them of their situation.

'How natural they are varies, and is partly influenced by how long they stay in the house. Our personalities are enduring, but we can mask them for a time. If you go to a party, for instance, a different side of your personality may be on show from the one your partner sees all the time at home. But you could not keep it up. And in the *Big Brother* house we are seeing people under conditions of boredom and stress, neither of which usually brings out the best in people; so we have to factor them in when we attempt to assess their behaviour and personalities.'

UNCUT 3 ON VIDEO AND

Look out for the official Big Brother video and , out to buy this autumn.
Features all of the funny, saucy and memorable moments from the 3rd Big Brother series.

            WARNER VISION
INTERNATIONAL